Demchinsky, Bryan.
Storied streets.

DATE			

STORIED STREETS

MONTREAL IN THE LITERARY IMAGINATION

STORIED STREETS

BRYAN DEMCHINSKY AND ELAINE KALMAN NAVES

Macfarlane, Walter & Ross
Toronto

Macfarlane Walter & Ross
An Affiliate of McClelland & Stewart Inc.
37A Hazelton Avenue
Toronto, Canada M5R 2E3

Canadian Cataloguing in Publication Data

Demchinsky, Bryan
      Storied streets: Montreal in the literary imagination

Includes bibliographical references and index.
ISBN 1-55199-044-X

1. Montréal (Quebec) in literature. 2. Literary landmarks–Quebec (Province)–Montréal.
3. Authors, Canadian (English)–Homes and haunts–Quebec (Province)–Montréal.*
4. Montréal (Quebec)–Description and travel. I. Naves, Elaine Kalman. II. Title.

PS8101.M65D45 2000   C810.9'3271428   C00-930719-2   PR9185.5.M65D45 2000

Macfarlane Walter & Ross gratefully acknowledges support for
its publishing program from the Canada Council for the Arts,
the Ontario Arts Council, and the Government of Canada through
the Book Publishing Industry Development Program.

BOOK DESIGN: ANDREW SMITH
PAGE LAYOUT AND COMPOSITION: ANDREW SMITH GRAPHICS INC.
MAPS: VISUTRONX–J. LOATES
PRINTED AND BOUND IN CANADA

CONTENTS

For Judy Kalman, Colleen Snipper, Ruth Richler, and Linda Schwartz, with love and gratitude.

EKN

For Stanley and Mary

BD

ACKNOWLEDGMENTS

IN 1996 CHAVA ROSENFARB heard Elaine give a talk at McGill University called "The Muse in Montreal." It was she who suggested that a book could be written on the subject. We thank her for a great idea.

We are grateful to Marvin Orbach of the Vanier Library of Concordia University for directing us to many specialized sources in poetry. Thanks as well to Eleanor London and the staff of the Côte St. Luc Public Library and to Frances Ackerman and the staff of the Fraser Hickson Library for their helpfulness. Appreciation to Aline Gubbay, Susan Bronson, David Homel, Glen Rotchin, Pieter Sipjkes, and Merrily Weisbord for their suggestions about sources and for the loan of books. Our editor, Jan Walter, deserves a special vote of thanks for her sound judgement and unflagging enthusiasm.

We also offer a note of appreciation to two stalwart historians whose dedication to Montreal's past has made our work easier and more enjoyable. Edgar Andrew Collard, editor emeritus of the Montreal *Gazette*, through his many books, monographs, and newspaper columns, has done more than anyone else to keep the city's history alive. And Kathleen Jenkins's *Montreal: Island City of the St. Lawrence*, published in 1966, remains the best history of the city, a source to be relied upon time and again.

ELAINE KALMAN NAVES AND BRYAN DEMCHINSKY

A NOTE ON PLACE NAMES: Just as a city is in constant evolution, so too are the names of the places in it. This is especially the case in bilingual Montreal, which in the course of 358 years has seen the names of streets change from French to English and back to French again. For the purposes of this book, we maintain an English style of spelling of names: for example, St. Antoine Street instead of rue St-Antoine. But in acknowledgment that certain names have become in recent years more recognized by their French designations, we use Avenue des Pins instead of Pine Avenue, St. Laurent Boulevard instead of St. Lawrence Boulevard, etc. Also in keeping with the more French aspect of present-day Montreal, names feminized in French appear as such: hence Ste. Catherine Street instead of St. Catherine. Finally, to retain the flavour of the writing in quoted material, styles were left as they were found in the publications they were taken from. So in Hugh MacLennan's writing St. Jacques is Saint James Street, and in Michel Tremblay's work, Fabre Street is rue Fabre.

INTRODUCTION

A GREAT CITY is twice built: once of wood, brick, and stone and once as an act of the imagination. The imagined city is configured in words and pictures, and exists in a more enduring realm.

Montreal belongs among the twice-built cities. For all its latter-day troubles – the divisive politics, the unyielding demographics, and sometimes faltering economy – it is a city bountifully, often brilliantly imagined. From the first description of the mountain at its centre, written before the city had been conceived, to the most recent postmodern evocation, Montreal continues to fascinate the beholder.

Home-grown writers and those from away, historians, and visitors have all contributed to building this Montreal. In a variety of languages, but mostly French and English, they have shaped the streets and neighbourhoods of the city over 350 years. The Montreal of the imagination has been a kind of talisman for the writers who contribute to the edifice. In literature, the city becomes a vast communion, a marketplace of the imagination.

But whose culture and whose nation? Especially for francophone writers, Montreal is home base. Even while much of the early literary production of Quebec was concerned with the countryside, the population needed to achieve society's accounting of itself lay in the city. And in the twentieth century, the city itself was the setting in hundreds of works of fiction and poetry. (Author and literary critic Monique LaRue has estimated that Montreal is the setting in whole or part for some 600 novels written in French between 1885 and 1985.) However, Montreal also has been and remains essential to English Canada's and anglophone Quebec's sense of identity. Before Confederation, Montreal was the largest city in British North America, and, being half English-speaking, it is also the cradle of Canada's English-language literature. As this book demonstrates, the city has been deeply ingrained in the imagination of writers in both of the country's founding languages. For some, such as Michel Tremblay and Hugh MacLennan, the city and the writer are inseparable. The interconnection of writer and place is so profound that each is identified by association with the other.

The writers of Montreal have created a particular geography of the city. This book maps that geography.

Opposite: *The view from Windmill Point on Île Perrot, just off the western end of Montreal Island. The restored windmill is typical of the type that dotted the island from earliest colonial times.*

MONTREAL

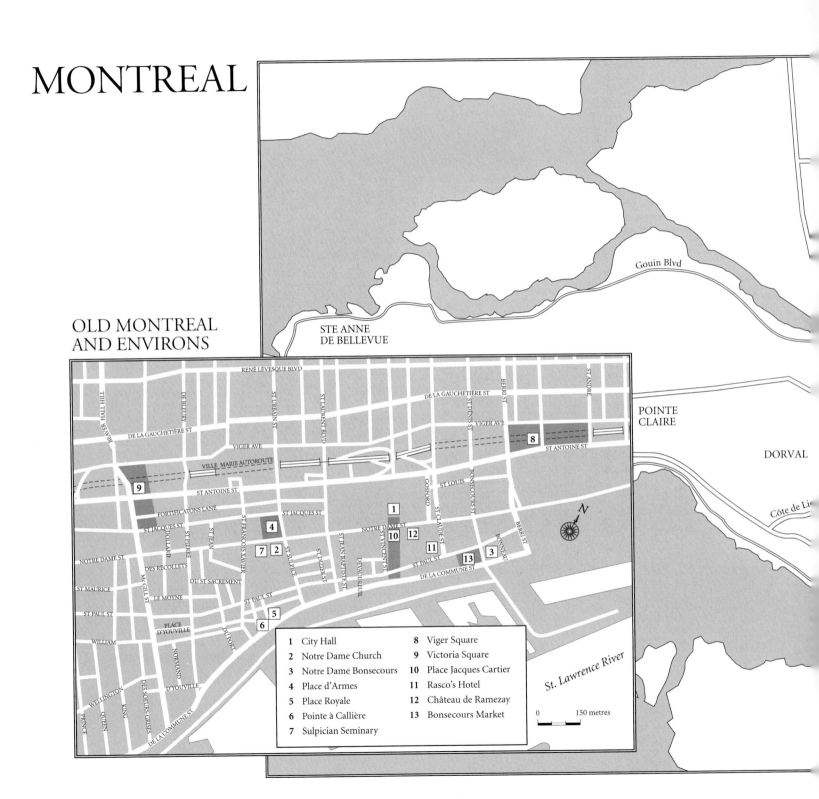

OLD MONTREAL
AND ENVIRONS

STE ANNE
DE BELLEVUE

Gouin Blvd

POINTE
CLAIRE

DORVAL

Côte de Li

RENÉ LÉVESQUE BLVD

DE LA GAUCHETIÈRE ST

DE LA GAUCHETIÈRE ST

VIGER AVE

VIGER AVE

VILLE MARIE AUTOROUTE

ST ANTOINE ST

ST ANTOINE ST

FORTIFICATONS LANE

ST JACQUES ST

ST JACQUES ST

NOTRE DAME ST

NOTRE DAME ST

DES RECOLLETS

DU ST SACREMENT

LE MOYNE

ST MAURICE

ST PAUL ST

ST PAUL ST

DE LA COMMUNE ST

ST. Lawrence River

PLACE
D'YOUVILLE

WILLIAM

WELLINGTON

PRINCE

QUEEN

KING

NORMAND

D'YOUVILLE

DES SOEURS GRISES

DE LA COMMUNE ST

BEAVER HALL HILL

DE BLEURY

ST URBAIN ST

ST LAURENT BLVD

ST DENIS ST

BERRI ST

ST ANDRE

GOSFORD

ST LOUIS

BONSECOURS ST

BERRI ST

BONNEAU

ST CLAUDE ST

DEVAUDREUIL

ST VINCENT ST

ST JEAN BAPTISTE ST

ST DIZIER ST

ST SULPICE

ST FRANCOIS XAVIER

ST JEAN

ST PIERRE

DOLLARD

McGILL ST

DUPORT

0   150 metres

1 City Hall	**8** Viger Square
2 Notre Dame Church	**9** Victoria Square
3 Notre Dame Bonsecours	**10** Place Jacques Cartier
4 Place d'Armes	**11** Rasco's Hotel
5 Place Royale	**12** Château de Ramezay
6 Pointe à Callière	**13** Bonsecours Market
7 Sulpician Seminary	

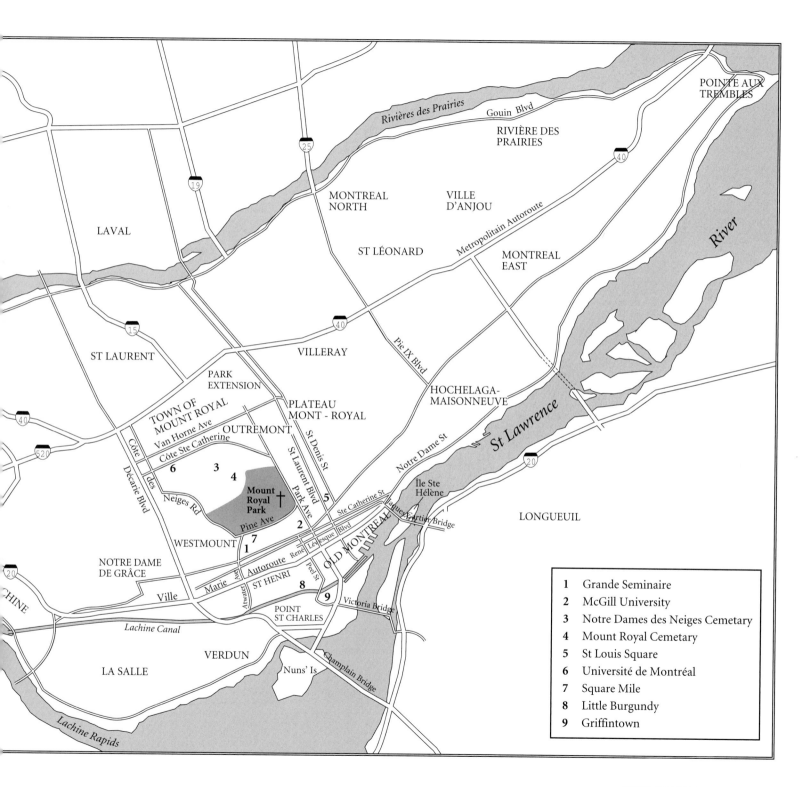

POINTE AUX TREMBLES

Rivières des Prairies

Gouin Blvd

RIVIÈRE DES PRAIRIES

River

MONTREAL NORTH

VILLE D'ANJOU

LAVAL

St LÉONARD

Metropolitain Autoroute

MONTREAL EAST

ST LAURENT

VILLERAY

Pie IX Blvd

HOCHELAGA-MAISONNEUVE

St Lawrence

PARK EXTENSION

PLATEAU MONT - ROYAL

Notre Dame St

LONGUEUIL

TOWN OF MOUNT ROYAL

Van Horne Ave

Côte Ste Catherine

OUTREMONT

St Denis St

St Laurent Blvd

Île Ste Hélène

Côte

des

Neiges Rd

3

4

6

Mount Royal Park

Park Ave

5

Ste Catherine St

Décarie Blvd

Pine Ave

2

Lévesque Blvd

Jacques Cartier Bridge

OLD MONTREAL

WESTMOUNT

7

1

René

NOTRE DAME DE GRÂCE

Marie

Autoroute

ST HENRI

Peel St

Ville

Atwater Ave

8

9

Victoria Bridge

LACHINE

POINT ST CHARLES

Lachine Canal

VERDUN

Champlain Bridge

LA SALLE

Nuns' Is

Lachine Rapids

1	Grande Seminaire
2	McGill University
3	Notre Dames des Neiges Cemetary
4	Mount Royal Cemetary
5	St Louis Square
6	Université de Montréal
7	Square Mile
8	Little Burgundy
9	Griffintown

Chapter 1
HOCHELAGA

Jacques Cartier as represented in a nineteenth-century drawing. Did the explorer embellish the account of his 1535 voyage?
Opposite: *Ramusio's drawing of Hochelaga has been the object of interpretation for more than a century.*

IN THE BEGINNING there was Hochelaga. Or was there?

An Indian village lingers like a ghostly presence in the story of Montreal. Hochelaga is indelibly etched into the historical record, yet remains ephemeral, as if carrying no weight at all. Its existence and fate have provided substance for both scholarly debate and the kind of ethno-political bickering that so much defines the character of the city. It is the first image of Montreal, and like so many since, what is seen depends a great deal on who is looking.

Hochelaga materializes for one brief, glorious moment, then disappears. This much seems certain: on October 2, 1535, Jacques Cartier, during his second voyage of exploration in the New World, landed on the shore of the island that today bears the city's name. A throng of native people greeted the French ecstatically:

"There came to meet us," Cartier writes, "more than a thousand persons, both men, women and children, who gave us as good a welcome as ever father gave to his son, making great signs of joy; for the men danced in one ring, the women in another and the children also apart by themselves. After this they brought us quantities of fish, and of their bread which is made of Indian corn, throwing so much of it into our long-boats that it seemed to rain bread."

The morning after an evening of feasting and gift-giving, the natives escorted Cartier and his companions to a nearby village:

"In the middle of these fields is situated and stands the village of Hochelaga, near and adjacent to a mountain, the slopes of which are fertile and cultivated, and from the top of which one can see for a long distance. We named this mountain 'Mount Royal.'"

The name has stuck, as has the image of benign first contact between the early inhabitants of the island and the explorers who preceded the European

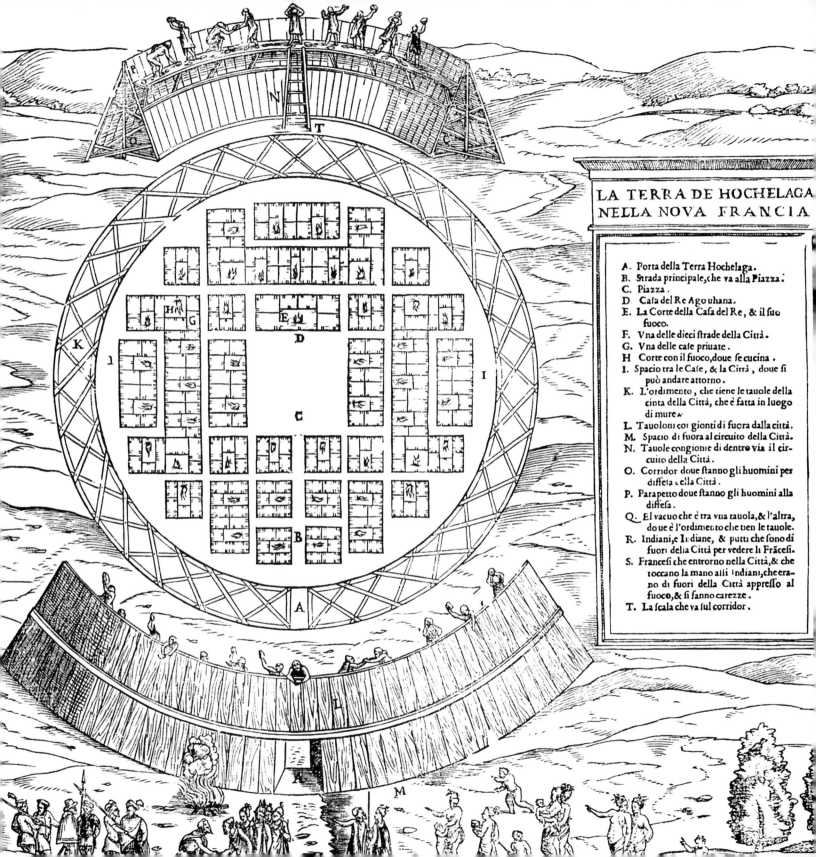

LA TERRA DE HOCHELAGA
NELLA NOVA FRANCIA

A. Porta della Terra Hochelaga.
B. Strada principale, che va alla Piazza.
C. Piazza.
D. Casa del Re Agouhana.
E. La Corte della Casa del Re, & il suo fuoco.
F. Vna delle dieci strade della Città.
G. Vna delle case priuate.
H. Corte con il fuoco, doue se cucina.
I. Spacio tra le Case, & la Città, doue si può andare attorno.
K. L'ordimento, che tiene le tauole della cinta della Città, che è fatta in luogo di mure.
L. Tauoloni coi gionti di fuora dalla città.
M. Spacio di fuora al circuito della Città.
N. Tauole congionte di dentro via il circuito della Città.
O. Corridor doue stanno gli huomini per diffesa della Città.
P. Parapetto doue stanno gli huomini alla diffesa.
Q. El vacuo che è tra vna tauola, & l'altra, doue è l'ordimento che tien le tauole.
R. Indiani, e Indiane, & putti che sono di fuori della Città per vedere li Fracesi.
S. Francesi che entrorno nella Città, & che toccano la mano alli Indiani, che erano di fuori della Città appresso al fuoco, & si fanno carezze.
T. La scala che va sul corridor.

settlers. In a 1942 history of the city, Stephen Leacock, who was then a McGill University professor, writes: "These are embalmed pages of Canadian history. They are almost sacred in the atmosphere they breathe of piety and mutual faith. No picture in all North American history is more inspiring. At least Montreal began well."

Cartier left the beauty of a Mount Royal autumn and sailed back down the St. Lawrence to spend a miserable winter at Stadacona, another Indian village near present-day Quebec City, before returning to France. The account of his explorations was published, and the portion of the text concerning Hochelaga was accompanied by a drawing by the Italian engraver Giovanni Battista Ramusio. The image purports to show the stockaded settlement described by Cartier and the surrounding fields and hills. These documents are the main evidence of the existence of Hochelaga. Cartier made no further mention of the place following a subsequent visit to the island of Mount Royal in 1541. Nor did Samuel de Champlain, who visited in 1611, clearing a spot for a future settlement. In less than a century Hochelaga had disappeared, leaving no trace, at least none recorded by the Europeans.

Sir John William Dawson believed he had rediscovered Hochelaga.

There has been much debate about who the Hochelagans were and what happened to the village. The two most likely theories are either that the village was destroyed by a competing tribe or that the inhabitants simply abandoned their settlement; this was a practice common among the woodland people of the time when they had exhausted the soil of the surrounding fields.

The fate of Hochelaga might have remained a footnote to the larger Montreal story but for a discovery by Sir John William Dawson in 1860. Workmen excavating a site a little to the south of the McGill University campus found skeletons and aboriginal artefacts, which they showed to Dawson, who was a geologist and the principal of McGill. After examining the site and relics, Dawson concluded that Hochelaga had been rediscovered. For many years, it was accepted that the so-called Dawson site, in the heart of the downtown, was the place Cartier had described and Ramusio had drawn, and, in 1925, this notion was memorialized when a plaque locating the village nearby was attached to a stone planted on the campus near the Roddick Gates entrance on Sherbrooke Street. The plaque remains there to this day.

But even as the Dawson site was being sanctified, doubts were being cast as to whether it was indeed the location of Hochelaga. The apparent size of the locale and the relative scarcity of artefacts suggested the settlement was much smaller than the large village described by Cartier (estimates put the population of his village at from 1,500 to 3,500). Conclusions about its whereabouts were made based on the two sixteenth-century documents by Cartier and Ramusio, so assuringly detailed in some aspects and frustratingly vague in others. In 1924, Aristide Beaugrand-Champagne, an architect and amateur historian, recorded the ideas of the even more impressively monikered Montarville Boucher de la Bruyère, who had proposed a radical new theory in a speech to an antiquarian society a few years earlier. Beaugrand-Champagne described how Cartier must have arrived on the island by way of the Rivière des Prairies, the current that flows around the north side of Montreal Island, and trekked to the mountain from there. If one correctly follows the clues given in Cartier's narrative and Ramusio's drawing, Beaugrand-Champagne said, it follows that Hochelaga was on the northeastern flank of the mountain, in present-day Outremont, and therefore in a francophone part of the city. (Abbé Lionel Groulx, the influential Quebec nationalist historian, was a supporter of the Beaugrand-Champagne thesis.)

W.D. Lighthall, a mayor of Westmount, favoured a west-end site for Hochelaga.

Not so, said W.D. Lighthall, another amateur historian. During his long life (1857–1954), Lighthall was a lawyer, briefly the mayor of Westmount (1900–3), and a passionate promoter of Montreal in poetry and historical sketches. In articles published in 1924 and 1932 in the *Transactions of the Royal Society of Canada*, Lighthall made his own analysis of Cartier's writing and Ramusio's drawing and concluded that Hochelaga occupied the Dawson site after all. Staking out his territory on the southwest side of the mountain, Lighthall says: "Undoubtedly the Hochelagans must have taken great pleasure in the magnificent woods, the immense trees, the beautiful flowers, the mosses and the dells and springs, of Mount Royal, which are such happy memories, also for many of us who have lived long in the neighbourhood."

About the same time, Stephen Leacock entered the fray with his own novel explanation of the Hochelaga conundrum. Leacock dismissed not only the authenticity of the Dawson site but the whole idea of the existence of the village. Considering how many logs it would have taken to build the number of houses recorded by Cartier, and the lack of evidence of them, Leacock concluded that "Hochelaga is like the farmer's giraffe. No such animal." He speculated that the whole Hochelaga episode might have been concocted by Cartier to promote to the French king the idea of opening up Canada.

Despite such reservations, the idea that the Dawson site was Hochelaga persisted and was repeated in history books – at least the English ones. And, to this day, it has remained an article of faith for others that Hochelaga was in the east. The debate developed along ethnic and linguistic lines, with both the French and English communities wishing to appropriate Hochelaga as its own by having the village located in its part of town.

It would probably be a larger burr under the saddles of the anglophone anti-revisionists if not for the work of Bruce Trigger and James Pendergast, leading authorities on eastern woodlands tribes. Pendergast is an archaeologist specializing in St. Lawrence Iroquoian culture and lives in Ontario, while Trigger is chairman of the Anthropology Department at McGill University. They re-examined the archaeological evidence from the Dawson locale, the writings of Cartier, and Ramusio's drawing, and in 1972 published a landmark work, *Cartier's Hochelaga and the Dawson Site*. Cautiously, it says that the downtown location must almost certainly be ruled out. Trigger also suggests that there may never have been a village called Hochelaga, that Cartier might have mistakenly applied the name to a settlement called Tutonaguy, which he visited on his third voyage to Canada. Hochelaga might be the name the inhabitants of the island gave to themselves. In the end, despite the rigours of the archaeological and anthropological analysis, apart from discrediting the Dawson site, Pendergast and Trigger seemed only to have deepened the mystery of Hochelaga.

Leacock's doubts aside, most writers have joined in the celebratory spirit that Cartier invoked when he spoke of Hochelaga. There could hardly be two more different sensibilities than those of Charles Sangster (1822–93), a Kingston-born poet whose work celebrates Canadian history and landscape, and Yolande Villemaire, a Montreal playwright, poet, and novelist, born in 1949. Both, however, have been inspired by the beauty implicit in an early fall journey to Hochelaga. In the poem "Jacques Cartier's First Visit to Mount Royal," Sangster writes:

He stood on the wood-crowned summit
  Of our mountain's regal height,
And gazed on the scene before him,
  By October's golden light....

In its gorgeous autumn beauty,
  Lay the forest at his feet.
With red and golden glory
  All the foliage seemed ablaze....

In her 1982 novel, *Amazon Angel*, Villemaire writes: "This is the dawning of the world. In my canoe I glide towards Hochelaga.... My canoe enters the Hochelaga archipelago, gleaming with October's flamboyant gold. Red rushes to the treetops like the red blood that surges in our veins. Hochelaga explodes in orange, ochre, purple and pink across the last traces of green on the blue and indigo of the sky."

Meanwhile, the ardent amateurs continue the debate. The most recent speculative foray is the work of Pierre Larouche, an urbanist and civil engineer, who wrote *Montréal 1535: La Redécouverte de Hochelaga* to coincide with Montreal's 350th anniversary in 1992. Larouche supports the back-river theory of Cartier's arrival, and through an arcane analysis of the elevations and positioning of the hills in Ramusio's drawing, concludes Hochelaga was where Notre Dame des Neiges and Mount Royal cemeteries are today – that is, on the northeast slopes of Mount Royal. Larouche condemns those who would have Hochelaga on the west side of Mount Royal, and in a curious epilogue to his book, he produces a map of Montreal, circa 1760, in which the conquering English armies of Generals James Murray and Jeffrey Amherst are depicted at the gates of the city. The circular stockade from Ramusio has been transplanted on to the map and stands on the mountain's northern flank cut off from the conquered town.

Will the mystery of Hochelaga's location ever be resolved? Probably not. Bruce Trigger says that to identify Hochelaga definitively, archaeologists "would have to find a site that is as big as Cartier's descriptions suggest it was, and if [this site] was dated from that era, then one could probably say, yes, it's Hochelaga." The anthropologist offers an explanation as to why such archaeological evidence has never come to light. Quebec, he says, lacked the tradition of people like farmers and builders collecting relics while plowing their fields and excavating building sites. Probably the evidence for the existence of Hochelaga has been lost forever. Still, Trigger defends the idea that the village was on the southern flank of the mountain. Here there was a longer growing season, good soil, and more shelter from the elements. And, he says, there remains one spot left that might contain evidence of the Montreal Eden. The grounds of the Grande Séminaire, the Sulpician estate on Sherbrooke Street West at the top of Fort Street, have never been thoroughly examined. Created as a fortified mission on the flank of the mountain a few kilometres from the Sulpician headquarters in Ville Marie, the outpost later became a summer residence, known as the Priests' Farm. The grounds have been continually settled by Europeans since the seventeenth century, and before that it was known to be a place visited by native people because of its favourable location.

If it were established that the Grande Séminaire grounds contained the Hochelaga site, there could hardly be a more appropriate place. True, it is on the west side of the mountain, in an as yet English-speaking part of town, but it has historical associations that extend to the city's beginning, and no pedigree is more impeccable than that of the Sulpicians, who were once seigneurs of the island. It would be a fitting conclusion to the Hochelaga mystery.

Chapter 2

POINTE À CALLIÈRE

Paul de Chomedey,
Sieur de Maisonneuve,
Montreal's founder.

Cᴵᴛɪᴇs ᴏꜰ ᴛʜᴇ Old World emerged from the distant past wrapped in legend; Rome, with its twins Romulus and Remus, suckled by a she-wolf, is the classic example. North American cities, by contrast, were founded by explorers or settlers who recorded their precise beginnings. In the case of Montreal, the time of its birth is known, but the aura surrounding the event is scarcely less mythic than that of Cartier's visit to Hochelaga.

The founding was in 1642, on May 17 or 18, depending on which of the early accounts you trust. After a strenuous upstream paddle from Quebec in small boats, Paul de Chomedey, Sieur de Maisonneuve, and a band of some fifty settlers landed on a still-identifiable spot on the south bank of an island in the St. Lawrence to found the colony of Ville Marie. De Maisonneuve, a soldier from Champagne, had been recruited by a group of French religious devotees whose goal was saving heathen souls in the New World. They could hardly have made a better choice than the energetic and resourceful young nobleman. De Maisonneuve and his followers – soldiers, sailors, farm hands, artisans, and, among them, three women – disembarked where a small creek flowed into the St. Lawrence River, forming a point of land that easily could be defended.

Two sources record what transpired on that day, and, as might be expected, they are at odds with each other. One was written by Father Barthélemy Vimont, a Jesuit priest who accompanied de Maisonneuve. His description appears in the Jesuit *Relations*, the record the order kept of their missionary work in the New World. Vimont has the de Maisonneuve party landing on May 17 and, after a brief religious service, setting about building the fort that would protect them from any hostile Iroquois who might be about. The second version of the founding comes from François Dollier de Casson, a Sulpician priest who wrote the first history of Montreal thirty years after the event. Dollier makes the historic day May 18 and says the whole of the first day was given over to "devotions, thanks-

giving and hymns of praise to the Creator." He offers the delightful image of the day as it drew to a close: An altar garlanded with wild flowers was set up; "there were no lighted lamps before the Holy Sacrament, but there were some fireflies which shone there very pleasantly day and night, hung by threads in a beautiful and marvellous manner." The flowers and fireflies were gathered by the women in the group, the nurse Jeanne Mance, who would in 1644 set up Hôtel-Dieu, the colony's first hospital; the noblewoman Madame de la Peltrie, who had come from the Ursuline Convent in Quebec City for the occasion; and de la Peltrie's maid, Charlotte Barré.

Later historians have suggested that Vimont's version is the likelier of the two, because he was there and because fear of attack would not have allowed the settlers a leisurely day of devotions. Both sources have Father Vimont conducting a mass in which he utters a memorable benediction for the city to be: "You are a grain of mustard seed, that shall rise and grow till its branches overshadow the earth. You are few, but your work is the work of God. His smile is on you, and your children shall fill the land."

A mid-nineteenth-century view of Pointe à Callière, drawn while the Victoria Bridge was under construction.

Louis Fréchette recounts the founding in "La Première Nuit," from his masterwork, *La Légende d'un peuple*.

It was the wilderness in austere splendour.
Nothing yet moving in this virgin corner of the earth
Where Montreal would one day put up its towers....

Downstream, following a winding course
That cuts between shadowy shores,
– Near the spot now called Pied-du-Courant –
Three boats laden under a mid-day sun,
Breasted the flow of the St. Lawrence.

LOUIS FRÉCHETTE

Born at Hadlow Cove near Lévis across the St. Lawrence from Quebec City, Louis Fréchette (1839–1908) became in the latter part of the nineteenth century the principal literary figure of French-speaking Canada, the only French-Canadian writer of his day to be well known outside this country.

In a life that included a stint in the proverbial garret and that was capped by a prestigious prize awarded by the Académie Française, Fréchette was for more than a quarter of a century the symbol of the ideal man of letters: a poet who had penned over four hundred verses, a playwright, essayist, folklorist, and short story writer.

Critics of his day called him "the Lamartine of Canada." His first collections were first romantically, then politically inspired. Many of his early lyrical poems were sparked by amorous adventures. He was radical in his politics, and his second book, *La Voix d'un exilé* (1868), was written in Chicago, where he exiled himself in 1866 in disgust over the approach of Confederation, which he believed would mark the end of French Canada.

A lawyer by profession, Fréchette made a stab at politics when he returned to Canada from Chicago in 1871. He sat in the House of Commons for four years but failed to get re-elected.

His marriage to a Montreal heiress in 1876 changed the course of his life. No longer obliged to worry about his financial future, he could devote himself to writing full time. His move to Montreal in 1877 also signalled the city's new status as the literary and cultural capital of the province.

In 1879 Fréchette published *Les Fleurs boréales*, the collection of stories that won him the Prix Montyon of the Académie Française and ensured his reputation. Upon his return from Paris, he was fêted at a public banquet and from this time was known as the unofficial poet laureate of French Canada. He may have been the first but would certainly not be the last Canadian for whom fame abroad meant recognition at home.

La Légende d'un peuple, a series of historical tableaux interpreting the emergence of French Canada, was published in 1887 and is regarded as Fréchette's finest work. A collection of epic poems reminiscent of Victor Hugo, it reflects the cult of great men popular in the nineteenth century. Several poems take as their subjects heroes of Quebec's history, such as Dollard des Ormeaux, Jolliet, and Papineau.

The Royal Insurance Company Building, seen in a photo by Alexander Henderson.

Who was making his way up the great river?
It was de Maisonneuve, the founder,
With de Montmagny, the brave soldier,
Vimont, the holy apostle, proud of his double mission,
And, gilding the era about to begin,
Two women, two grand hearts: de la Peltrie and Mance;
Two souls ready for any sacrifice.

While the location of Hochelaga remains an enigma, there is no mystery about where the settlers disembarked. It was the place Champlain had visited thirty years earlier and called Place Royale. "In all I saw, I found no place more suitable," he writes in the record of his voyages. "[It] is as far as barques and boats can easily come up, unless with a strong wind or by a circuit, because of the great current; for higher than that place (which I named Place Royale), there is a little river which goes some distance into the interior, all along which there are more than sixty acres of deserted land, which are like meadows, where grain can be sown and gardens made. Formerly the savages tilled these, but they abandoned them on account of the wars they had here."

The Petite Rivière St. Pierre, as the creek flowing into the St. Lawrence was named, was channelled underground in the nineteenth century, but its course remains visible in the angle Place d'Youville forms with de la Commune Street. This historic ground appears frequently in the visual and written record of the city, and it has been much studied, thanks to the museum of archaeology that today stands on the spot. The earliest image of Ville Marie to have survived dates from 1647, just five years after its founding. It shows de Maisonneuve's house, a small church, a storehouse, and a number of dwellings. The marshy, low-lying area was prone to flooding, and it was rising water in the spring following the settlers' arrival that prompted de Maisonneuve to erect the first cross on the heights of Mount Royal in thanksgiving for the colony's survival. By 1654 the settlers had moved Ville Marie to higher ground across the Saint Pierre creek, and the first fort was abandoned. Toward the end of the seventeenth century, part of the point was ceded to Louis-Hector Callière, a French governor who built a residence there. The present-day name, Pointe à Callière, commemorates him, while Champlain's Place Royale lives on as the name of the adjacent square which contained the city's first marketplace.

In the early eighteenth century, the point was a common outside the gate of the wooden stockade that enclosed the new settlement. Here, in front of the Callière house, Indians from upriver came to trade furs, beginning a commerce that eventually spread along the length of the river bank now occupied by de la Commune Street.

Toward the end of the century, the Callière house was demolished and other buildings were erected on the point, at first houses, but by the nineteenth century, inns and storehouses, since the area was just a few steps away from the marketplace across the creek. During this period, much of the point belonged to Pierre Berthelet, one of Montreal's largest landowners. The storehouse he built on the site can be seen in several mid-century images of the port.

Another view of the area during this period takes shape in the words of Thomas Storrow Brown, who came to Montreal from New Brunswick in 1818. Brown was a prominent nineteenth-century Montrealer, successful in business and a founder of the newspaper *The Vindicator*, which supported the Patriote side in the rebellion of 1837–38. Before his death in 1888, Brown's recollections were gathered for a series of newspaper articles. He recalled the day he entered the city by way of the port, a few metres from where the first settlers had landed nearly two hundred years earlier: "I came into the city through a narrow passage leading to the Custom House Square, then 'the Old Market,' a low wooden shed-like building; and along the south side of the square was a row of old women seated at tables with eatables for sale. Capital Street was a succession of drinking houses, carrying on an active business from morning till night; for in those anti-temperance days drinking appeared one great object of life and daily occupation." And not just drinking, but fighting, too. The fur trade no longer brought natives to the town, but instead the roughest of voyageurs in need of a spot of recreation. "Rare sport it was, " reported Brown, "to see the whole [market] square filled with these people – a dozen fights going on at the same time – fresh men stepping into the ring, as the vanquished, in their blood, were led off – all as gay as if it were merely a dance."

Pointe à Callière today, showing the archaeological museum, which echoes the form of the insurance building.

Later in the nineteenth century, a more sophisticated kind of business was conducted at Pointe à Callière by the Royal Insurance Company, whose flatiron-shaped building fit snugly into the apex of the point. Its neoclassical detailing and elegant tower made it a landmark for nearly a century. The building was converted into a customs house before being damaged by fire and demolished in 1951. It can be seen in wonderfully evocative photographs by the great nineteenth-century Montreal photographer Alexander Henderson, and its form has been echoed by the Pointe à Callière archaeological museum, which today stands in its place. The museum's postmodern style has been criticized as being out of context with the old neighbourhood in which it stands. Nonetheless, its shape, tracing the contours of the point, and radically contemporary design suggest continuity between past and present over three and a half centuries.

Chapter 3
OLD MONTREAL

MONTREAL IS A far-flung affair. Its metropolitan population of three and a half million occupies an island of almost five hundred square kilometres, as well as off-island communities extending in all directions. So it is remarkable that half of the city's history is accounted for in a riverside strip of land a mere three and a half kilometres in length and less than a kilometre's width. From Berri Street on the east to McGill Street on the west, de la Commune Street on the south, and St. Antoine Street on the north: these are the boundaries of Old Montreal. Although fire and thoughtless demolition have battered the architectural integrity of the old quarter, its streets and dimensions are true to the earliest days when Montreal was a walled town. The remnants hint at a world of stories. The most memorable of these concern the early years of the colony.

De Maisonneuve's followers were motivated by religious zeal, sent to convert the natives to Christianity. Things turned out differently. The settlers spent as much time defending themselves against the Iroquois as they did converting them and less hostile Indian peoples. The harrowing accounts of living under constant threat of kidnap, murder, and scalping form a motif in the earliest writing about the city.

One of the most famous stories concerns de Maisonneuve's fight with an Iroquois chief in 1644. After months of harassment and being forced to stay close to their fort, some of the more rash among the men wanted to venture forth for a showdown with the natives. De Maisonneuve resisted the idea until his courage became suspect. One morning in early spring, when the barking of the settlers' dogs warned of the presence of the Iroquois, de Maisonneuve led thirty men out of the fort and almost immediately into an ambush at a spot that has since been designated Place d'Armes. Several of the French were killed, and the patrol was forced to return to the fort under fire with de Maisonneuve, a pistol in each hand, covering the retreat. An

Opposite: *The face of Old Montreal today: The domed Bonsecours Market Building has been a prominent landmark since it was built in 1842.*

Our Lady of the Harbour, the statue of the Virgin Mary atop the Bonsecours Church referred to in Leonard Cohen's song "Suzanne."

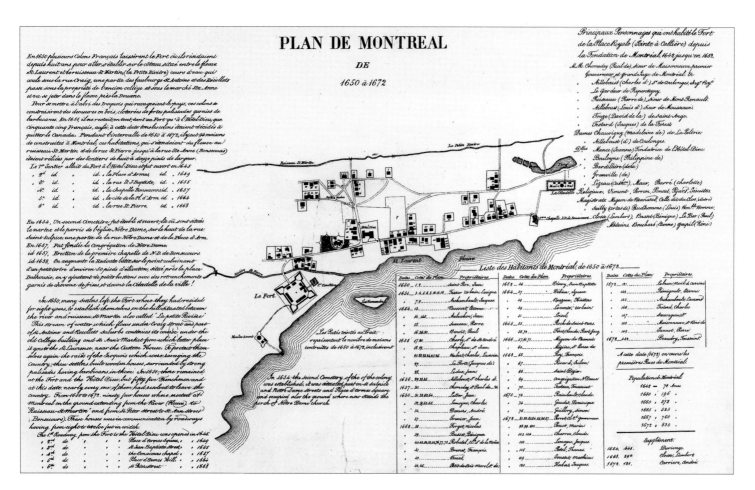

An early map of Montreal lists the names of the settlement's landowners.

enemy chief singled out the governor as the leader of the French side and approached for personal combat. De Maisonneuve's first pistol misfired, but he killed the chief with a shot from the second.

Two plaques attached to the wall of a building on the north side of the square, one in French, the other in English, commemorate the bloody occasion: "Near this square afterwards named la Place d'Armes the founders of Ville-Marie first encountered the Iroquois whom they defeated Paul Chomedey de Maisonneuve killing the chief with his own hands March 1644."

The incident has resonated in the work of writers who in the twentieth century sought to soften the image of the people whose land was taken from them. One was the poet F.R. Scott, who writes in the poem "The Founding of Montreal":

A pistol went bang bang for Christ and France.
Another Indian died a Christian death.
That night red women wept white women's tears.
And white men snored like any Indian braves.

Robert Majzels makes reference to the incident in his 1997 novel, *City of Forgetting*: "Single-handed, pistol-packing hero. L'exploit de la Place d'Armes. He has solved the morale problem, and wasn't that the objective of the exercise? Three of his men dead. And the other. The dark eyes full of intelligence and strength, the hand outstretched."

Sulpician, Récollet, and Jesuit priests were the principal missionaries in the early years of New France, the latter keeping a comprehensive if sometimes lurid record in the *Relations* of proselytization and martyrdom. But, in the case of Montreal, a more vivid picture of the colony was provided by François Dollier de Casson. He was a remarkably energetic man whose accomplishments were equal to those of any of Montreal's founding figures. Dollier was born in 1636 and was a soldier in France before taking vows with the Sulpicians, the order which brought him to Canada. He spent months travelling deep into the heart of the continent with the explorer René-Robert Cavelier, Sieur de La Salle, seeking native tribes in need of conversion. In 1671, Dollier was appointed superior of the Sulpician seminary in Montreal. By then the community had grown to about eight hundred people and was as likely to be called by the name of the island on which it stood, Montreal, as by Ville Marie. Dollier was aware that the colony's heroic age was passing, and he wanted to capture some of the flavour of the early years. He set about writing the first history of the town, relying on the testimony of the remaining founders, Jeanne Mance among them.

Dollier was a worldly character who revelled in the earthy details of the stories he recorded. Like the Jesuit *Relations*, his history was much concerned with the predations of the Iroquois, no doubt because they were never far from the minds of his witnesses. But the *Relations* would never have offered the ribaldry of *Histoire de Montréal*. An example is Dollier's account of an incident in which a settler working with some others in a field "went to perform the functions of nature, placing himself at the edge of [an] enemy ambush, to which he turned his back...." Indignant at the insult, an Iroquois pricked the settler with his weapon, sending him dashing back to his companions.

The Sulpician father was not above fashioning a quip at the expense of his old comrade, Sieur de La Salle. He remarked upon the latter's obsession with finding a passage to China by way of the St. Lawrence: alluding to the little settlement at the western end of the St. Lawrence rapids that became the village Lachine, he writes that it would be "a great consolation to those who come to Mount Royal when they find it is only three leagues from la Chine [China]."

Another example of Dollier's storytelling skills is his account of the Iroquois attack on a settler. It is found in *A History of Montreal, 1640-1672*, the 1928 English translation by Ralph Flenley of *Histoire de Montréal*.

> "A woman of virtue, called today the goodwife Primot, was attacked within two gunshots of the château. As soon as she was attacked she shouted loudly.... The woman defended herself like a lioness, but as she had no weapons but hands and feet, at the third or fourth blow they felled her as if dead. Immediately one of the Iroquois flung himself upon her to scalp her and escape with this shameful trophy. But as our amazon felt herself so seized, she at once recovered her senses, raised herself and, more fierce than ever, caught hold of this monster so forcibly by a place which modesty forbids us to mention that he could not free himself. He beat her with his hatchet over the head, but she maintained her hold steadily until once again she fell unconscious to the earth, and so allowed this Iroquois to flee as fast as he could, that being all he thought of at the moment, for he was nearly caught by our Frenchmen, who were racing to the spot from all directions."

Dollier has been called Canada's first local historian, but he was much more than that. Near the spot where de Maisonneuve killed the Iroquois chief, he oversaw the building of the colony's first parish church, Notre Dame, in 1673, and adjacent to the church, the Sulpician seminary, begun about 1685. Part of the latter building remains, the oldest structure in central Montreal. Although the name Place d'Armes wasn't applied until the following century, the square that developed next to these religious institutions became the heart of the old city.

Dollier was also responsible for laying out the first streets, St. Paul and Notre Dame, and some of the cross streets that run between these two thoroughfares of the town. The course of the streets, still largely empty of buildings, was indicated with stones, which bore the stamp of the seminary and the words "to remain there untouched for ever and aye." The stones have disappeared, but the streets are much as Dollier had planned them.

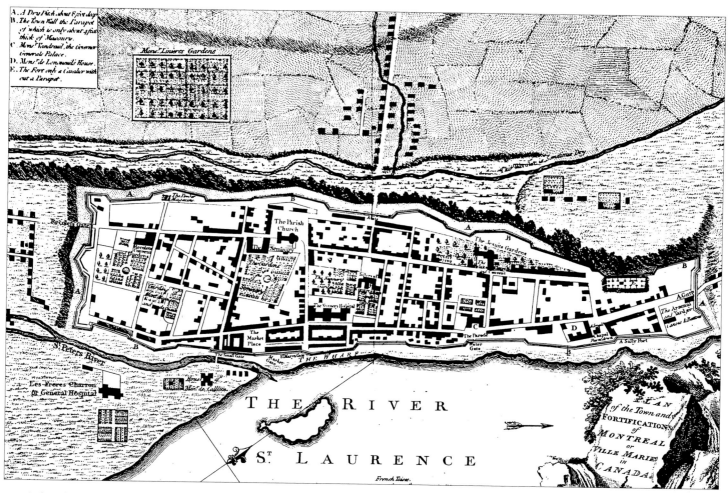

Mons. Linieres Gardens

The Recolets

Recolets Gate

The Parish Church

The Seminary

The Jesuits Gardens

THE WHARF

Peters River

Les Freres Charron or General Hospital

The Market Place

Water Gate

A Gate

The Arsenal and Yard for Canoes & Boats

A Sally Port

THE RIVER ST. LAURENCE

French Toises.

PLAN of the Town and FORTIFICATIONS of MONTREAL or VILLE MARIE in CANADA

The threat posed by the Iroquois waxed and waned during the seventeenth century. Dollard des Ormeaux's heroic defence of the colony in 1660, in which he and sixteen comrades were slain, and the Lachine massacre in 1689, in which the Iroquois killed at least twenty-four settlers, were the most memorable confrontations. The acts of cruelty were not restricted to the native side of the conflict. W.D. Lighthall records the following anecdote from 1696 in his book *Montreal After 250 Years* (published in 1892). He does not provide a source for the story:

"An eyewitness of the burning of the four Iroquois on what is now Jacques Cartier Square thus describes:
'When I came to Montreal for the first time, it was by the St. Francis

A map of Montreal from the 1760s. Houses appear along the road that has become St. Laurent Boulevard.

Gate. I there saw a man of my province, who came up to embrace me, which he did and after some compliments, informed me that he was of our company. As we were speaking together, he perceived that I was much distracted because of a large crowd that I saw on the Place des Jésuites. Thereupon my new comrade exclaimed: "Upon my word! You've just come in time to see four Iroquois burnt alive. Come on as far as the Jésuites; we'll see better." It was immediately in front of their door that this bloody tragedy was to take place. I thought at first they would throw the poor wretches into a fire; but on looking around on all sides, I saw no faggots for the sacrifice of the victims, and I questioned my new friend about several small fires which I saw at certain distances apart from each other. He answered me: "Patience; we are going to have some good laughing." For some, however, it was no laughing matter. They led out these four wild men, who were brothers, and the finest looking men I have ever seen in my life. Then the Jesuits baptized them and made them some scanty exhortations; for, to speak freely, to do more would have been "to wash the head of a corpse." The holy ceremony finished, they were taken hold of and submitted to punishments of which they were the inventors. They bound them naked to stakes stuck three or four feet in the ground, and then each of our Indian allies, as well as several Frenchmen, armed themselves with bits of red-hot iron, wherewith they broiled all parts of their bodies. Those small fires, which I had seen, served as forges to heat the abominable instruments with which they roasted them. Their torture lasted six hours, during which they never ceased to chant of their deeds of war, while drinking brandy, which passed down their throats as quickly as if it had been thrown into a hole in the ground. Thus died these unfortunates with an inexpressible constancy and courage. I was told that what I saw was but a feeble sample of what they make us suffer when they take us prisoners.'"

Despite the predations on both sides, Montreal was growing. The outlines of Old Montreal took shape as spaces and institutions still on the map were created. As noted, the marketplace stood opposite Pointe à Callière, its north side opening on to St. Paul Street. East along St. Paul Street was Jeanne Mance's Hôtel-Dieu hospital, while farther east, beyond the limits of the town was Notre Dame de Bonsecours Church, which began as a wooden structure built under the direction of Marguerite Bourgeoys in 1657. Rising several times from the ashes of fire, a church has been on the site ever since. Placed atop the church during an 1894 renovation is a statue of the Virgin of Bonsecours, which looks out toward the St. Lawrence River, giving rise to the church's nickname as the Sailor's Chapel. In his song "Suzanne," Leonard Cohen refers to the statue with the words "And the sun pours down like honey on our lady of the harbour."

On Notre Dame Street, the notable structures were the parish church of Notre Dame and the Sulpician seminary. The Récollets built a substantial church and convent on Notre Dame Street as did the Jesuits. In 1687, the colony was enclosed by a wooden stockade that served as a defensive perimeter. By then, attack was more likely to come from France's English rivals in the New World than it was from the natives. In 1701, the year of Dollier's death, Governor de Callière concluded a treaty with thirty-eight chiefs whose people lived in French territory. The era of the Indian wars had ended. In its place began a period of growth and prosperity. Streets were extended and new buildings went up, among them, in 1705, a new governor's mansion, the Château de Ramezay, a building that remains a jewel among the city's historical properties.

Montrealers were discovering that their true vocation was commerce, and in its early form this meant the fur trade. It changed the town radically. The fur-trading fairs attracted natives who came from far to the west and could be seen striding the streets in traditional garb, sometimes more naked than clothed. While good for the economy, the trade with the Indians had a corrupting effect, especially on the natives. Abbé François Belmont, Dollier's successor as head of the Sulpicians, commented sourly that Montreal had become "a little Babylon which has overwhelmed and intoxicated all the [Indian] nations with the wine of its prostitution." Many years later, in the poem "Montreal 1945," Earle Birney noted the peculiar amalgam of religious and capitalist conviction that continued to characterize the city:

> *This is New France the oldest France alive*
> *where Church is more than state*
> *and less than stock-exchange....*

With the surge in activity came growing pains. Filth was thrown into streets constructed without proper drainage. When it was wet the avenues were turned into muddy bogs, while in dry weather the passage of wagons and horses raised clouds of dust. After mass at the parish church of Notre Dame, there was such a crush of traffic in the street that it posed a hazard to pedestrians.

The preference for sleighs rather than snowshoes for getting around in winter was taken as a sign that people were not as hardy as in former times. Ordinances forbade allowing pigs and other livestock from running free in the streets – but the nuisance problem continued until it was decreed that owners of stray pigs might literally lose their bacon to fellow citizens who corralled the animals.

Fire was a more serious problem. Buildings were still constructed of wood and most of them burned down at one time or another. The Hôtel-Dieu burned in 1695, 1721, and 1734, being rebuilt each time until it was finally demolished for good in the mid-nineteenth century when the hospital moved to its present location on Avenue des Pins.

Marie Morin, a Quebec-born nun who became head of the Hospitalières nursing order in Montreal, vividly describes the 1695 fire in her memoir *Histoire simple et véritable : les annales de l'Hôtel-Dieu de Montréal, 1659–1725:*

> "One of our friends in the faith, a Sulpician priest, told me that upon rising during the night, between midnight and one a.m., he saw a light in the spire of the church and thought that a hospital servant had gone up there for some reason, not considering the unlikely hour. The guard at the door of the governor's home also saw the light, which was getting brighter, not realizing that a fire was about to burn our home, until the flames began shooting from the gable of the church on the Saint-Paul Street side, which was heavily thatched. That led the guard to cry loudly 'fire!', but because everyone was sleeping, no one heard him; so he had to knock loudly on the door of the hospital. The nurse and several patients ran out into the yard announcing the fire. Sister Maumousseau, who was at the end of the dormitory, heard their voices and dashed from her cell in a panic, running along the corridor, yelling as loudly as she could, 'We're on fire, sisters, we're on fire. Get up quickly and save yourselves.' I don't believe the church bell could have got us up more promptly than her voice."

With houses closely packed together in the manner of European towns, a fire in one building might turn into a general conflagration. The 1721 blaze that consumed the Hôtel-Dieu was one of these, burning down half the town. As a result, regulations were imposed requiring houses to be built of stone with thick firewalls and slate or tile roofs. As the new houses were erected, inhabitants began adapting the building styles they had brought from France to local

MARIE MORIN

A prototype of the kind of stalwart pioneering woman New France is renowned for, Marie Morin was the first Canadian-born nun. She can also be called our first home-grown historian if the concept of history is stretched to include annals of a narrow variety.

She was born in Quebec in 1649, into a family of twelve children. As a boarder at the Ursulines in Quebec, the little girl formed a passionate desire to come to Montreal to be a nurse after a visit by Jeanne Mance and three nursing nuns who had been chosen to found the Hotel-Dieu Hospital of Ville Marie.

With the Iroquois steadily pounding away at them, Montrealers clearly needed a hospital. Marie's parents, however, wouldn't hear of sending their daughter off to the perils of the frontier when she could join a safe nursing order in Quebec. Thirteen-year-old Marie prevailed by convincing Bishop Laval himself to issue her a special authorization.

After she took her vows, she proved a capable leader and businesswoman, elected financial manager and Mother Superior of her order over many terms. Her memoirs are written in a blunt style for which she apologized in the preface, citing her many responsibilities for the overseeing of the building's construction and reconstruction after fire. "The carpenters, masons, stone-cutters, and joiners needed to speak to me often, and that distracted me from my subject...." She writes of the city's early founders, of English attacks, of the looters during two serious fires who sampled the hospital's strong medicines, and even of a personal visit by the devil.

Of special interest is her attention to domestic detail. Morin's description of Canadian winters before the advent of central heating is particularly chilling. "You must know that the cold in this country can be understood only by those who are subjected to it. Their houses having holes in more than 200 places, the wind and snow easily passed through them ... so that when there had been wind and snow during the night, one of the first things to be done in the morning was to take wooden shovels and the broom to throw out the snow around the doors and windows ... and the water that was put on the table for drinking froze within a quarter of an hour."

conditions. It was the beginning of a Quebec vernacular architecture that created an image of the city still discernible today in its greystone walls, pitched roofs, and dormer windows.

Epidemics were another unhappy consequence of the town's growth. Smallpox broke out in 1733, killing hundreds in the Montreal region, including the governor, M. de la Chaissagne. As with runaway fires, contagions periodically struck Montreal until well into the nineteenth century.

The population grew steadily if unspectacularly, from 1,200 in 1700 to about 4,000 in 1750. With everyone struggling to make a living, there are few accounts or images from the French colonial era that present an impression of the town itself. For this reason, the writings of the priest Pierre de Charlevoix and the Swedish naturalist Peter Kalm have always intrigued readers.

Charlevoix, a Jesuit, spent the winter of 1720–21 in Montreal. "This town," he writes in *Histoire et Description générale de la Nouvelle France*, "has a pleasing appearance. It is well situated, well laid out and well built. The charm of its surroundings and its streets inspire a certain gaiety." But he noted the lack of protection offered by the wooden stockade erected in the previous century and now crumbling. "For some years there had been a project afoot to surround it with walls but it will not be an easy task to induce the inhabitants to contribute to its expense. They are brave and they are not rich." (In fact, work began on stone fortifications in 1722 under the supervision of the French engineer Chaussegros de Léry.)

As others were to do after him, Charlevoix noted the rise in elevation between what he described as the "lower" and "upper" town. The lower town, along the river and St. Paul Street, contained the king's storehouses, the Hôtel-Dieu, the merchants' quarters, and the public square. The upper town, around Notre Dame Street, housed the headquarters of the religious orders – the Sulpicians, Récollets, and Jesuits, and the Sisters of the Congregation of Notre Dame. After three centuries of building and levelling, the distinction between an upper and lower town in Old Montreal is less pronounced. But you can still get a feel for it looking northward up the slope from St. Paul Street to the top of Place Jacques Cartier toward City Hall, where the Jesuits' property once stood atop a low hill.

Peter Kalm toured North America for two and a half years, studying the flora and fauna of the New World, arriving in Montreal in 1749. He kept an entertaining record of the places he visited that described the customs of the locals. Kalm astutely assessed Montreal's prospects when he compared it with Quebec. Montreal, he says, was "the second town in Canada in regard to size and wealth; but it is the first on account of its fine situation and mild climate."

Kalm provided a detailed description of the town and, good Protestant that he was, notes, "It has got the name of Montreal from a great mountain about half a mile westwards of the town, lifting its head far above the woods.... The priests, according to the Roman Catholic way, would call every place in this country after some saint or other, calling Montreal Ville Marie, but they have not been able to make this name general, for it has always kept its first name."

He describes the houses as "neatly built," and "the streets are broad and straight, and divided at right angles by the short ones; some are paved, but most of them are very uneven. The gates of the town are numerous; on the east side of the town toward the river are five, two great and three lesser ones; and on the other side are likewise several."

From the description of the produce grown on the island, the reader might conclude that the climate was milder than today: grapevines and apple, pear, and plum trees bore abundant fruit, and on three sides of the colony, in an area that would now comprise much of present-day downtown, were well-tended fields of grain. Curiously, there were no potatoes.

Most fascinating was Kalm's description of the Montreal women, who met with his approval :

"In general [they] are handsome here; they are well bred and virtuous, with an innocent and becoming freedom.... They dress very fine on Sundays.... They wear a neat jacket and short petticoat, which hardly reaches the mid-leg and in this particular they seem to imitate the Indian women. The heels of their shoes are high and very narrow, and it is surprising how they walk on them. In their knowledge of economy they greatly surpass the English women in the plantations, who indeed have taken the liberty of throwing all the burden of house-keeping upon their husbands, and sit in their chairs all day with arms folded."

Soon after the prosaic scenes described by Peter Kalm, Montreal was plunged into the turbulent era of the Seven Years War. For its entire history, the town, situated near the confluence of several rivers, was vulnerable to attack from all directions, at first from the Indians, then from the British, and later the Americans. When Quebec fell to the British at the Plains of Abraham in 1759, Montreal was left isolated and it was only a matter of time before it, too, was captured. Thousands of French soldiers were gathered on or near the island, straining the town's resources. Hunger and unrest spread as the French army prepared to make a last stand here. But the situation was hopeless. Surrender to the approaching armies, on September 9, 1760, was the only sensible response.

The capitulation ended more than a century of solitude for the town. Before the Conquest, Montreal was an outpost, the last community of consequence on the edge of the vast wilderness that made up most of French North America. While Quebec had been the gateway to New France and its administrative centre, Montreal was more preoccupied with the hinterland, whence its livelihood came by way of farming and the fur trade. Now, an invading army brought a flood of new people and influences. No longer was Roman Catholicism the only faith. Within weeks of the occupation, the Catholic churches were lending their buildings to the occupiers so that Anglican and

Artist B. Cole's schematic rendering of Montreal in 1760.

Presbyterian services could be held. With the British troops came provisioners who stayed on as merchants. Scots and Americans from Britain's southern colonies added to their ranks.

During the French regime, Montreal had been little visited by outsiders and was a curiosity. Almost immediately upon the arrival of the British, pictures began appearing in London, the first being a rather crude effort from 1760 by an artist named B. Cole. More schematic drawing than realistic depiction, it features a large British flag hoisted above the citadel, a military emplacement on the town's east side. Another image, by Thomas Patten and published in 1762, offers a more realistic view, though Mount Royal looms in a backdrop as huge and rugged as Gibraltar.

What some visitors drew, others rendered in words. In the late eighteenth century and into the nineteenth century, there was an outpouring of memoirs, journals, diaries, and letters that offer images of Montreal. One of the first of these writers was John Knox, a captain in the occupying army, who left a detailed account of the town as he found it in 1760:

"For delightfulness of situation," Knox writes, "I think I never saw any town equal to it; besides the advantages of a less rigorous climate, it is infinitely preferable to Quebec.... It stands on the side of a hill sloping down to the river...with many gentlemen's seats thereon together with the island of Saint Helen, all in front; which forms a most agreeable landscape.... The streets are regular, the houses well constructed, and in particular the public buildings far exceed those of the capital of Canada [Quebec City] in beauty and commodiousness."

Knox was less impressed with the stone fortifications, which he describes as "mean and inconsiderable...calculated to awe the numerous tribes of Indians who resort here at all times from the most distant parts for the sake of traffic, particularly at the fair, a kind of carnival, held every year, and continuing near three months, from the beginning of June till the latter end of August." By the

Thomas Patten's 1762 view of Montreal is more realistic than Cole's but Mount Royal looms larger than life.

end of the French regime, the fur fairs were in decline, though, considering the popularity of today's jazz, comedy, and film festivals, occurring during the summer months, it would appear that Montrealers' love of a "carnival" during these months has not diminished.

Like Kalm before him, Knox was charmed by the inhabitants, whom he found "gay and sprightly, much more attached to dress and finery than those of Quebec.... From the number of silk robes, laced coats and powdered heads of both sexes, and almost all ages, that are perambulating the streets from morning to night, a stranger would be induced to believe Montreal is entirely inhabited by people of independent and plentiful fortunes."

Another writer, Frances Brooke, echoed the sentiment about Montreal being a more enjoyable place than the town of Quebec, a notion as prevalent

Governor Guy Carleton reviews British troops on Place d'Armes in 1775 on the eve of the American invasion of Canada. Behind them is the parish church of Notre Dame.

among Montrealers today as it was in the eighteenth century. Brooke was the first writer to portray the town through a fictional lens, in *The History of Emily Montague*, which has been called the first Canadian novel. Montreal is, Brooke says through one of her characters, "a very lovely spot; highly cultivated and though less wild and magnificent, more smiling than the country around Quebec." The speaker is Ed. Rivers, a British officer and "man of adventure," who eventually marries the heroine of the title. Brooke was the daughter of an Anglican minister. She had already written a novel when she arrived in Canada in 1763 to join her husband, a chaplain with the British garrison. In Rivers, Brooke echoes the blunt prejudices of the day, when he describes the habitants in quite different terms than Knox had. They are "ignorant, lazy, dirty, and stupid beyond all belief," Rivers says. But as they had done for other visitors, the Canadian women turn Rivers's head: "What is particularly agreeable, [the men] leave their wives and daughters to do themselves the honours of the house.... Their conversation is lively and amusing; all the little knowledge of Canada is confined to the sex; very few, even of the seigneurs, being able to write their own names." In such lines, readers discern why Brooke has been championed as a Canadian proto-feminist.

When it was ruled by the French, Montreal was mostly neglected as a military

Richard Dillon made this drawing, published in London in 1803, when the stone walls still surrounded the city. The view is from Île Ste. Hélène. The hill at right, called the Citadel, has since been levelled. Montreal's city hall stands there now.

An 1824 view of Montreal looking south from the Citadel.

Rosanna Leprohon wrote about a misalliance between a British officer and a French girl.

outpost. The British, ever mindful of the threat of invasion from the south after the American Revolution began, were more energetic in defending the town. Thousands of troops were quartered within its walls or nearby in places like Île Ste. Hélène. The presence of so many soldiers had a powerful impact on the small town's social structure. The officers exuded exoticism and worldliness, attracting the young women even as the soldiers were being drawn through loneliness and boredom to mix with the local population. Sleigh rides, balls, and other social occasions provided the opportunity for contact. The occasional dalliance between French and English was one of the risks and attractions of the new social order. The young women who consorted with the officers became known – somewhat disparagingly – as "muffins."

Almost a century later, one of Canada's first home-grown writers of fiction used the post-Conquest era and a Montreal setting for her best-known novel. Rosanna Leprohon was born in 1829 to a wealthy merchant of Irish Catholic background. She married a French-Canadian doctor, bore thirteen children, and became one of those admirably bilingual, bicultural people that Quebec produces generation after generation.

Her best-known novel, written in English but more read in its French translation, was *Antoinette de Mirecourt*. It takes place in and around a "substantial-looking stone house, situated towards the east extremity of Notre Dame Street, then the aristocratic quarter of the city." A French-Canadian heiress secretly marries a British officer stationed in Montreal. The unhappy consequences of the mixed alliance is the major theme and is reflected in the subtitle: *Secret Marrying and Secret Sorrowing*. Published in 1864, *Antoinette de Mirecourt* encouraged the kind of ethnic and religious separation that came to characterize Montreal in the nineteenth century and which had its roots in these early encounters. It is ironic that Leprohon should have chosen to defend a position that was contrary to her own biculturalism, but her outlook was a reflection of the times, when keeping order in a newly heterogeneous society was paramount.

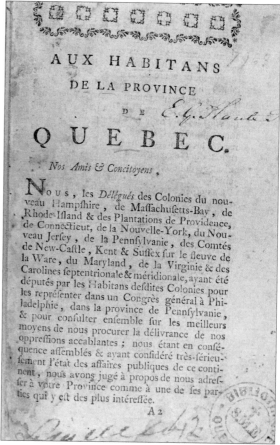

Fleury Mesplet's call to arms to the citizens of Quebec during the American Revolution. A Frenchman stuck in Montreal after the Americans abandoned the city, Mesplet went on to found the forerunner to The Gazette.

Montrealers had only a few years to enjoy the return of peace before troubled times again beset them. The new threat was the revolution that convulsed the colonies to the south and threatened to spread to Quebec. The strenuous efforts of the Catholic clergy, the seigneurs, and the British administrators barely managed to keep the habitants in line. But the town, still strategically placed for anyone wishing to control the continent, was once again invaded. Choosing to make their main defence at Quebec, the British abandoned Montreal to the Americans who arrived in November 1775. A small but vocal group of republicans, mostly Yankee traders, welcomed the Americans as liberators. The French population watched the newcomers, at first warily and then with growing hostility. Lack of discipline among the American troops, an incompetent commander, and the issuing of paper money of dubious value all quickly served to make the Americans unpopular. Benjamin Franklin came to Montreal to assess the situation the following spring, but the game was up. The Americans were forced into an ignominious retreat. There was one lasting benefit of the American presence: the founding of the first newspaper in Montreal by Fleury Mesplet. Mesplet, a Frenchman recruited by Franklin to spread the gospel of revolution among French Canadians, was left behind with his printing equipment when the Americans departed. Within a couple of years, he was able to start the *Gazette du commerce et littéraire de Montréal*, the ancestor of today's Montreal *Gazette*, providing a spark of intellectual life in the community that had been absent.

With the American adventure ended, Montreal's development picked up

Opposite: *A colonial-era house at the corner of St. Vincent and Ste. Thérèse Streets in Old Montreal, photographed early in the twentieth century. The house, since demolished, illustrates the fire-prevention features noted by Captain Anburey.*

Washington Irving visited Montreal as a young man engaged in the fur trade.

where it had left off. Again visitors, often British soldiers, provided the most lively and informative impressions of the place. One such was Captain Thomas Anburey. He examined Montreal in that peculiarly anthropological way of an Enlightenment gentleman, meticulously detailing its layout and appearance, the climate, and the habits of the local populace. He was intrigued by the house construction, noting the fire-prevention building techniques, such as the thick stone walls and fire breaks between buildings. The doors and window shutters, he wrote, were made of plate iron nearly half an inch thick, and this would ordinarily give buildings an oppressive appearance were it not for the fact the ironwork was painted green, making for a pleasing contrast with the walls.

Anburey was much taken by the French-Canadian sleighs, or carioles as they were called. "The carioles are fashioned after different devices to imitate birds and beasts, but in general they are of one construction, with this difference, that the common people have theirs close upon the ice or snow, while those of their superiors are raised upon what are called runners.... They paint them of various fantastical colours; many of them, as a contrast to this season of the year, are coloured in imitation of thunder and lightning. It is certainly a very easy and expeditious method of travelling, for the horses of the country will go with ease fifteen miles an hour upon the ice. The inhabitants think nothing of a journey of forty or fifty miles to see a friend, returning the same day."

Discussion of the severity of Montreal winters has probably gone on as long as people have lived on the island. Anburey contributed his reflections on the subject when he concluded that far from suffering from the effects of the cold, "people...seem to be perfectly in their element; there's nothing but carrolling, feasting and other amusements."

At the turn of the nineteenth century, amusement might be found in carousing with the fur traders, many of whom were partners in the North West Company. One visitor who observed the traders in action was the New Yorker Washington Irving. As a young man, years before "Rip Van Winkle" brought him fame, Irving came to Montreal on business. Recalling the experience in later life, Irving writes, "Few travellers that have visited Canada...in the days of the M'Tavishes, the M'Gillivrays, the M'Kenzies, the Frobishers, and the other magnates of the North West, when the company was in all its glory, but must remember the round of feasting and revelry kept up among these hyperborean nabobs."

Alexander Mackenzie, William McGillivray, Joseph Frobisher, Alexander Henry, Simon McTavish, and James McGill – Scotsmen all – had made fortunes following in the wakes of the coureurs de bois of an earlier time. They

left a lasting imprint on the city. McGill, of course, provided land and funding for the founding of a university, and McTavish is recalled by a street adjacent to the McGill campus. Frobisher's log mansion, constructed on the rise of land above the old town, was known as Beaver Hall, a name that has stuck to the street that today climbs the escarpment rising from the river. All the traders had wintered at one time or another in the wilderness that supplied their wealth. They were a hardy breed for whom the town was a place to relive their exploits in convivial surroundings like the Beaver Club.

George Landmann was another who fondly remembered the exploits of the nabobs. Like Thomas Anburey, Landmann was a British officer, but while Anburey put Montreal under a microscope, Landmann's reminiscences of being stationed in Quebec in 1797–98 were those of a retired soldier at his ease among his club mates, telling tales that grew taller over the years. Landmann, whose temperament matched that of the traders, was happy to spend his time drinking and carousing. The boisterous atmosphere of Montreal's fur-trading days is captured in his account of a drinking session at the Beaver Club:

Simon McTavish was one of the Scots who made a fortune from the fur trade.

"I had not been twenty-four hours at Montreal before I was invited to dine for every day in succession, during a week or ten days…. After many days of feasting and hard drinking, I was engaged…to dine with Sir Alexander Mackenzie and [William] McGillivray…. In those days we dined at four o'clock and after taking a satisfactory quantity of wine, perhaps a bottle each, the married men, viz. Sir John Johnson, McTavish, Frobisher, O'Brien, Judge Ogden, Tom Walker and some others retired, leaving about a dozen to drink to their health. We now began in right earnest and true highland style, and by four o'clock in the morning, the whole of us had arrived at such a degree of perfection that we could all give the war-whoop as well as Mackenzie and McGillivray, as we could all sing admirably, we could all drink like fishes, and we all thought we could dance on the table without disturbing a single decanter, glass or plate by which it was profusely covered; but on making the experiment we discovered that it was a complete delusion, and ultimately, we broke all the plates, glasses, bottles, etc., and the table also, and worse than all, the heads and hands of the party received many severe contusions, cuts and scratches."

Landmann recounts making his way back to his hotel near the waterfront, answering "all the challenges of the sentinels, in a soldier-like manner." His hotel keeper, Pat Sullivan, detects that his guest is in no great shape and decides to keep an eye on him.

"I locked the door and without delay proceeded to get into bed. I deposited each article of my dress in a proper manner on a chair, with the same regularity as usual, but with this small difference, I was far more litigious, and folded and unfolded each article some ten or twelve times, before I felt satisfied that I had done it in the best manner. Nevertheless, in the morning I discovered that several of them had become dispersed about the floor in a most unintelligible manner. Having completed these important arrangements to my satisfaction, I jumped into bed, and went off to sleep, without forgetting to place my famous horse pistols, which I had purchased at New York, by the side of my bed. How long I remained in that happy state, I do not find recorded in my journal, but I remember having been disturbed during the night by some suspicious noise, that upon looking about me, I perceived a man working his way through an

Simon McTavish's house on St. Jean Baptiste Street in Old Montreal. It still stands but has been much altered since this 1920s photo was taken.

aperture about a yard square which had been made in a boarded partition, separating my room from the one adjoining; and which opening was commonly filled by a close cast iron stove, so that two rooms should be warmed by one fire.

"Immediately on my satisfying myself that a man was actually endeavoring to force an entrée into my apartment, I snatched up one of my trusty companions; and before I could obtain any very clear answer to my brief interrogatory, I fired at his head; upon which a loud screech, followed by a hollow groan was heard, and the man fell. A general confusion very soon afterwards spread itself throughout the house; every individual it contained, came stumbling over each other, all directing their hurried steps to the point whence the report of a pistol had issued, and I was compelled to allow them a free admission into my room.

"It was now ascertained that Pat had been most fortunately but slightly wounded, the ball having merely scratched the skin of his bald head. After dressing his wound with a piece of court-plaister, Sullivan related that, having observed I could not have walked along two yards of a single board, he had remained on the alert to watch my movements, and that having perceived I had got into bed without extinguishing my candle, he had tried in vain to draw my attention to that important fact by battering on my room door. At length it had occurred to him that he could make his way to my candle by squeezing his corpulent body through the hole in the partition already mentioned, without disturbing me; but unfortunately I had been sufficiently aroused by the battering, and the result I have described."

If the rowdiness of the fur traders suggests Montreal was as yet a frontier town in the early years of the nineteenth century, the impression was not diminished by the appearance of the place. Situated on an island, the town was still difficult to reach. Montreal was impressive when seen from the river, with its metal-roofed stone buildings and spires glinting in the sun, but once visitors had disembarked, they were sometimes disappointed. "The interior of Montreal is extremely heavy and gloomy. The buildings are ponderous masses of stone, erected with very little taste and less judgment," wrote John Lambert, a Scottish traveller in 1806.

Years after he had taken up residence in Montreal in 1816, J.H. Dorwin was asked by a newspaper to sketch his first impressions of the town: "The river margin [was] almost lined with rafts and logs, but otherwise was in its natural state. There were no wharves; passengers walked ashore on planks, goods were landed on the beach, whether it was muddy or dry. In some places, carts were driven into the river to obtain loads of driftwood.... Over [the river's] banks was thrown all the filth and refuse of the city, to be washed away once a year by the spring freshets."

The following year, Englishman John Palmer recorded this picturesque scene on the river bank: "The manner of washing pursued by many of the women is similar to that pursued in the West Indies. I every day saw thirty or forty soldiers' wives, and other women, standing up to their knees in water in different parts of the river, washing and beating the clothes on large stones."

For many visitors, the impression Montreal made was according to their prejudices. Some were charmed or impressed at finding a town already old by North American standards and in which French was heard in the street. "It required no powerful effort of the imagination to conceive that we were arrived in Europe," wrote Benjamin Silliman, an American who visited in 1819. "A town, compactly built of stone, without wood or brick, indicated permanency, and even a degree of antiquity, presenting some handsome public and private buildings, an active and numerous population, saluting the ear with two languages, but principally with the French – every thing seems foreign, and we easily feel that we are a great way from home," Silliman said, echoing the impression of many tourists who have since arrived from his homeland.

Europeans were less likely to be awed, as was the case with Edward Allen Talbot, who after sailing from Ireland in 1824, complained that "it is impossible to walk the streets of Montreal on a Sunday or other holiday, when the shops are all closed, without receiving the most gloomy impressions. The whole city appears one vast prison; and at every noise which salutes the ear of the passing stranger he imagines that he hears the clankings of a malefactor's chains, or the pitiful moaning of an incarcerated debtor." Some found as much to dislike as Talbot, among them the British actress Fanny Kemble, who, following a North American tour, fumed in an 1834 letter: "The heat, while we were in Montreal, was intolerable – the filth intolerable – the flies intolerable – the bugs intolerable – the people intolerable – the jargon intolerable. I lifted up my hands in thankfulness when I set foot again in 'these United States.' "

As the nineteenth century progressed, the town's centre shifted from the riverfront and the old market square to Place d'Armes, Notre Dame Street, and St. James Street. In the 1830s and '40s, Montrealers witnessed the construction of the new Notre Dame Church on the south side of the square. It was at the time the biggest church in North America and the largest building in Montreal, and it created a focal point for the town that invited comment from visitors and locals alike.

Among those whom the building impressed was the sage of Walden Pond, Henry David Thoreau, who came to Montreal in 1850. One would not have expected Thoreau, an advocate of individualism and a critic of priestly intercession in spiritual affairs, to have a revelatory moment inspired by a Catholic church. Soon after stepping ashore in the harbour, Thoreau and a companion found themselves on Place d'Armes, at the entrance to the church:

"Coming from the hurrahing mob and the rattling carriages, we pushed aside the listed door of this church and found ourselves instantly in an atmosphere which might be sacred to thought and religion, if one

Henry David Thoreau was impressed by Notre Dame Church in spite of his prejudice against Catholicism.

had any.... It is true, these Roman Catholics, priests all, impress me as a people who have fallen far behind the significance of their symbols. It is as if an ox had strayed into a church and were trying to bethink himself. Nevertheless, they are capable of reverence, but we Yankees are a people in whom this sentiment has nearly died out, and in this respect we cannot bethink ourselves even as oxen."

The poet Joseph Lenoir (who was also a mayor of St. Henri) in *Poèmes épars*, published after his death in 1861, echoes Thoreau's sense of the church as a place of refuge in his description of Notre Dame:

> *It is a house of peace amid the tumult,*
> *An oasis where from unruly wilderness,*
> *Or the floodtide of faraway seas,*
> *Comes he who is weary of the Earth's empty roar,*
> *The traveller, sitting devout and alone,*
> *Whose days the world has embittered!*

While peace reigned within, such was not always the case outside the doors of the church. A formerly isolated, unilingual community was being transformed into a diverse and bilingual one, and the stresses began to show. Since the Conquest, French Canadians had been guaranteed the right to their religion, language, and civil law, first under the Quebec Act of 1774 and then the Constitutional Act of 1791. These measures were undertaken more out of expediency than benevolence, but, combined with the compact formed by British administrators, the French clergy, and seigneurs, peace had been kept, even during the tumult of the American Revolution. Recalling the unhappy experience of American rule, the renewed threat of invasion from the south in the War of 1812 drew all sides together. But in the wake of that conflict, the rapid changes taking place in Lower Canada, especially in Montreal, could no longer be ignored. Montreal's population, a mere 9,000 in 1800, grew five-fold by mid-century. Almost all of these were non-French speakers – Britons, United Empire Loyalists, Yankees from New England, Scots traders and merchants, and Irish labourers. By 1831, most Montrealers were English-speaking, and anglophones would remain the majority until Confederation. Some who had lived in England or the former southern colonies, where democracy had been achieved, wanted to be governed in similar fashion in Quebec. Others on the English side were dyed-in-the wool Tories, who were content to have all governmental power vested in a hand-picked legislative council. Meanwhile, among the French-speaking population, many were inspired by Enlightenment ideals that had fired the American and French Revolutions, while others, especially the clergy, were conservatives of the ultramontane variety. Whatever their political outlook, francophones viewed with growing unease the influx of new people and the customs they brought with them.

Battle lines were drawn between English-speaking Tories and the Patriotes, mostly French-speaking promoters of representative government. Although the Patriotes had supporters among liberal-minded anglophones, the movement was mainly francophone and represented the first major manifestation of French-Canadian nationalism. The cleavage between English and French, in Montreal, and indeed all of Canada, began here. Street disturbances and slanderous attacks in the press were the order of the day. The climax of the fractious period came in the uprising of 1837–38. In the aftermath of the rebellion, order was not fully restored and hostility remained intense, especially after the execution of twelve rebels and the exile of hundreds more.

The execution of twelve Patriotes in 1838.

During the Lower Canada Rebellion of 1837–38, the fighting took place outside Montreal, but the town, filled with both supporters and opponents of the uprising, was rife with intrigue and anxiety. The pent-up atmosphere was neatly captured by a journalist. John Richardson is remembered today for his novel *Wacousta* and its sequel, *The Canadian Brothers*, set in Upper Canada and in the United States, where the author was a prisoner during the War of 1812. Toward the end of his life, Richardson lived in Montreal, where he served as a correspondent for *The Times* of London. Richardson arrived in Montreal in early 1838, a year of unrest that led to the arrest of hundreds of people in a roundup reminiscent of the one that took place in the city more than a century later during the 1970 October Crisis. Richardson wrote about his Montreal experiences in the memoir *Eight Years in Canada*; here he describes the scene at Place d'Armes, which was in turmoil:

JOHN RICHARDSON

One of the earliest of Canada's novelists, John Richardson (1796–1852) was born in Queenston, Upper Canada, the son of a British medical officer and a mother of native ancestry. For much of his life a career soldier, from the mid-1820s he also pursued a parallel career as a writer and journalist, producing poetry, novels, memoirs, pamphlets, polemics, and at times flirting with pornography.

During his service as a gentleman volunteer in the War of 1812, Richardson was taken prisoner by the Americans during Tecumseh's last stand at Moraviantown in 1813. Tecumseh, about whom he subsequently wrote a lurid epic poem, remained a lifelong hero to Richardson, and many of his later writings reflect the violence he witnessed in forest warfare.

Richardson's peripatetic soldierly life took him to the West Indies, London, Paris, and Spain. Returning to Canada in 1838, he tried various brands of journalism in Montreal and Ontario. Arrogant, short-fused, and intemperate, he died starving and penniless in New York.

John Richardson witnessed first hand the unrest in Montreal produced by the Lower Canada Rebellion in 1838.

Opposite: *Place d'Armes in 1836. The new Notre Dame Basilica is under construction behind the original parish church.*

"It was nearly twelve o'clock, when, following the rue Bonsecours from the neighborhood of the bishop's church, I reached a corner of the rue Notre Dame, and yet there was no change in the gloom of the atmosphere. Bodies of dark forms, which were soon discovered to be regular troops, were to be seen posted at various distances along main streets, which moreover, were filled with small knots of inhabitants conversing earnestly in a low tone. Parties of volunteers were also busied in entering the houses of such French Canadians as were suspected, and securing what arms and ammunition were to be found in them.... The most imposing part of this lugubrious spectacle was in the Place d'Armes, which seemed to be the principal theatre of interest. Here their guns facing the Catholic cathedral, the *boudonnement* of the bells which had summoned the people to mass as usual and among these a number of individuals of influence and high standing in the city, whom having been included in the list of those denounced to the chief magistrate, it was intended to seize as they issued from the sacred edifice. The guns were on the ground to awe down any attempt at rescue on the part of the people.... When the service was concluded, the arrests were made, much it will be presumed, to the dismay of those who perceived their designs were discovered; and by one o'clock numerous persons, including those taken from their own residences, were lodged on that and the following day, in the gaol of Montreal."

Another decade of on-and-off unrest produced a final spasm of violence in 1849 when a riotous Tory mob, protesting a bill that would give compensation to those, including French Canadians, who had suffered losses during 1837–38, burned down the parliament building. (The Constitution Act of 1791, which joined Lower and Upper Canada, had established Montreal as the capital. The legislature was housed in the St. Ann's market building. It stood in what is today Place d'Youville.) Montreal now was considered too volatile a place to maintain a parliament, and it has never had one since.

Since the mid-nineteenth century, the church and seminary on Place d'Armes, symbols of spiritual questing, have faced on the opposite side of the square the grandiose neoclassical façade of the Bank of Montreal, whose concerns are more temporal. The bank, on the square's north side, links two sections of St. Jacques, or St. James Street as it was known during its heyday, when it contained the banks, trusts, and insurance companies that represented the financial might of a young, growing country.

St. Jacques was one of the streets laid out by Dollier de Casson in 1672, named for Jean-Jacques Olier, the founder of the Sulpician monastic order. Running along the northern wall of the town, the street was largely vacant until the mid-eighteenth century, and for a hundred years after that, it was a residential street. But as the town's population grew and moved beyond the boundaries created by the fortifications, the street took on a commercial character with some of Montreal's best stores located there. The banks and other financial institutions followed. By the 1920s, St. James, as it had become known during the period of English ascendancy, had taken on its present form, a canyon of stout stone and brick buildings. "Pile upon pile, buildings we should call skyscrapers...succeed one another," a visitor reported in the *Liverpool Daily Post*. "Each has a great banking hall on the ground floor, culminating in the finest banking hall in the world, that of the Bank of Montreal."

While it was never a match for Wall Street and has since been eclipsed by Toronto's Bay Street, nonetheless St. James "ranked uniquely high," as Hugh MacLennan writes in *Two Solitudes*.

No author writing in English represented Montreal more often or more faithfully than MacLennan and nowhere are theme and the symbolic elements of setting more deftly combined than in *Two Solitudes*, where the title as well as the story summed up Montreal's (and Canada's) fundamental duality. The novel, published in 1945, takes in the conscription crisis of World War I and ends on the eve of World War II. In it, St. James Street epitomizes the wealth and status attained by the city's anglophone élite, which had supplanted the seigneur class represented by Athanase Tallard, whose efforts to pull his village into the twentieth century fail tragically.

"There was tenacity in Saint James Street," MacLennan writes. "They knew how to keep their mouths shut and take the cash and let the credit go. They were bothered by no doubts."

These cold and remote men with their interlocking directorates are the undoing of Tallard. Just prior to his death by a heart attack, he finds himself on St. James Street. "It was a gaunt, scarred cavern, hideously cold and ugly, this street where the English made their money. How could a man like himself have hoped to be successful here?"

Writing at about the same time as MacLennan and setting his novel *Le Poids du jour* roughly contemporaneously with *Two Solitudes*, the novelist Ringuet seems to answer Tallard's question. Ringuet (1895–1960) was the pen name of Philippe Panneton, a Trois-Rivières–born doctor who spent much of his career in Montreal. In *Le Poids du jour*, the protagonist is an ambition-driven small-town boy, Michel Garneau. He embodies the sense of purpose of a class of French Canadians who prospered during the early

Philippe Panneton, writing as Ringuet, was not only a prolific author but a doctor too.

RINGUET

"I am first a doctor and then a writer," wrote Philippe Panneton in 1939. "Literature... is a distraction in my leisure time." A distinguished physician who taught in the faculty of medicine at Université de Montréal, under the pseudonym of "Ringuet," he carried on a parallel literary career which might well excite the envy of most single-track professional writers.

He produced journalism, verse, drama, and parodies. His greatest achievement, the novel *Trente arpents* (*Thirty Acres*), won the Prix de la Province de Québec, the Governor General's Award, and a prize from the Académie Française. When *Trente arpents* appeared in 1938, it was immediately acclaimed on both sides of the Atlantic as the first great French-Canadian novel and lauded as a masterpiece of literary realism.

Set firmly in the genre of the *roman de la terre québécois, Thirty Acres* recounts the story of a family over four decades, from its rural roots in the Laurentians to chosen exile in the mill towns of New England. But it was a literary tour de force precisely because it transcended the tradition in which it was grounded. Whereas previous rural novels romanticized the countryside and vilified the city, *Thirty Acres* drew a tragic portrait of a farmer beset by the forces of urbanization and technology and in conflict with a harsh and unforgiving land.

Ringuet also produced two other novels, several works of non-fiction, and a posthumously published memoir.

years of the twentieth century when the great mercantile fortunes were made in Montreal:

"He knew that his power lay in his will. For the next fifteen years he had but one object: to make his fortune, as had done so many others he knew or at the very least whose story he knew. Captains of industry, princes of Saint James Street, many of them had started out even lower than him. Ludger Constantineau, a plain messenger at the Stock Exchange twelve years ago, today ruled over the stock market. Edmour Saint-Denis, director of half a dozen companies and president of the Montreal Club, a future senator. Norman T. McDiarmid, son of a grocery clerk in Griffintown, who left school at the age of twelve to make bicycle deliveries and who, at thirty-eight, monopolized the wholesale grocery business. Alberto Marchioni, come from Italy in steerage around 1902, today a builder of ports – nearly illiterate, but five times a millionaire. And others!"

By the time Hubert Aquin wrote his groundbreaking first novel, *Prochain épisode*, in 1965, the ambitions of an earlier generation of French Canadians to conquer St. James Street on its own terms had changed. Money, and even political power within the compact that favoured the wealthy on both sides of the French-English divide, was not enough for a young urban middle class radicalized by the Quiet Revolution.

Prochain épisode, arguably the most important novel of the independence movement, is the story of a young separatist awaiting trial and writing an espionage story in the psychiatric ward of the Montreal prison where he has been detained. The plight of Aquin's narrator was in the main that of the author, who wrote the book during four months that he was under observation in a psychiatric institute while waiting for his case of alleged terrorism to come to trial (he was acquitted). The climax of the novel, which was instantly hailed a masterpiece, takes place in Place d'Armes.

"The next day, I emptied my savings account at the Toronto Dominion Bank, 500 St. James St. West. I pocketed $123 in all, enough for one week's modest living. From the telephone booth outside, opposite the Nesbitt Thompson building, I called M again, as arranged. We made a rendezvous for exactly noon-hour in the aisle of Notre-Dame Church, close to the tomb of Jean-Jacques Olier; certainly, we didn't name either

For Hubert Aquin, Old Montreal represented the weight of history.

HUBERT AQUIN

On March 15, 1977, Hubert Aquin (1929–77) – variously described as "the greatest novelist of modern Quebec," "a literary saint," "a national hero," and "the most intelligent writer in the Francophone world" – took a shotgun and, in the peaceful grounds of Villa Maria, raised it to his mouth and killed himself.

It was perhaps the only imaginable ending for the darkly brilliant artist of paradox and contradiction whose last and greatest novel, *Hamlet's Twin* (1974), begins with a quotation from Kierkegaard, "I must now both be and not be."

Aquin's extraordinary first novel, *Prochain épisode*, burst upon the literary scene in 1965 with the force of the bombs that were in those days exploding from Montreal mailboxes. Aquin had become a member of the Ralliement pour l'Indépendance Nationale five years earlier and, after announcing to the press in 1964 that he was about to join an underground terrorist movement, was arrested in possession of a gun in a stolen car. Upon pleading temporary insanity, he was transferred from jail to the Albert Prévost Psychiatric Institute for observation, where he wrote *Prochain épisode*.

The author of this disturbing, angry, and obsessed novel was a slender, quiet man with sensitive features and a demeanour difficult to reconcile with terrorism.

He grew up in the Parc Lafontaine area of Montreal and studied philosophy at the Université de Montréal. He later attended the Institut d'Études Politiques in Paris. When he returned from Paris at the age of twenty-six, he pursued a varied career as a journalist, a producer at Radio-Canada, and a scriptwriter and film director for the National Film Board. All his novels bear strong cinematographic influences: he strove to incorporate into literature the full force of visual, sound, and mythic evocation that would seem to be the preserve of film.

In 1969 he became the first francophone writer to refuse the Governor General's Award. A tortured genius who saw his life as a conscious metaphor for Quebec history, Aquin left a suicide note claiming his death to be a free and positive choice. "I have lived intensely and now it is over."

that illustrious abbey, or the ancient church whose presbytery adjoins the Montreal Stock Exchange."

As a child, Aquin had attended École Olier, a school in the Plateau Mont-Royal, named after the Sulpician cleric. The narrator of *Prochain épisode* is apprehended by the police in the church that recalls the spiritual foundations of Montreal, even as Aquin reminds us that the stock exchange is next door. Like nearly everything else in *Prochain épisode*, a novel obsessed with suicide, the associations of the arrest scene are pregnant but not explicit, and history haunts a present rife with irony. Twelve years after writing *Prochain épisode*, Aquin killed himself in the grounds of the Villa Maria school for girls in Notre Dame de Grâce. Villa Maria is itself a historic locale. Formerly known as

Place d'Armes in the nineteenth century, with the Bank of Montreal at right and St. Jacques Street at left.

Monklands, the mansion that is the school's centrepiece was the governor general's residence at the time of the 1837–38 rebellion and its aftermath. On the day the parliament was burned in 1849, the governor, Lord Elgin, had been forced to flee to Monklands, then his home in the country, after being pelted with stones and eggs by a mob in Place d'Armes. Elgin later wrote in a letter to the colonial secretary in London: "Montreal is rotten to the core, and if all Canada be like it, the sooner we have done with it, the better."

At about the same time as Aquin was enlisting Old Montreal's history in his fiction, so was an English-language writer from Toronto. Scott Symons was born in 1933 to a wealthy family of Loyalist ancestry, and, after being educated at a series of distinguished schools, he married and became curator of the Canadiana collection at the Royal Ontario Museum. He abandoned his wife and child to live in Montreal, where he wrote *Place d'Armes*, an avant-garde novel, much heralded when it was first published in 1967, but now largely forgotten. In *Place d'Armes*, the old city and and its environs are a sanctuary for Hugh Anderson, an exiled Upper Canadian WASP who explores his homosexuality while absorbing the quarter's historical resonance. While for Aquin history is part of the landscape, a ballast that weighted the surroundings with significance, for Symons, Old Montreal is a place of liberation from the strictures of conformist, Upper Canadian conventions:

> "I stumble my faith down la rue Notre Dame, blinkered, saving me again for La Place d'Armes. Past la rue Bonsecours with its church, and La Maison Papineau, and the Château Ramezay, and the Hôtel de Ville, and the Court Houses, old and new.... To La Place. And only there open my eyes, wide opened, to embrace La Place...mumbling 'I've come...I've come...look, I've come back, I promised.'"

The second half of the twentieth century saw the decline of the part of Montreal that was its centre for 250 years. From the mid-nineteenth century onward, it lost most of its residential population. As businesses moved "uptown" above the Dorchester Street escarpment, much of Old Montreal became a rundown warehouse district, thanks to the port, and it was not until the rediscovery of the area by tourists in the 1970s that a revival began. Capturing its latter-day aspect in verse, poet and journalist Mark Abley writes in "Montreal":

> *The chartered streets*
> *grow narrower towards the port. It harbours*
> *tourists now.*

Today, Old Montreal is a jumble of relics – a few houses and institutional buildings from the colonial era, nineteenth-century warehouses and shops, grand financial establishments from the city's glory days, and twentieth-century condominiums and office buildings filling in the gaps where the earlier structures have burned down or been demolished. A new residential population is settling into old buildings converted to lofts and apartments, suggesting it will again be a good address. Sometimes grey and gloomy, especially in winter, it is not the most handsome of historical districts, but like a much-mended coat, it fits the city well.

Chapter 4

THE FAUBOURGS AND THE MOVE UPTOWN

An 1820s view looking north from Haymarket Square (later Victoria Square). Although the town's walls had been recently demolished, the gate in the centre left of the picture was still standing.

AS PRIMITIVE AS Montreal appeared in the opening years of the nineteenth century, changes were afoot that would banish its backwater image. The stone fortifications of 1722, never of much use in the defence of the city, were in ruin. Their demolition began in 1801 and proceeded by fits and starts into the next decade. By then the town had already burst the boundaries demarcated by the walls. Since about the time of the Conquest, Montreal had begun to spread to the east, west, and north of the fortifications, forming "faubourgs," or sub-urbs. To the east was the Faubourg Québec, so called because it was along the road that led to the capital. To the west was Faubourg des Récollets, named for

the religious order which had owned the land where this neighbour-hood grew up. To the north was the Faubourg St. Laurent, which grew up around the road that in the nineteenth century became St. Lawrence Main Street, more recently known simply as the Main. To the northwest was a less developed neighbourhood, Faubourg St. Antoine. Later in the century other faubourgs would be added – Ste. Anne's, St. Louis, and St. Joseph.

Most of the town and almost of all its commercial activity and institutional buildings remained within the old city walls. So did the residences of the wealthier families, except for a few who moved beyond the suburbs to the lower slopes of Mount Royal, beginning the migration that led to later development of Montreal's most resplendent neighbourhood, the Golden Square Mile. Farther abroad were occasional small villages such as Lachine and Pointe Claire and farms strung out along the country roads that criss-crossed the island – the "côtes" that to this day are the main thoroughfares of the metropolis.

The faubourgs were densely built and mainly composed of wooden structures, which were inhabited by artisans and labourers, mostly the poor who could not afford the better-built stone houses of the old quarter. A vivid picture of the working-class existence in the Faubourg St. Laurent in the mid-nineteenth century is found in a seminal work of fiction, *La Terre paternelle*, by Patrice Lacombe (1807–63), a Montreal writer and accountant. Published in serial form in 1846, it recounts the story of the Chauvin family, which, through the father's greed and mismanagement, loses to the "anglais" its land in the rural Rivière des Prairies part of Montreal island. The family is forced to move to town, where father and son work as carters of water until a younger son returns from the fur trade to buy back their land. In Lacombe's novel, Montreal is the place of perdition, the punishment that comes after the fall from grace that the bucolic countryside represented. The passage below describes the Chauvins' life in town:

"The two men finished their day's work: thoroughly exhausted and chilled to the bone, they made their way back to their home in the impoverished and lonely Faubourg Saint-Laurent. Arriving in front of a

The Parting Hour, an 1832 cartoon published in London, was unflattering to emigrants.

low, miserable-looking house, the older man hastened in, leaving the younger to take care of the horse and sledge. Everything in their reduced surroundings spoke of their misery. In one corner, a straw mattress with patched-up bedspread; on the other side of the room, a crude pallet, some chairs with the stuffing gone, a little wobbly table, an old trunk, some tin utensils hanging from a mantel – this was all the furniture. The door and the windows were badly sealed, letting the wind and snow steal in. A little iron stove in which a few sticks burned barely heated the single room that made up this house, which had not even the luxury of a chimney: the stovepipe went right up through the ceiling and roof.

"Near the stove, a woman was on her knees. Poverty and bitterness had added to her years. Two deep furrows on her cheeks marked the track of many tears. Near her, pale and suffering in appearance, could easily be recognized a woman who was her daughter, preparing a few scraps for her father and brother who had just arrived."

An 1838 view looking north from the Faubourg St. Laurent, or St. Lawrence suburb.

In the early nineteenth century, Montreal's infrastructure, despite some improvements, failed to keep up with its burgeoning population. Street lighting was introduced with lamps being fuelled with whale oil and, later, kerosene. An early police force was created when men equipped with batons were hired to light the lamps and patrol the streets. A harbour commission began rebuilding the riverfront. Some of the wharves and stone embankments of today date from the time of the commission. The first aqueduct was built. Until then, the town's drinking water came from wells or the St. Lawrence, both sources prone to pollution. And the fetid streams that flowed on the edge of the old town were covered over. But crowded and unsanitary conditions remained, especially in the faubourgs, and given the primitive state of medical practice, death by disease was never far off. Before mid-century the infant mortality rate was one baby in four.

In 1832, a cholera epidemic broke out, the disease having been carried to the city by newly arrived immigrants. With political tensions already high, the population was set further on edge as the Patriote faction accused Britain of "vomiting" its sick immigrants on Canada. Two thousand people died in the 1832 epidemic, which was followed by smaller ones in 1834 and 1854. The worst outbreak of disease was to come in 1847 with a typhus epidemic, which claimed the lives of 20,000 immigrants throughout Canada, most of whom were incoming Irish.

Two sisters who passed through Montreal at different times during the 1832 epidemic have left their impressions of the fever-afflicted town. Catharine Parr Traill and Susanna Moodie were on the way to join husbands on farms in Upper Canada. Moodie's *Roughing It in the Bush* and Traill's *The Backwoods of Canada* are classics of pioneer literature. In Montreal, both women noted the filthy conditions of the streets and the miasmic stench issuing from the open sewers. Traill writes:

> "We were struck by the dirty, narrow, ill-paved or unpaved streets of the suburbs, and overpowered by the noisome vapour arising from a deep open fosse that ran along the street from the wharf. This ditch seemed the receptacle for every abomination, and sufficient in itself to infect a whole town with malignant fevers.
>
> "I was greatly disappointed in the first acquaintance with the interior of Montreal.... I could compare it only to the fruits of the Dead Sea, which are said to be fair and tempting to look upon, but yield only ashes and bitterness when tasted by the thirsty traveller."

Catharine Parr Traill was appalled by the poor sanitary conditions in Montreal when she passed through the town in 1832.

Rebellion, social unrest, disease, primitive living conditions – given all that had happened, the city's prospects at mid-century might have seemed bleak to some. Nothing could be farther from the truth. As if by some sort of unspoken but mutual consent among hostile factions, the political trouble faded, helped along by the prosperity brought by such innovations as steam power and the railways.

The *Accommodation*, Canada's first steamship, built for the brewer John Molson, was launched in 1809. It made its maiden voyage from Montreal to Quebec in an astonishing sixty-six hours. Everyone rejoiced at the prospect of a new era in transportation, but few realized that the steamship was the beginning of Canada's industrial revolution. The next step came with the construction of the Lachine Canal in the 1820s. The waterway finally conquered the rapids that had hindered travel and transportation into the interior of the continent since Cartier's time. Montreal would remain a place where lake boats transferred their cargoes to ocean-going ships, but henceforth the volume of traffic would be vastly increased, making the city one of the great inland ports of North America. The canal spurred the development of industry along its banks, and the industrialization was further stimulated by another technological advance – the railway. The earliest in Canada, built in 1836, was the Champlain and St. Lawrence railroad, joining Saint-Jean, Quebec, with La Prairie, the terminus used to connect the South Shore with Montreal. Within a few years another line followed the canal and was eventually extended to Toronto. One more essential ingredient remained to be added before the city's destiny was set. There was as yet no bridge across the St. Lawrence from the South Shore. When that engineering feat was accomplished in 1859, the consolidation of rail, canal, and steamship technology positioned the city for a great leap forward.

The population was growing at a faster rate than it had at any time in its previous two hundred years. The form and styles of British cities were superimposed on a French town, but everyone was proud of sophisticated new buildings, including the Bonsecours Market, the Customs House, and the Bank of Montreal on Place d'Armes. Also admired were two huge new Gothic churches, Notre Dame on Place d'Armes, and St. Patrick's, mother church of the city's growing Irish community. The latter, completed in 1847, was built above de la Gauchetière Street in the St. Antoine suburb, indicating that the old city was no longer the only section with important buildings in it.

With the fortifications gone, there was no distinct boundary between the

An 1830s view of the new and improved harbour.

old town and the adjacent neighbourhoods. Nonetheless, as in other industrializing cities in the nineteenth century, Montrealers were being separated by class, language, and ethnicity. The English-speaking population generally favoured the western side of town in the St. Antoine and Récollets districts, while francophones settled on the east side. Wealthy anglophones took to mansions on the lower slopes of Mount Royal. The francophone élite settled the area around the lower part of today's St. Denis Street, and later the eastern portion of Sherbrooke Street.

Two of the city's great squares began to take shape. Viger Square, at the southeastern edge of the old city, was celebrated as one of the most beautiful spots in the city, and Victoria Square, created from a hay market on the western side of town, became the first important business district outside the cramped confines of the old city. New neighbourhoods developed in the city's present downtown. At first this area was primarily residential, but as the century progressed, merchants, continuing the flight from Old Montreal and the environs of Victoria Square, began setting up on Ste. Catherine, in what was described as "the move uptown."

Opposite: *This Faubourg St. Laurent house was on its last legs when it was photographed in early 1920s. The Royal Bank Building on St. Jacques Street is under construction in the background.*

The rapid change provoked dismay as well as admiration. In a refrain heard since Dollier's era, some lamented the end of simpler times: "The expansion of our city is mostly toward the western side of the mountain," noted an article in an 1845 edition of the newspaper *La Revue canadienne*. "The fine country properties have not been spared by the recent building craze. An orchard, to the eyes of the owner, is good for nothing but building lots.... The most respectable and oldest families have given up, and are giving up, every year, the patrimony of their fathers...to the encroachments of progress."

Montreal at mid-century was thriving, poised to become a major metropolitan centre. As the old gave way to the new, another visiting military man, Lieutenant-Colonel B.W.A. Sleigh, in 1846 provided a colourful sketch of a city with one foot in the past and another in the future:

"At seven o'clock we approached Montreal, which stood out boldly in the distance, presenting one mass of glittering steeples, domes and massive stone wharves, fully a mile in extent, and the most costly and substantial in North America. Shipping of every size and nation, crowds of steamers, American and English, bateaux, canoes, timber rafts, schooners in full sail, all covered the surface of the river; and the city with its dark stone buildings and iron shutters, gave an impression of ancient grandeur; while towards the west rose the Mountain, above six hundred feet high, along whose base, and upward, were charming houses and villa residences of the gentry.

"Indeed, in Montreal you cannot fancy you are in America; everything about it conveys the idea of a substantial, handsomely built European town, with modern improvements of half English, half French architecture, and a mixed population of the two races. The habitants' strange dress, with their grey cloth capots, with the scarlet sash tied round the waist, and *bonnet bleu*, with Indian moccasins, tastefully worked in beads of various colours, is certainly foreign. The Canadian women look very pretty, with the mantelet of grey-coloured cloth, stuff petticoat, and head-dress – mob or Normandy caps; and their feet, which are very small, look so saucy in those elegant little moccasins.

"There are also to be seen stalking about numbers of Indians, with their squaws, their children tied to their backs in wooden cases, almost invariably sucking a piece of pork fat, tied with a string to avert the chance of suffocation. Canadian voyagers formed another motley group,

with their half-Indian dresses, bronzed faces and flaringly striped cotton shirts. Hunters, from the Hudson's Bay Company's regions, come in with peltries, to return with provisions for some distant fort. Then there is your regular Yankee 'b'hoy,' belonging to the river steamers, or on tours of trade with the natives. Throw into this crowd an odd monk, in his sombre vestments, a lady of charity, hidden by a veil from vulgar gaze, swiftly proceeding with head bended, on a tour of mercy or kindly mission, and Highland soldiers in the kilt, infantry soldiers with the Prince Albert chacos, artillerymen, sappers and miners, rifles, officers, aides-de-camp, gold-lace, cocked-hats and feathers, and you have a fair description of the motley masses, who every day swarm the streets of Montreal."

Still, there were reminders of the bad old days. The city suffered several more huge fires, one, in 1852, proving to be the largest in its history. It consumed 1,200 buildings in the east and southeast districts and left one-fifth of the population homeless. But such events, astonishing in their magnitude when seen from the present, were only temporary setbacks during a period in which Montreal's expansion was unstoppable.

The crowning achievement of the era was the completion, in 1859, of the Victoria Bridge. It was heralded as an engineering feat equal to any in the world, and when the Prince of Wales, the future King Edward VII, inaugurated the bridge the following year, to many it seemed the city was becoming, in the over-worked terminology of a later day, world class. Like many construction projects, it was not an immediate financial success, prompting one visitor, the novelist Anthony Trollope, to muse: "There are schemes which seem to be too big for men to work out with any ordinary regard to profit and loss." (A future mayor, Jean Drapeau, might well have heeded Trollope's remark as he set about building the Olympic Stadium.)

With Montreal's coming of age, a steady trickle of writers passed through, variously on lecture tours, for business, or tourism. The young Charles Dickens arrived in 1842 as part of a North American tour from which he hoped to draw material for a book. He rather cryptically described Montreal as a "heart burning town," but by all accounts enjoyed his stay. Although his best work lay ahead of him, Dickens was already a star, as was noted by *The Gazette*, which recorded that he was staying at Rasco's Hotel, a building still standing on St. Paul Street near the Bonsecours Market.

A young Charles Dickens visited Montreal in 1842.

"Montreal Market: Habitans [sic] Purchasing Cloth," a drawing that appeared in The London Illustrated News, *published in 1859, is in keeping with B.W.A. Sleigh's 1846 description of Montreal.*

Dickens was persuaded to appear in a play mounted by officers of the Montreal garrison – the tradition of soldiers staging theatrical performances in Montreal extended back almost as long as the British army had been in the city. Dickens was both stage manager and actor for the performance and acquitted himself handsomely in both roles. "This was THE performance of the evening, and was most admirably acted," a critic wrote. In a letter written from Rasco's, Dickens says, "We have experienced impossible-to-be-described attentions in Canada. Everybody's carriage and horses are at our disposal, and everybody's servants; and all the government boats and boats' crews."

Some visitors were struck by the extent to which the city had become stratified by class and partitioned by language. Captain Horton Rhys, yet another British officer and an actor travelling with an amateur troupe in 1861, detected the split personality: "The principal hotels, of which there are but two, are enormous edifices, the others mere pot-houses. The principal streets, of which there are but two, are wide and handsome, the rest mere lanes. The people, of whom there are but two, the rich holding high estate, the poor, holding nothing. There is nothing *middling* in Montreal. One of the said two people, the high, are dissatisfied that they can't be higher; the other, the low, are striving to be lower; and it is probable that half a century will see them attain their object."

The captain's words are strikingly similar to those of two writers who collaborated on a sketch of the city for the book *Picturesque Canada*, published in 1882. Edited by Dr. George Monro Grant, principal of Queen's University in Kingston, the book is a description of Canadian places, rural and urban. Montreal contributors were A.J. Bray, a minister of Zion Congregational Church and editor of *The Canadian Spectator*, and Jean Talon Lespérance, journalist and editor of *The Canadian Illustrated News* and of *The Dominion Illustrated News*.

"Montreal abounds with striking contrasts," they write. "It has had only one or two hundred years of history; and yet everything is here – the antique and the modern – while hostile oddities lie cheek-by-jowl on every hand. Here are frame houses, some of them scarcely better than an Irishman's hovel on his native bog, and ignorance and squalor and dirt; close at hand are great streets of great houses, all of fine-cut stone. Here are thousands of French who cannot speak one word of English, and thousands of English who cannot speak one word of French. Unthrift and thrift come along the same thorough-fares. Some are content with a bare existence and some are not content with colossal fortunes."

The writers identified the divisions as chiefly stemming from ethnicity: "There is no fusion of races in commercial, social or political life; the differences are sharply defined, and appear to be permanent.... It is easy to trace the two main divisions of the population of Montreal. Taking St. Lawrence Main Street as a dividing line, all that is east of it is French, and all that is west of it is English-speaking." By century's end, it had become an over-simplification to say the east side of the Main was French and the west English. Central and East European immigrants began to fill up the area that would become known as the Plateau Mont-Royal, east of the Main, while traditionally francophone villages, like Côte des Neiges, on the west side, were being swallowed up by the expanding city. Nonetheless, the idea of a city divided down the middle persisted, and only in the past few decades has the mixing of French, English, and other populations become so extensive as to render the notion anachronistic.

It took an outsider, in 1889, to provide the most penetrating analysis of the city's character with regard to its linguistic and cultural makeup. C.H. Farnham, a journalist for the *Harper's New Monthly Magazine*, wrote:

> "Montreal is a striking exception to the text that a house divided against itself cannot stand. Its divisions are so fundamental and persistent that they have not diminished one iota in a century, but rather increased. The two irreconcilable elements are Romanism and Protestantism; the armies are of French and English blood. The outlook for peace is well nigh hopeless, with two systems of education producing fundamental differences of character, and nourishing religious intolerance, race antipathy, social division, political antagonism and commercial separation.
>
> "Nevertheless, this city of disunion flourishes as the green bay-tree, with a steady if not amazing growth, which is due chiefly to the separate, not the united, efforts of the races."

Farnham accurately depicted what he saw, and, like many Americans since, concluded the arrangement should not work – hence his notion that peace was unlikely. But he failed to detect the essential difference between the society he came from and the one he was observing. During the time of troubles in the first half of the nineteenth century, the folly of confrontation had been made clear. As prosperity beckoned at mid-century, strife was a drag on everyone's well-being. But how were the antagonisms, once kindled, to be dampened? In the answer to this question lay not only an accounting for the kind of city that Farnham and others described, but also, by extension, the way in which Quebec came to operate vis-à-vis Canada. The solution was a kind of benign, voluntary apartheid. Each community developed its own institutions: separate school systems, hospitals, and cultural institutions operated side by side with a minimum of contact. The élites might keep lines of communication open in certain public forums – the charity ball, a royal visit – and in the political arena, as would the working classes on the athletic fields, but essentially the two solitudes were entrenched. It was an arrangement that was based on the common desire of each community to get ahead. It was the great Canadian compromise, and it would endure for a century until the Quiet Revolution demanded a new status quo.

While observers like Farnham managed a certain detachment in their assessment of the city's distinctiveness, others found it stirred their native prejudices. H. de Lamothe, a worthy republican from Paris, admired some of what he saw in Montreal in 1880, but concluded that a bicultural city was detrimental to the advances French culture had to offer. He was particularly put out by Victorian (or in his words, "Puritan") customs. "In Montreal," he writes, "Sunday is a middling term, a sort of compromise between the Puritan 'Sabbath' of New England and the day of recreation enjoyed by the French worker and peasant. As in New England, the trains stop, the telegraph office is closed; the Protestant districts take on the air of a necropolis; the bar rooms, even, hypocritically lock up their fronts while a secret door is discreetly left ajar under the policeman's nose to accommodate a clutch of needy drinkers. Fortunately, the French Canadians – though the habits of their neighbours have infected them somewhat – as yet don't feel obligated to stay indoors pretending to commune with Ezekiel and Jeremiah."

It was an era when religion and the mores that attended it were pervasive, in Montreal, with its many ethnic groups, maybe more so than elsewhere. Churches of all denominations as well as other religious institutions – convents, orphanages, asylums, schools, etc. – flourished everywhere, and prompted one of the most quoted remarks about the city, made by Mark Twain during an 1881 speaking engagement: "This is the first time I was ever in a city where you couldn't throw a brick without breaking a church window." Less known but more fulsome were the words of Harriet Beecher Stowe, the author of the anti-slavery classic *Uncle Tom's Cabin*: "Montreal is a mountain of churches," she wrote in 1869. "Every shade and form of faith is here in wood or stone, and the gospel feast set forth in every form and shape to suit the spiritual appetite of all inquirers."

Not only in religion was Montreal becoming a city of some sophistication. A lively theatre scene operated in both languages, bringing international celebrities such as Sarah Bernhardt to town. The Art Association, the forerunner of the Montreal Museum of Fine Arts, was founded in 1858. There were various athletic clubs, and a series of winter carnivals began in 1880s. ("By next year, we expect that the Czar will have adopted our plan as the sovereign cure for Nihilism," a reporter wrote of the success of the 1883 carnival.)

For a proper English gentleman, however, the city still lacked refinement and exhibited entirely too much vice. After staying in 1865 at St. Lawrence Hall, one of the two big hotels of Captain Rhys's quip, Englishman George Tuthill Borrett wrote: "You must not mind smoke, for you will be smothered

Samuel Butler ridiculed the provincialism he found in Montreal.

with it; you must learn to tolerate chewing, or you will get bilious; you must be indifferent to spitting, or you will die of nausea."

Such cultural influences as might penetrate came mostly from abroad, and the English-speaking community was particularly ready to ape the old country in matters of taste. The philistinism of the colonials must sooner or later come under scrutiny. It fell to the novelist and poet Samuel Butler to take note following an 1875 visit.

We hesitate to dust off yet again the story of the Discobolus, grown hoary in the retelling, but not to do so would be an oversight, since it perfectly represents the contradictory impulses the upwardly mobile faced between cultural aspiration and moral constraint. That it was a failing business venture in which Butler had invested heavily that brought the author of *The Way of All Flesh* to Montreal probably contributed to his splenetic assessment of the city. While prowling the streets, Butler discovered a copy of a Greek statue of a discus-thrower – the Discobolus – in a neglected corner of the Montreal Natural History Society. A taxidermist working in the building at the time told him the figure was stowed away because, in its nudity, it was considered too vulgar to be openly displayed. The encounter prompted Butler's satiric jab "A Psalm of Montreal."

Stowed away in a Montreal lumber room
The Discobolus standeth and turneth his face to the wall;
Dusty, cobweb-covered, maimed and set at naught,
Beauty crieth in an attic and no man regardeth:
    O God! O Montreal!

Quoting the taxidermist, Butler continues:

"The Discobolus is put here because he is vulgar –
He has neither vest nor pants with which to cover his limbs;
I, Sir, am a person of most respectable connections –
My brother-in-law is haberdasher to Mr. Spurgeon."

We can only imagine the mortification in Montreal when word of the poem, published in 1878 in London, reached the city. The Natural History Society rose to the hapless taxidermist's defence, calling Butler the Heathen Londonee. Butler's poem put Montreal on the map in a rather unflattering way and made a celebrity of the Discobolus. More than thirty years later, in 1913, when the English writer Rupert Brooke was in the city, he made a point of going to see the statue, at the time residing at the Art Association of Montreal gallery. "I have to report that the Discobolus is very well, and, nowadays, looks the whole world in the face, almost quite unabashed," Brooke said.

Montreal writers, too, had begun to discover their hometown as a useful setting. From the time of Patrice Lacombe and Rosanna Leprohon, novels began to appear, serialized in the popular press. Among them are no less than three titled *Les Mystères de Montréal*. Inspired by the same source, there was a fourth book, in English, called *The Mysteries of Montreal*. The explanation for the copy-cat titles lies in the novel *Les Mystères de Paris*, by the French writer Eugène Sue, an immensely popular work of fiction that portrayed the underworld of the French capital.

Appearing between 1855 and 1893, the three Quebec *Mystères* were potboiling adventure-romances designed to bolster newspaper sales. Of the three, the one by Montreal journalist Hector Berthelot is more literarily advanced and, with its string of low-life characters and street language, reflected the dynamism (and the social problems) of the city in the later nineteenth century.

Its opening scene takes place in Viger Square and gives some of the insouciant flavour of the book. The short, choppy paragraphs reflect the newspaper format in which the book first appeared, but also indicated that this was a new kind of fiction, a departure from the wordy, moralizing works that ruled the day:

"It was 1879.

"May had strewn flowers and greenery all over Place Viger in Montreal.

"The breeze was mild, the park filled with confused squawking and chirping of sparrows.

"The grass was up, green and thick; the daisies and blue bells were blooming, one by one, amid the poison ivy and the Queen Anne's lace.

"The fountains babbled in their basins, and all of nature seemed to intone a hymn praising the heavens.

"A young woman could be found in this Eden, sitting on a bench in the shade of a sycamore tree.

A view of Viger Square from about the time of Hector Berthelot's Mystères de Montréal.

"She was tall, willowy, with well-formed shoulders and thighs, her face pale, suggesting frailty, even though her sturdy arms were outlined by a clingy dress set off by a 'pull-back' in black silk, which fortunately countered her wan expression.

"The sun was at its zenith, the park becoming unbearable in the scorching heat.

"Great droplets of sweat appeared on the alabaster forehead of the girl. She drew from a satchel an issue of *Nouveau-Monde* and began using it as a fan. Suddenly, a steam engine's raucous whistle sounded just as the clock at St. Jacques Church spire began sounding the Angelus."

The unlikely appearance of poison ivy and weeds amid the flowers in the city's most elegant square, like the coinciding blast of the steam engine and the melodious chiming from the church, sets the tone for a series of contrasts that run through Berthelot's novel – between refinement and coarseness, the doings of high and low society, and comedy and tragedy.

Ursule, a young working-class woman, waits in the park for a rendezvous with her admirer Benoui, who works in a shoe repair shop. Benoui is unhappy because he has heard that Ursule has been seen in the company of a carriage driver touring around Saint-Jean-Baptiste village. (In 1879, the village, in the area of present-day Rachel and St. Denis Streets, was still on the edge of town.)

Berthelot's work is topical and loaded with geographical references to the city his readers lived in. Ursule returns to her home on Dorchester Street in the city's east end, where the reason for her sweats in the Viger garden soon becomes clear. She has contracted smallpox, at the time a predator sweeping through the city's poor neighbourhoods. Benoui's rival, the carriage driver Cléophas, lives in a boarding house on Sanguinet Street. At the other end of the social spectrum, the Count de Bouctouche and his family live in a bourgeois neighbourhood, on St. Denis Street near the "carré Saint-Louis." These locations, representing the spectrum of French-Canadian society, are all within about a couple of kilometres or so of one another and reflected the still-compact size of the city.

Meanwhile, the English entry into the mysteries is by Charlotte Führer, a German-born immigrant who arrived in the city in 1859. Her *Mysteries of Montreal: Being Recollections of a Female Physician* (1881) is based on her experience as a midwife, an occupation that provided plenty of material for behind-the-curtains peeks at the sexual habits of Victorian anglophone society. Führer constructs a series of morality tales with such chapter titles as "A Blighted Life," "A Wolf in Sheep's Clothing," and "The Frail Shop Girl."

"A Disciple of Satan," the story of a young widow's fall from grace, is typical. After the woman's garrison-officer husband is killed in a sleigh accident

Bertholet's themes were taken from the day's headlines. A cover from an 1875 Canadian Illustrated News *bears the caption "Montreal's Night-Mayor on His Nightly Rounds (Dedicated to the Board of Health)." The magazine was reporting on the continuing struggle against infectious diseases.*

while crossing the St. Lawrence, she marries an elderly farmer whom she does not love. She meets the narrator-author whom she visits for a "lying in." The child born is not her husband's, but that of a young man in whose family she served as governess. She manages to quell the scandal only to embark on another series of misadventures with several other men. The story ends with the woman drowning in a ferry boat accident while crossing Lake St. Louis with a Russian nobleman with whom she is running away to escape her most recent husband.

En route to her anti-heroine's destruction, Führer provides a postcard-pretty view from Mount Royal that stands in contrast to Berthelot's coarser (and wittier) rendering of Viger Square:

> "After about twenty minutes climbing they arrived at the 'view point' immediately over Sir Hugh Allan's residence.... At their feet lay the beautiful city, the rows of shade trees, clothed with verdure, lending a gorgeous setting to the elegant limestone buildings. In front rolled the mighty Saint Lawrence, nearly two miles wide, the vast expanse being relieved by St. Helen's Island, with its luxuriant foliage. On the right the Victoria Bridge, that monument of engineering skill, stretched across the mighty river towards the picturesque village of St. Lambert; while further westward might be seen Nuns' Island with its shady groves, at the head of which rushed the boiling waters of the famous rapids of Lachine."

Führer's romanticized morality lessons take in the city from above and represent the aspirations of a newcomer trying to fit in to the city's tightly knit English-speaking society. Berthelot's social realism offers a closer-to-the-streets view of Montreal. Both writers depict a city still intimate in scale. That version of Montreal was about to change.

Chapter 5
STREETS OF DREAMS

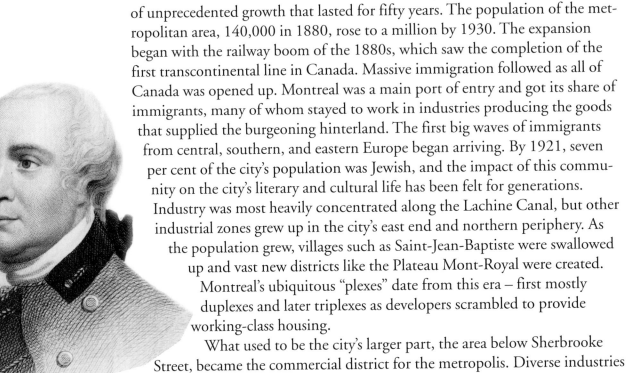

Guy Carleton, Lord Dorchester, was sympathetic to French-Canadian aspirations, but he also represented the conquerors.

In the final decades of the nineteenth century, Montreal entered a period of unprecedented growth that lasted for fifty years. The population of the metropolitan area, 140,000 in 1880, rose to a million by 1930. The expansion began with the railway boom of the 1880s, which saw the completion of the first transcontinental line in Canada. Massive immigration followed as all of Canada was opened up. Montreal was a main port of entry and got its share of immigrants, many of whom stayed to work in industries producing the goods that supplied the burgeoning hinterland. The first big waves of immigrants from central, southern, and eastern Europe began arriving. By 1921, seven per cent of the city's population was Jewish, and the impact of this community on the city's literary and cultural life has been felt for generations. Industry was most heavily concentrated along the Lachine Canal, but other industrial zones grew up in the city's east end and northern periphery. As the population grew, villages such as Saint-Jean-Baptiste were swallowed up and vast new districts like the Plateau Mont-Royal were created.

Montreal's ubiquitous "plexes" date from this era – first mostly duplexes and later triplexes as developers scrambled to provide working-class housing.

What used to be the city's larger part, the area below Sherbrooke Street, became the commercial district for the metropolis. Diverse industries and businesses congregated in various parts of the central city – the garment industry along the Main, financial services on St. James Street, and shopping on Ste. Catherine. With the gathering clouds of World War I on the horizon, the economic boom came to an end in 1913, but resumed during the 1920s. In these latter years of the great expansion, the first skyscrapers made their appearance in the new downtown.

The downtown area can be defined as extending from St. Antoine Street on the south to the foot of the mountain on the north, and from Atwater

Avenue on the west to about Berri Street in the east. The twentieth-century image of the city can be discerned by following the development of the three great east-west streets that run through the area: Dorchester/René Lévesque, Ste. Catherine, and Sherbrooke.

Dorchester is the oldest of these streets, extending along the edge of the escarpment that is the first step up toward Mount Royal. The street was named after Guy Carleton, first Baron Dorchester, who was twice governor of Quebec in the eighteenth century, once as military ruler shortly after the Conquest. Carleton was sympathetic to the concerns of French Canadians, and he played a strong role in the formulation of the Quebec Act in 1774, which guaranteed their rights. But he was, after all, the embodiment of the conqueror nation, and so perhaps his name was the most dispensable when in 1987 it was decided to name a major thoroughfare for the beloved and recently deceased Quebec premier, René Lévesque.

Dorchester was originally a narrow residential street, in its west and central part lined with houses and churches of the anglophone bourgeoisie, while east of the Main it ran through a more working-class French-Canadian district. Its

A bird's-eye view of Montreal in 1889, near the beginning of the city's transformation into a metropolis.

residential character was not to last long. In the burgeoning years of the later nineteenth and early twentieth centuries, the central part of Dorchester became the most desirable real estate in the city, thanks to the railways. The Canadian Pacific Railway established its grand Windsor Station just south of the street and the equally monumental Windsor Hotel on the north side of Dorchester. The street bisected an old burying ground, which, after the Catholic and Protestant cemeteries were moved to the back of Mount Royal, became Dominion Square. By the turn of the century, the square had become the new heart of the city, displacing Place d'Armes in that role. The Sun Life Building, built in stages between 1913 and 1927, became the signature structure on Dominion Square and had the distinction of being the largest office building in the British Empire.

Real estate speculation reached its most fevered pitch in the years leading up to World War I as the Grand Trunk, Canadian Pacific, and Canadian Northern railways waged a war to gain access to the city centre. Although Canadian Pacific was the eventual winner, Canadian Northern, a forerunner of Canadian National, also had a tremendous impact as it boldly bought up large tracts of land northwest of Mount Royal and tunnelled under the mountain in preparation for building a huge station and office complex. The 1913 real estate bust and the onset of World War I ended the dreams of the Canadian Northern's magnates. The downtown entrance to the tunnel was left an open ditch, an unsightly gash on both sides of Dorchester that lasted until mid-century. Place Ville Marie, the Queen Elizabeth Hotel, and several of the other large office towers were finally put in place in the early 1960s, consolidating the area around the Dominion Square as the present-day city's centre.

Most of the imposing homes were demolished during downtown development and the widening of the street into a boulevard in the 1950s, but a particularly fine example remains at Fort Street in Shaughnessy House, home of the former railway magnate, Baron Thomas Shaughnessy. Today it is the centrepiece of the Canadian Centre for Architecture.

The Winnipeg-born poet Miriam Waddington captures the flavour of the street in a 1966 poem. Commemorating the end of a love affair, she sets the scene in lyrical and painterly words:

> *At the end of the street is buff-coloured fog,*
> *the red rubies of traffic lights hang*
> *in smoky overtones while emeralds shine*
> *against the dark licked pavement.*

A fine description of the downtown segment with its present-day landmarks is found in Roger Fournier's novel, *Moi, mon corps, mon âme, Montréal, etc.* Lucie, the narrator, marches to work along Dorchester on a June morning in 1970, in a mood of ecstatic elation, having recently given birth.

"We're all going to work!... We're all going to build!... I belong to this sidewalk I'm trampling between Peel and University. I belong to the old Windsor Hotel, to the Queen Elizabeth Hotel, to the big modern buildings like the Canadian Imperial Bank of Commerce…. Even that frightful Mary Queen of Angels Cathedral, under which I walk, makes me happy to look at it because it's part of my world. Those thousands of windows in Place Ville Marie reflect the sun back to the sky and everything explodes with light."

When Yves Beauchemin began writing his best-selling novel *Juliette* in the early 1980s, Dorchester had not yet become René Lévesque Boulevard.

The west end of Dorchester Street was lined with mansions at the turn of the century.

Beauchemin situated the house in which his vastly proportioned heroine, Juliette, was brought up on the corner of Dorchester and Lambert Closse near the Montreal Children's Hospital. By the time he completed the novel some eight years later, the premier had died and the street was renamed after him. Beauchemin has joked that, with the use of the word processor, the extensive revision required in changing the street name in his manuscript was achieved with one simple key stroke.

Beauchemin's description of the magnificent heritage property that was Juliette's childhood home in the 1930s bears the hallmark of his precise, documentary style:

"The former residence of Joséphine Deslauriers, a magnificent two-storey red-brick house built in 1887 by Télesphore Latourelle, stood at the corner of boulevard René Lévesque and rue Lambert Closse. The cornices and stringcourse, the window arches, sills, and piers, were of worked granite, while vermiculated embossing emphasized the building's outer corners.

The main entrance was surmounted by a full semicircular arch with a decorative lion's head in the middle, and flanked by splendid pink sandstone columns embedded in the façade. The house had twenty-two rooms, those on the top floor with sloping ceilings, but spacious and bright."

A later passage from the same book sets out a René Lévesque Boulevard of proliferating skyscrapers at afternoon rush hour – "a huge windswept canyon filled with carbon dioxide" – but where, toward the western extremity of the street, restoration and gentrification are at hand. "Dead trees, or those cut down when the boulevard was widened in the early fifties, were being replaced. But dozens of hideous structures, or vacant lots strewn with debris half-hidden by snow, showed that in many places, help had come too late."

Like Dorchester, Ste. Catherine began as a residential street early in the nineteenth century, but the origins of its name are obscure. It may have started out as Ste. Catherine's Road, leading to the convent of the Sisters of the Congregation of Notre Dame. It's also possible that it honours the memory of a Frenchwoman, Catherine de Bourbonnais (1749–1805), who lived on the road in the eighteenth century. Or perhaps Jacques Viger, inspector of roads and subsequently first mayor of Montreal, named it after one of his daughters.

YVES BEAUCHEMIN

Born in Noranda in 1941, Yves Beauchemin grew up in the northern Quebec logging community of Clova. He was a voracious reader from early childhood, and some critics have found seeds of the raciness and episodic quality of his novels in his early love of American comics such as *Archie* and *Batman*. More commonly, however, his sprawling and densely written works are compared to nineteenth-century greats, such as Dickens, Balzac, and Zola.

Beauchemin began to write in his teens while attending classical college in Joliette. His arrival in Montreal in 1962 to attend university had a profound effect on him. "A great city is an inexhaustible subject," he has said, and Montreal and its suburbs spring to vivid life in novels such as *The Alley Cat* (1981), *Juliette* (1989), and *The Second Fiddle* (1996).

Montreal was also the crucible of his political awakening. Confronted in the early 1960s by unilingual English signs and a French-language majority, Beauchemin became a committed and vocal *indépendantiste*. (His brilliant analogy of Quebec as a cube of sugar next to a gallon of coffee has been widely quoted.)

Beauchemin is one of Quebec's most celebrated novelists. His two blockbusters, *The Alley Cat* and *Juliette*, were respectively the best- and third best-selling Quebec books of the 1980s. (*The Alley Cat* has sold over a million copies in fifteen languages.) His immense popularity can be traced to his marvellously inventive plots and highly original characters, who are defined through their actions, not their psyches, and who are frequently drawn from life.

Mrs. Lovell, wife of the John Lovell who created the city directories bearing his name, has left this description of a bucolic Ste. Catherine, dated 1837:

"There were gardens and fields throughout what is now the city. My aunt's garden was on the east side of the Main Street (Saint-Laurent Boulevard), near Sainte-Catherine. There the delicious Fameuse apple was in perfection, also the Bourassa, and Pommes Grises, apples that kept throughout the winter. A friend's garden was situated on Mountain Street below Sainte-Catherine. Grapes were cultivated, and there were luscious strawberries. Our greengage plums and egg plums were far superior to those from California, for they had a richer flavour, when picked off the trees."

For most of the nineteenth century the street was crowded with greystone dwellings and houses of worship within walking distance of the residents. The Anglican Christ Church Cathedral and St. James United Church in the heart of present-day downtown are among a handful of surviving examples.

Ste. Catherine became the city's consumer emporium in the 1890s with the establishment of the Henry Birks jewellery shop and Henry Morgan's (now the Bay) department store facing Phillips Square. Eastward and westward, stores replaced houses on the street as it rapidly turned into the major shopping and entertainment strip that it remains today. A 1921 visitor to the city reported in *The Gazette*: "Soon I was lost in St. Catherine Street, and after excursions into many stores and 'movies,' the first impression I received was of your interiors as compared with exteriors. The Capitol and Allen theatres – who would think that such inconsequent entrances were but the prelude to such splendours as they are? In England I have not seen such splendid 'cinemas.'"

As the effervescent 1920s gave way to the Depression, a grimmer view of the street appeared. The St. Henri pharmacist Émile Coderre (1893–1970), who wrote under the pseudonym Jean Narrache ("j'en arrache" translates as "I have a hard time making ends meet"), begins his Depression-era poem "Soir d'hiver dans la rue Ste-Catherine":

Evenin' on Ste. Cath'rine
Ev'ryone shufflin' along, mutt'rin'
As they bump into themselves in the windows
Standin' foot-deep in choc'lit snow.

Hugh MacLennan, summoning memories of the Depression in the 1959 novel *The Watch That Ends the Night*, writes: "Never before was Montreal as it was in the Thirties and it will never be like that again." MacLennan's narrator, George Stewart, is far from rich, but nevertheless has a job and feels guilt-ridden as he witnesses the suffering of those who don't. "The unemployed used to flow in two rivers along St. Catherine Street, and I used to see eddies of them stopping in front of shop windows to stare at the goods they could not buy." There was plenty of hunger, too: "There was a restaurant that used to roast chickens in its windows over electrically-operated spits, and there were always slavering men outside staring at the crinkling skin of the chickens and the sputtering fat."

The longing unleashed by the unobtainable goods behind the street's plate glass façades is also evoked in Gabrielle Roy's *The Tin Flute*. Roy depicts a Saturday night scene, in the imagination of the impoverished but hungrily ambitious

The down-and-outers MacLennan saw in the 1930s and Leonard Cohen in the '60s are no less prevalent today.

St. Henri waitress, Florentine Lacasse. To Florentine, even in wartime Ste. Catherine Street represents the epitome of her dreams and of worldly sophistication, "the department store windows, the elegant Saturday night crowd, the florists' displays, the restaurants with their revolving doors and tables set almost on the sidewalk behind gleaming bay windows, the brightly lit movie theatres.... Everything she desired, admired and envied floated there before her eyes."

Though prosperity returned after the war, the contrast between Ste. Catherine's glittering storefronts and the grittiness found on the sidewalks continued to fascinate writers. In *Let Us Compare Mythologies*, Leonard Cohen's first poetry collection (1956), "Les Vieux" evokes the down-and-outers Cohen calls "the public men...speaking all the languages of Montreal,"

with rotting noses and tweed caps
huddling in thick coats...in Phillips Square,
   on newspaper-covered benches,
unaware of St. Catherine Street
or grey and green pigeons
      inquiring between their boots.

Opposite: *Ste. Catherine, looking east from Stanley Street in 1928, where soon the unemployed would "flow in two rivers" on either side of the street.*

Perhaps the strongest poetic evocation of east-end Ste. Catherine Street comes from the Toronto poet Raymond Souster writing in the 1960s:

Beer on a hot afternoon? – what else
in this Bon Marché of the World,
earth's narrowest, most crowded rabbit-run,
sweating under loud sunshine that glints off
baby carriages, tin cups of beggars,
silver balls of pawnshops, making
the rouge-layered, powder-dipped girls
squint hard but not taking anything off
their free-swinging walk on the stilt heels.

While the beggars of Ste. Catherine Street suggested an unappealing continuity between the Depression era and the 1960s, in fact post-war Quebec was swiftly evolving, coming of age in the modern world. With the prosperity of the 1950s, people aspired to a materially better life and more political control over it. For French Canadians, no longer would the church dictate mores and conduct with the same authority as it had. And no longer would the compact between church and state, which had allowed the English-speaking minority to play a disproportionate role in the ordering of society, be allowed to continue. The Quiet Revolution was under way.

Just as more than a century earlier politics had played out in the streets of Old Montreal and in Place d'Armes, now there was a new locale for the dramas to be staged in the latter-day city centre. Descriptions of Ste. Catherine Street from francophone writers of the period are often highly politicized. Describing an event that was later seen as a precursor to the nationalist fervour to come, *Les Vivants, les morts et les autres,* Pierre Gélinas's novel about trade unionism and class struggle in the 1950s, carries a vivid, almost blow-by-blow account of the Maurice Richard riot of St. Patrick's Day, 1955, sparked by a suspension of the hockey superstar by NHL president Clarence Campbell.

The riot began in the hockey arena and spread onto Ste. Catherine Street: "From one end of the city to the other, thousands of people were drawn to the Forum by a kind of suction to which each and everyone contributed separately." Gélinas's hero, the young labour organizer Maurice Tremblay, "had smelled the odour of powder and of bullets; the screeching of sirens intoxicated him." After the riot, the rumour is bandied about "that the first concern of the authorities had been to protect the English residential district of Westmount

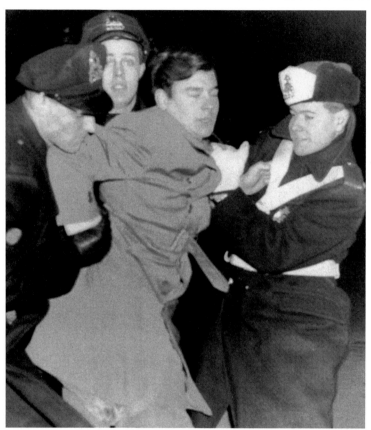

which extends a few streets west of the Forum; they had been worried about the lawns and windows of rich doctors, lawyers and industrialists. But, aside from the employees of bakeries, dairies and laundries…, the great majority of French-Canadian demonstrators had never in their lives crossed the boundary of Atwater Avenue westward; the Forum was their only point of reference in that unknown part of the city; they reached it via the long corridor of Ste-Catherine Street from the natural eastern boundary, St-Laurent Boulevard, as Dantzig had been reached before the war via Germany."

The formless rage of the 1950s coalesced into an organized challenge to the political establishment in the form of the separatist movement, both in its democratic and revolutionary guises. The first separatist party, the Ralliement pour l'Indépendance Nationale, or RIN, was formed in 1960, its manifesto proclaiming, "At the present time when, the world over, peoples emancipate themselves from the colonial yoke and nations demand their full independence, French Canada can no longer accept to remain under the eco-

The Richard Riot was seen as an event that stirred Quebec nationalism back to life.

nomic and political trusteeship of the outsider." While the majority of nationalists chose the democratic path of René Lévesque's Parti Québécois, at the fringes of the movement, more militant groups like the Front de Liberation du Québec emerged. The FLQ's campaign of bombings and robberies culminated in the kidnappings in 1970 of Quebec cabinet minister Pierre Laporte and British diplomat James Cross, provoking the October Crisis. The murder of Laporte at the hands of the kidnappers and the federal government's show of force in sending troops into the streets of Montreal seemed an echo of the long-ago uprising of 1837–38, and as was the case then, it was a reminder of the consequences of violence and repression.

In 1963, shortly after the first wave of FLQ bombings, a group of budding francophone writers in their twenties founded the short-lived (it folded in 1968) but influential literary journal *Parti pris*, advocating a sovereign and socialist Quebec. One of their number was the twenty-one-year-old André Major, whose 1963 poem "O rue Ste-Catherine" pulses with rage, disillusionment, and angry love and ends with a call to arms:

Ste Catherine Street, shifting shadow of the coming battle cry
a nation's sword has already etched on you
the disquiet of its love.

In what may be the oddest piece of erotic writing in Canadian literature, novelist Evelyn Dumas has her female protagonist enact an exhibitionistic fantasy at Montreal's best-known intersection. Her novel *Un Événement de mes octobres* is an extravagant allegory about the October Crisis, playing on the theme that terror and celebration of becoming a nation are one and the same. The narrator declares, "I want to run nude on my Catherine, to stretch, legs spread, on the corner of Peel. I want to expose myself, perfumed, lotioned, and talced at the 'crossroads of Canada,' offering each of my seven orifices to all living things."

A quarter of a century later, the landscape has changed for Barney Panofsky, in Mordecai Richler's novel *Barney's Version*. Panofsky roams the downtown streets on the eve of the sovereignty referendum of 1995, the bleakness to which he is witness reflecting the wasteland of his own heart:

"Squatters had appropriated the crumbling building that had once been the art-deco York Theatre. Every lamp-post on St. Catherine Street was adorned with both OUI and NON placards. Scruffy, shivering teenagers with sleeping bags were camped outside the Forum, where the tickets would go on sale in the morning for a Bon Jovi concert. A greasy, bearded old man, wild-eyed, muttering to himself, and wheeling a supermarket cart before him, was rummaging through a wastebin, searching for empty cans that could be redeemed. A plump rat skittered out of the lane behind an Indian restaurant."

Opposite: *The 1968 St. Jean Baptiste Day parade turned into a riot.*

So much had happened during the twenty-five years between the ecstatic dance of Dumas's heroine and the jaundiced observations of Richler's aging protagonist. The election of the Parti Québécois as the provincial government in 1976 had once and for all legitimized the nationalist agenda and ensured it would remain close to the centre of political debate in Quebec and Canada for decades to come. Language laws and restricted access to English-language education ensured a dominant place for French in the day-to-day life of Quebec. While the outcome of the 1980 sovereignty referendum was not really close, it shook the confidence of the English community. People and businesses left. Quebec society in the 1980s and '90s seemed confronted by a series of contradictions enveloped in irony. The more the aspirations of the majority to be "*maîtres chez nous*" were met, the more ambivalence there seemed to be about seeing the evolution through to the final goal of independence – sovereignty-association, the best of both worlds, was a more palatable end. At the same time, each advancement toward political and cultural autonomy carried a price. The stagnation of the post-referendum period in the early 1980s and a recession in the early 1990s stalled the material advance of Quebec, and nowhere was this more apparent than in Montreal, the engine that drives the province's economy. And nowhere was the cost of Quebec's fractious debate on its destiny more evident than on Ste. Catherine Street. Only in the waning days of the century, with nationalist fervour and anglophone backlash both for the moment quiescent, was there a revival of Gabrielle Roy's street of dreams.

If there is one street in the city that all Montrealers have taken pride in, regardless of language or political outlook, it is Sherbrooke. Hugh MacLennan called it "the best loved street in Canada" while the novelist Régine Robin, who views Montreal with more reserve, perhaps even with suspicion, describes Sherbrooke as "that endless street, a chameleon street, a jungle street."

Sherbrooke is one of the longest streets of Montreal – Robin estimates it at "two or three universes where you don't belong" – extending from the anglophone bastion of Montreal West, through Notre Dame de Grâce, Westmount, downtown, and a crazy quilt of francophone and ethnic neighbourhoods until it ends on the island's eastern tip. The street traces its origins to the beginning of the nineteenth century and its name to a British soldier named Sir John Coape Sherbrooke. He was a career military officer who distinguished himself in India and Europe before becoming a colonial administrator. A contemporary described Sherbrooke in 1807 as "a short, square, hardy little man, with a

countenance that told at once the determined fortitude of his nature. Without genius, without education, hot as pepper, and rough in his language...." Not, on the face of it, the ideal mediator between French and English interests in Lower Canada when he arrived in 1816 as governor-in-chief of British North America. But the same officer who had described Sherbrooke as "hot as pepper" had also added that he possessed "a warm heart and generous feelings" and was "true, straight forward, scorning finesse and craft and meanness." All were characteristics that in the end enabled Sherbrooke to steer clear of partisan politics, to sustain a cordial relationship with the young firebrand speaker of the legislative assembly, Louis-Joseph Papineau, and to win the trust and regard of colonists of all parties. That the street named after him runs two-thirds of the length of the island of Montreal, binding together neighbourhoods French and English, seems entirely apt.

The poet Claude Beausoleil says in "Endless Montreal," Sherbrooke is the city's "celestial centre/Lordly Sherbrooke like a slippered scar."

Situated on the last terrace below the heights of Mount Royal, the street during most of the nineteenth century marked the limits of the city. By 1900, Sherbrooke had become the most exclusive residential street in the city. It was the main thoroughfare of the Golden Square Mile, the district that straddled its western end, so called because the residents, grown wealthy during the railway boom and the period of pre-World War I expansion of the city, were reputed to control seventy per cent of the wealth in Canada. Here there were, Hugh MacLennan writes, children of affluence "coasting down Peel Street on sleds while their nannies were stationed at the corner of Sherbrooke to warn of approaching sleighs." Fewer in number but not necessarily less wealthy, rich francophone families occupied Sherbrooke east of Bleury to St. Denis Street.

Sherbrooke Street was the victim of both the Square Mile's success and its failure. As real estate values rose during the boom years before World War I, the pressure to build something other than mansions on the street became unstoppable. Square Mile residents opposed having commerce in their backyards, but an exception was made for prestigious buildings like the Linton and the Château apartments and the Ritz-Carlton Hotel. The hotel got its stamp of approval from the neighbourhood a few years after its opening in 1912, when it became the preferred lodging place in Montreal of the Prince of Wales, the ill-fated Edward VIII, who gave up his throne for the love of a woman in 1936. The prince preferred the glamour of the Sherbrooke Street hotel to that of the Windsor, where royalty had until then stayed while in town.

Today, the Ritz-Carlton is considered a vestige of that gilded age, when Sherbrooke was dubbed "Montreal's Fifth Avenue." Recalling the period of transition, Linnet Muir, Mavis Gallant's fictional alter ego, visualized the street "as a moat I was not allowed to cross alone; it was lined with gigantic spreading trees through which light fell like a rain of coins."

The Depression relegated the Square Mile to history. When the industries that built the capitalist fortunes fell silent, the grand houses were left behind and were demolished in favour of high-rises, turned into boarding houses, or bought up by institutions such as McGill University. But Sherbrooke, now more commercial than residential, remained one the city's best addresses.

Jean Basile, in the 1970 novel *Les Voyages d'Irkoutsk*, compares Montreal to a glacial San Francisco of the north and flash-freezes an image of Sherbrooke Street shop windows during an early morning

Mavis Gallant in 1948. Gallant remembers Sherbrooke Street as "lined with gigantic spreading trees."

MAVIS GALLANT

"Only personal independence matters" was the epigraph to Mavis Gallant's 1981 Governor General's Award-winning collection of short stories about Canada, *Home Truths*. If four words can sum up a life (they were written by Boris Pasternak), these would be the ones to encapsulate Gallant's.

One of the finest living fiction writers of English, Gallant was born in 1922 in Montreal. When she was four, her parents sent her to a French Catholic boarding school, an unusual decision at that time for English Protestants. Her father died when she was ten; her mother soon remarried. By the time she had completed her schooling at eighteen, she had attended seventeen different schools in Quebec, Ontario, and the United States.

She returned to Montreal in 1940, determined to survive on her own. She obtained a job as features reporter for the *Montreal Standard*, in the meantime writing stories which she kept in a large picnic basket. In 1950 in pursuit of independence, Gallant left marriage, job, and country, and took the plunge to full-time professional fiction writing. She settled in Paris, but has maintained her Canadian citizenship and comes home on average twice a year.

Gallant's work is permeated with historical events and with politics whose shocks are seen and felt in the destructive personal relationships of her characters. Her own favourite among her books, *The Pegnitz Junction* (1982), which deals with post-war Germany, explores the processes by which the past continues to haunt the present. The Linnet Muir stories, six interrelated loosely autobiographical tales in *Home Truths*, recreate in language of utter purity and economy a younger self from the point of view of a mature woman.

"I think the difference between a writer and everyone else is the ability to put yourself in someone else's place completely," Gallant has said. On every page of her masterful stories, Gallant demonstrates that she possesses this ability.

Opposite: Sherbrooke Street when it was dubbed "Montreal's Fifth Avenue."

stroll: "diamonds and gold in Lucas, lace and silk in Holt-Renfrew, ivories in the Petit musée."

The haven of privilege represented by the street is brusquely shaken in Alice Parizeau's 1967 novel, *Rue Sherbrooke ouest*. In it, Parizeau's Polish-born narrator, Yves Stanski, tries to make sense of the multiple contradictions of the Montreal of the 1960s and of his own fractured identity. When a bomb goes off maiming a man, it's no coincidence that the terrorist act takes place on Sherbrooke Street in front of the apartment of Yves' patrician mistress,

Polish-born Alice Parizeau wrote the novel Rue Sherbrooke ouest.

Thérèse Delatour. Yves analyzes the reasons for Thérèse's panic. "What strikes her is that they've dared to set off a bomb on Sherbrooke Street West. In this quiet neighbourhood inhabited by genteel people. Had it gone off on Laval Avenue or on Coloniale Street, that would have made far less of a difference. It's normal that events of that kind take place on sad streets."

The street's transformation continued apace in the 1950s and '60s as glass towers replaced mansions, especially on Sherbrooke West. In Jacques Benoît's semi-fantastical novel, *Gisèle et le serpent*, the narrator, Grégoire Rabouin, also ruminates on the changes taking place as the skyscrapers supplant the older buildings. "I have always loved Sherbrooke Street, and I love it still despite the hammering it has received from the construction

ALICE PARIZEAU

A journalist, novelist, and lawyer, Alice Parizeau (1930–90) was born Alice Poznanska in Poland, where she lived until 1945. Her participation in the Polish Resistance as a child forms part of the background of her best-known novel – the only one to be translated into English – *Les Lilas fleurissent à Varsovie* (1981) (*The Lilacs Are Blooming in Warsaw*), which won a prestigious French prize, the Prix Européen. As a teenager, she was incarcerated during the war in the Bergen-Belsen concentration camp; her future books would often deal with the subject of alienation and exile.

Upon liberation in 1945, Parizeau relocated in Paris, where she received her university education. She immigrated to Canada in 1955 and subsequently married Jacques Parizeau, the future separatist premier of Quebec.

Alice Parizeau's first two books were journalistic travelogues about Poland and eastern Europe. She then wrote several novels, setting them in her homeland and in her adoptive country, with common underlying themes related to the overthrow of oppressors and dreams of independence. Indeed, some critics have read her Polish-inspired fiction, much of which was written during the time when the Solidarity Movement was making headlines around the world, as an elaborate allegory for Quebec.

Nationalist fervour resulted in a statue of Sir John A. Macdonald in Place du Canada, formerly Dominion Square, losing its head in 1992.

of discordant buildings. Less than twenty years ago," he observes around 1980, "this was a majestic street, relatively free of traffic, an open invitation for a stroll. A street for shooting the breeze with friends, for philosophizing. Today it's swarming with cars, but by some miracle even now, though it's hard to converse on account of the racket of the traffic, you can still string together a thought or two."

In the same period, Régine Robin's narrator in *The Wanderer* takes the No. 24 bus from its western terminus in Notre Dame de Grâce all the way to the east end, often making comparisons to Paris, where like the author, she used to live. In its downtown stretch, she finds "a Sherbrooke that's the Avenue de l'Opéra and Rue Saint-Honoré all in one.… A Place de la Bourse Sherbrooke, a Sherbrooke of the *grands boulevards.* Then the high-rise buildings thin out, giving way to town-houses and posher restaurants as you approach Rue St-Denis – this town's Latin Quarter – and Rue St-Hubert. Farther east, the fabric gets shabby. It's the Sherbrooke of the poor, of molasses, of the lower city, of petroleum, of factories. The Sherbrooke where no one ever goes, where only French is spoken, the sad Sherbrooke where the snow is grey even right after a storm, where thoughts are as grey as life."

Let's not leave Sherbrooke Street on this depressed note, however. In an essay in *Aura d'une ville : Montréal des écrivains*, poet and novelist Nicole Brossard is energized by present-day downtown, particularly the sections centred on Sherbrooke Street:

"My senses suddenly come alive when I'm strolling down Sherbrooke Street, absorbing the galleries, boutiques, the Ritz, and the way Mountain Street slices through de Maisonneuve Boulevard, letting me slip, transparent and multiplied, amid the icy glass towers with their ochre and silvery reflections refracting civilization. Something there inspires me to write, to break through a barrier to a higher level…. It's then that I see a Montreal that works, in profile between the curves of Mount Royal and the flatness of the river: Place Ville Marie, the striking Maison des Coopérants, the audacious angles of the Banque Nationale de Paris, their verticality repeated by bits of neon as night falls, little luminescent commas in the dusky blue expanse of a continent."

Since becoming a radical feminist, Nicole Brossard has used language as a political weapon.

NICOLE BROSSARD

A poet, essayist, and novelist, Nicole Brossard was born in Montreal in 1943. In the mid-1960s, she attended the Université de Montréal where she was involved in the ferment of nationalist politics; she published her first poetry collection in 1965. In the same year, she co-founded *Barre du jour*, an avant-garde literary journal with a strong commitment to the development of Quebec literature.

Dissociating herself from mainstream trends in Québécois poetry, Brossard decided to devote herself to full-time writing and, since the late '60s, has produced a body of work of some twenty-five books. Full of word play, foreign terms, and typographical devices, her work taxes the ingenuity of translators, yet, to date, about half of her books have been translated into English, including the novels *Mauve Desert* (1987) and *Baroque at Dawn* (1995), the poetry collection *Daydream Mechanics* (1973), for which she won a Governor General's Award, and the essay collection *The Aerial Letter* (1985). Brossard won a second Governor General's Award in 1985 and has received numerous other prizes, including the Prix Athanase-David, the highest literary recognition in Quebec.

After the birth of her daughter in 1974, Brossard's life and work assumed a radical feminist and lesbian orientation. Heavily influenced by the Austrian philosopher Ludwig Wittgenstein, by the French deconstructionist philosopher Jacques Derrida, and by feminist writers Gertrude Stein, Adrienne Rich, and Kate Millett, Brossard has used language as a political weapon in her later writings. Her novels, which deliberately subvert the familiar conventions of narrative techniques (judged to be patriarchal), are an extension of her experiments in poetry. But they also go well beyond the aims of realism that define much of traditional literature. "You have to write two kinds of pages almost at the same time," she said in an interview in 1991, "one on which you try to understand and uncover the patriarchal lies; and another on which you try to give your new values, your utopias, and everything you find positive about yourself and about women."

Chapter 6

THE MOUNTAIN
AND THE RIVER

M OUNT ROYAL AND the majestic St. Lawrence – the mountain and the
river – are the dominant symbols of Montreal. The city lies near the confluence of the Ottawa and St. Lawrence Rivers, its landscape defined by the fact
that it is an island and that it holds at its heart a small mountain of volcanic
origin. Both mountain and river figure in the major events of the city's history
and are referred to repeatedly in its literature.

Of all the writers intimately associated with Montreal, perhaps none has
done more to popularize in print its landscape and in particular its two great
symbols, the mountain and the river, than Hugh MacLennan. An urbane
Montrealer for most of his adult life, MacLennan (1907–90) was born in Cape
Breton Island (he always preserved a slight Gaelic lilt in his speech) and arrived
in Montreal in the mid-1930s, to take up a teaching position at Lower Canada
College in Notre Dame de Grâce.

*A view of Montreal, from
atop Mount Royal in 1784.*

A well-travelled and refined man (he studied classical Greek and Latin at Dalhousie, Princeton, and Oxford, where he was a Rhodes scholar), he considered Montreal to be one of the most beautiful cities in North America and its "subtlest and most intricate." His writing bears witness to his awe at the splendour of the St. Lawrence – he called it "an imperial river" – but his profoundest love was reserved for Mount Royal: "Of all the cities I have seen around the world Montreal is the only one with a mountain in its heart – a mountain that rises higher than the tallest skyscraper in the business district, a mountain on whose top a forest, as Europeans would understand a forest, has been preserved for the pleasure of the people who love it."

The mountain and the river are the primary symbols of *Two Solitudes*, MacLennan's novel centred on archetypal conflicts between English and French Quebecers. Set against the conscription crisis of World War I, the book, at the time of its publication in 1945, had powerful contemporary echoes for Canadians enduring yet another wartime national unity imbroglio that turned on compulsory military service. Yet MacLennan had deliberately set out to write a work that not only would ring powerfully for Canadians but would also resonate for an international readership unfamiliar with Canadian issues and settings.

He had originally begun writing a decade earlier in the style of Hemingway and using cities in the United States as backdrops. It was at the suggestion of his American wife, Dorothy Duncan, that he began to use Canadian settings. In 1937, fired by a spirit of experimentation, the impoverished schoolmaster began working on *Barometer Rising*, a tightly knit novel about the explosion that devastated Halifax in 1917. When the book appeared in 1941, it became a runaway success and established MacLennan on the course he followed for the rest of his life: exploring in novels and essays the meaning of being Canadian. He won five Governor General's Awards and became a Canadian literary icon, having come to realize that "the novel is such an intimate form that you're stuck with your own country."

MacLennan's second and most famous novel was *Two Solitudes* and in it his need to portray his adopted city – "this covetous, bawdy, exciting place" – is palpable. The book begins with a powerful image of the converging of the Ottawa and the St. Lawrence:

"Northwest of Montreal, through a valley always in sight of the low mountains of the Laurentian Shield, the Ottawa River flows out of

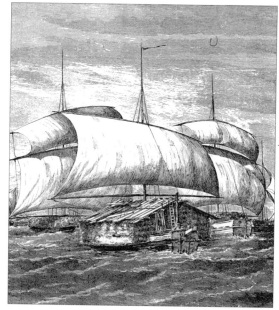

Barges on the St. Lawrence River, making their way against the St. Mary's Current. The image appeared in The Canadian Illustrated News *in 1879.*

Protestant Ontario into Catholic Quebec. It comes down broad and ale-coloured and joins the Saint Lawrence, the two streams embrace the pan of Montreal Island, the Ottawa merges and loses itself, and the mainstream moves northeastward a thousand miles to the sea....

"Down in the angle at Montreal, on the island about which the two rivers join...two old races and religions meet...and live their separate legends, side by side. If this sprawling half-continent has a heart, here it is."

Visions of the mountain or of the panoramas seen from its summit recur frequently in the novel. In one scene set in 1921, Paul Tallard, the chief protagonist and a kind of alter ego for the author, scales the mountain after the death of his father. The whole city lies below him:

"It looked magnificent in the sunshine.... The upper part hugging the mountain was beautiful, soft lights and shadows lying among trees and the roofs of various houses quiet in the shade. But the central and eastern parts were a raw waste of masonry with an occasional square building jutting high above the flat roofs around it. In all parts were the spires and domes of churches, more to the acreage than any other commercial city in the world. About the oval shore of the island the river curved in a great distant sweep out of the Lachine Rapids under the Victoria Bridge, folded the slip of Nun's Island and the green bluff of Saint Helen's. Factory smoke from Verdun drifted downstream on a light southwesterly breeze, but through it he could see the plain spreading to the mountains across the American border, sloping so gradually that at this height it even seemed to be tilted downward."

A coupling of the mountain and the river has been a common conceit for writers situating their stories in Montreal. More than half a century after the publication of *Two Solitudes*, Trevor Ferguson, writing under the pseudonym John Farrow in his 1999 thriller *City of Ice*, echoes MacLennan's descriptions of the geography of the city, emphasizing the mountain and the river as he sets the scene for a vast international criminal conspiracy centred on Montreal:

"The St. Lawrence River flows from West to East, out of the Great Lakes to the Atlantic Ocean, connecting the industrial heartland cities of Chicago and Detroit, Cleveland, Buffalo and Toronto to the sea.... Where the river bends up and begins to widen toward the Atlantic, it is

Opposite: *Hugh MacLennan. In his fiction, Montreal's mountain and river were primary symbols.*

joined by the waters of the Ottawa, and there divides around a city established upon an ancient volcanic island. At one time the volcano soared above the clouds. Over eons it was worn away, rubbed down by nature's relentless chafe.... Time eroded the lava crust, the river carried the dust away, and all that remained of the immense volcano was the hardened, tenacious core, the crater's plug.

"A faint replica of its former glory, the plug is called a mountain now."

Rather than one "plug," the mountain consists of three hills joined together, the highest being the crest above where the downtown lookout is located. As well, there are two lesser summits: one in Westmount, where the appropriately named street Summit Circle is found, and one on the northern slopes by the mountain's cemeteries.

One of the most appealing aspects of the mountain is that though it sits in the centre of a metropolis, it has never been entirely tamed. For most of Montreal's history, it served as backdrop to the human drama at the river's edge. Many climbed it for the view it presented, and its lower slopes were exploited for timber, pasture, and orchards. But it was not built upon until the mid-nineteenth century, and except for a handful of properties, the upper reaches were never settled.

The encroaching city would have certainly overrun the mountain had it not been for the far-sighted actions of municipal leaders, who in the 1870s expropriated land to the tune of one million dollars ("an astronomical sum at the time," writes urbanist J.-C. Marsan in *Montreal in Evolution*) for the cre-ation of Mount Royal Park. Designed by Frederick Law Olmsted, the 182-hectare park was inaugurated in 1873. Marsan notes that Mount Royal Park accounts for only fourteen per cent of the mountain's surface and is relatively small by comparison with, for example, the Bois de Boulogne in Paris, which is more than eight hundred hectares. (Montreal's paucity of green space during the era of its industrialization is borne out by another statistic offered by Marsan. In 1912, all the parks in the city totalled 326 hectares, an area smaller than New York's Central Park.)

Olmsted, North America's premier landscape architect, worked on Mount Royal between 1873 and 1881. As is often the case with projects undertaken on large tracts of land and over the course of many years, the completed enterprise differed from what he had originally contemplated. He had, for instance, wanted to include a residential component in the northeast corner to help pay for the park's development, had never planned for the Chalet that now exists, and would

The Montreal skyline and the mountain in the mid-1920s, during the era of MacLennan's Two Solitudes.

have been appalled at the idea of a giant glowing cross on the mountain's brow, not to mention the unsightly communications towers nearby. Even Beaver Lake, a small artificial pond in the southwest corner of the park off Remembrance Road, was an idea implemented long after Olmsted's day, in the 1930s.

Nonetheless, Olmsted's conception of the mountain's symbolic value and of how a park could add to it hit the mark. As his biographer, Witold Rybczynski, writes in *A Clearing in the Distance*, the mountain park remains "natural and magical; healthful and healing." One can detect both disparagement and pride in the way Olmsted himself viewed the project in his description of the master plan for the park, addressed to municipal leaders – and by extension to all Montrealers – in 1881: "You have chosen to take a mountain for your park, but, in truth, a mountain barely worth the name. You would call it a hill if it stood a few miles further away from the broad, flat, river valley. Its scenery, that is to say, is but relatively mountainous. Yet, whatever of special adaptation it has to your purpose lies in that 'relative' quality. It would be wasteful to try to make anything else than a mountain of it."

From the beginning, Montrealers took great pride in the mountain. Let no one call it a hill! When Oscar Wilde appeared in Montreal on a lecture tour in 1882 at the height of his notoriety, he provoked less of a stir for his ideas on aesthetics than he did when he told his audience that he had taken a tour and "went up the hill behind your lovely city." The *Montreal Star* plaintively commented: "It was not nice to hear our cherished mountain reduced to a hill.... You can say nearly anything you like of Montreal and the people will not bother their heads about it, except when you belittle their mountain. It is high treason to speak ill of that, or to attempt to lessen its size or grandeur by as much as a spadeful."

Though Olmsted and Wilde were correct in calling it more hill than mountain, Mount Royal has remained both the city's signature landmark and a cherished recreational haunt. Poets, short story writers, novelists, and memoirists have all lavished attention on it, depicting it by turns as parkland, wilderness, lover's lane, or, because of its association with the great cemeteries on its flanks and with the cross, a site of either transcendence or of grim finality.

As we have noted, many of the aspects currently associated with the mountain were not integral to Olmsted's design. The bridle path was an original Olmsted feature, but the monument in honour of George-Étienne Cartier, one of the Fathers of Confederation, was added later. Inaugurated in an unusual way on September 6, 1919, it was unveiled by King George V at the push of a button in Balmoral Castle, Scotland, the King, according to *The Storied Province of Quebec*, sending along a congratulatory cable: "In unveiling the Cartier monument, which ceremony, thanks to the marvelous agency of electricity, I am able to perform at a distance of three thousand miles, I am glad to join with the people of Canada in commemorating the centenary of their illustrious citizen whose name will ever be closely associated with the consolidation, progress and prosperity of the Dominion."

The poet A.M. Klein, who grew up in the second decade of the twentieth century on streets in the shadow of the mountain (his schooling, in fact, began at Mount Royal School on Clark Street), had a great fondness for it. His poem "The Mountain" is replete with nostalgic moments for "all the amber afternoons" of "my youth, my childhood," and contains this droll recollection of the Cartier statue:

> *And Cartier's monument, based with nude figures*
> *still stands where playing hookey*
> *Lefty and I tested our gravel aim*
> *(with occupation flinging away our guilt)*
> *against the bronze tits of Justice.*

A.M. KLEIN

Born in Ratno in Ukraine, A.M. Klein (1909–72) came to Montreal as a baby in 1910 with his family. He grew up in the heyday of Yiddish culture in the ghetto of Montreal, rooted in Jewish tradition from which, though he eventually modified his orthodoxy, he never broke away. After attending Baron Byng high school, Klein went on to McGill University, where he was associated with the McGill Movement of poets. The 1920s were his most prolific period, and his first poems were published in the *McGill Daily*. Upon graduation, he chose law school at the Université de Montréal. His poetry would later show a deep sympathy and understanding of French-Canadian society, and in diction and cadence poems like "Montreal" bear the obvious stamp of the French language:

> Splendour erablic of your promenades
> Foliates there, and there your maisonry
> Of pendant balcon and escalier'd march,
> Unique midst English habitat,
> Is vivid Normandy!

Klein graduated from law school to the financial woes of the Depression. In the late 1930s, his law practice languishing, he took over the editorship of the *Canadian Jewish Chronicle*, then the leading English-Jewish weekly in Canada. But his greatest achievements were as a poet and visionary novelist: his masterpiece, the innovative novel *The Second Scroll* (1951). The writer of this impassioned and triumphant poetic narrative battled despair and self-disgust for large chunks of his life. In 1954 he suffered a nervous breakdown from which he never fully recovered. For the last eighteen years of his life he did not write a word.

A.M. Klein grew up in the shadow of the mountain.

Nostalgia also animates a passage about the Chalet written by Michel Tremblay. Patterned on the model of a Swiss mountain lodge, the Chalet was built in 1931–32. It became notable for the commanding view of the city from its terrace and from the nearby lookout, and in the 1930s and '40s it was the site of many open-air performances. Tremblay alludes to these outdoor recitals in his 1986 novel *The Heart Laid Bare*. In a scene in the unfolding romance between a thirty-nine-year-old CEGEP teacher named Jean-Marc and his much younger love interest, an aspiring actor named Mathieu, Jean-Marc recalls his childhood when the Chalet was a rather recent innovation.

"I told Mathieu that when I'd started going up to the lookout at the

Opposite: *The Cartier monument with cross in the background.*

Chalet on the mountain...the Sun Life Building was the highest in town....

"We'd take the trolley up to Beaver Lake, along the Camillien-Houde Parkway which didn't have a name back then, I think, then we'd walk here. Every Tuesday night in summer the symphony orchestra gave a concert. They'd put chairs out all around the Chalet and the orchestra played on the steps. The kids in my gang didn't have any money, so we'd bring blankets and lie around the lookout.... We'd look down on the city while we tried to hear a few bars of the 'Danse macabre' or the 'Capriccio Italien.'"

Yves Thériault wrote in the 1920s and '30s of a park "where the owl sings and fox yelps."

Yves Thériault, perhaps Quebec's most prolific and versatile author, devoted poetic passages to Mount Royal in *Aaron*, widely regarded as his finest novel (it won the Prix de la Province de Québec in 1954). *Aaron* is the story of a young, orthodox Jewish immigrant to Montreal who, in order to become assimilated into Montreal's English community, rejects his heritage and the influence of the grandfather who has raised him. In one scene, the grandfather sends an adolescent Aaron to the mountain to find peace of mind there.

"A park where the owl sings and where the fox yelps, while from below sounds the synthetic noise of a modern city....

"Every day a multitude of people ascends in search of peace. Lovers stroll beneath the leaves. Others, older, more serene, come to dream close to nature. They listen to the birds and watch the squirrels; they are wary of skunks, and, if it's a lucky day, maybe they'll glimpse a ferret lying in wait for its prey or a yellow fox, head low, taking to its heels, or beyond the tall trees, the flight of a hawk."

Whereas Thériault stressed the mountain's fauna, Jacques Godbout in his 1965 novel *Knife on the Table* emphasized its flora. "Summer would be torrid in a city which, for me, had become silent and empty (storms followed the course

of the rivers and we on our island were inundated daily just like a tropical country. Unusual, luxurious vegetation flourished on the Mountain, as if Mount Royal were a huge garden set down in the middle of the city to guarantee the necessary amount of chlorophyll to children, grasshoppers, to those who, despite soot, daily rounds, the exactitude of boredom, still resembled men)."

By contrast, in Leonard Cohen's semi-autobiographical novel of 1963, *The Favourite Game*, the mountain is identified with a much grimmer idea, the finality of death. The invalid father of Laurence Breavman, the hero of *The Favourite Game*, "lived mostly in bed or a tent in the hospital. When he was up and walking he lied.

> "He took his cane with the silver band and led his son over Mount Royal. Here was the ancient crater. Two iron and stone cannon rested in the gentle grassy scoop which was once a pit of boiling lava....
> "'We'll come back here when I'm better.'
> "One lie.
> "Breavman learned to pat the noses of horses tethered beside the Chalet, how to offer them sugar cubes from a flat palm.
> "'One day we'll go riding.'
> "'But you can hardly breathe.'
> "His father collapsed that evening over his map of flags on which he plotted the war, fumbling for the capsules to break and inhale."

The mountain's association with death is made most explicit by the cemeteries that flank its back slopes and that actually predate the park. (An Irving Layton poem titled "Cote des Neiges Cemetery" speaks of "A ghost city where live autumn birds flit.") The idea of putting the cemeteries on the northern flank of Mount Royal came about as the growing town below began crowding its graveyards in the mid-nineteenth century. Mount Royal Cemetery, the Protestant one, was created in 1852 (with a small Jewish presence immediately next to it a few years later), and Notre Dame des Neiges, the Catholic, in 1855. The cemeteries became tourist attractions. Pamphlets invited the public to come and visit, though the clergy denounced the practice strenuously. J.-C. Marsan writes in *Montreal in Evolution*, "The superb landscaping of this realm of death made it the most romantic and picturesque place in Montreal, especially on the Protestant side."

A century later, Trevor Ferguson wrote in *City of Ice*, "The mountain provided a sprawl of cemeteries, English and French and Jewish, as though the

LEONARD COHEN

Leonard Cohen was born in 1934 in Montreal and grew up on Belmont Avenue in Westmount. Despite an economically privileged childhood, tragedy touched him early in life. His father, a semi-invalid as a result of injuries suffered in World War I, died when Leonard was nine. Thirteen years later in 1956, the young poet would dedicate *Let Us Compare Mythologies*, his first book, "To the memory of my father."

The *New York Times* has called Leonard Cohen "a kind of rock and roll Lord Byron." By now, his international renown as a singer-songwriter has largely obscured his earlier writing successes. But before his gravelly croak of a voice ever assaulted an ear, Cohen was a rebel poet and avant-garde novelist, the author of *Beautiful Losers* (1966), perhaps the most daring experimental novel in Canadian letters. Religion, sex, death, violence, beauty, and the search for ecstasy have been the touchstones of his work.

Cohen's most prolific writing period was the 1960s, during which he published four volumes of poetry and two novels and launched his first recording. In 1969 he turned down a Governor General's literary award for his *Selected Poems: 1956-1968*, saying, "Much in me strives for this honour but the poems themselves forbid it absolutely." A quarter of a century later, he graciously accepted a Governor General's Award for the performing arts, given for lifetime achievement, adding it to his honorary degree from McGill University, his rank as an Officer of the Order of Canada, and his membership in the Juno Hall of Fame.

Montreal, Cohen's "Jerusalem of the North," has been an all-important inspiration from the earliest poems such as "Saint Catherine Street" and "Had We Nothing to Prove," through his first published novel, *The Favourite Game*, and through songs such as "Suzanne Takes You Down," which held the status of an anthem for a whole generation. He still maintains a residence in the core of the city, off the Main, and returns frequently from Los Angeles.

Leonard Cohen in 1963. His semi-autobiographical The Favourite Game *was about growing up in Westmount.*

A Monique Proulx story underlines the mountain's wilderness quality.

height gained an advantage on heaven, shortening the journey upward, and brought those who visited nearer the realm of their departed."

One of those visitors is the narrator of Monique Proulx's story "Baby" in Proulx's 1996 collection, *Aurora Montrealis*. The narrator, who shares Proulx's year of birth – 1952 – walks up Mount Royal Boulevard and through the woods to the cemetery in search of a gravestone she had discovered earlier, marking the burial plot of a five-year-old child who had died in 1952. The approach through the woods to this sad memorial underscores the fact that, despite the bustling city around and below, parts of the mountain remain a wilderness. "As the woods close about you, you strip off your factory-made skins and you recognize members of your essential family in these roots and trunks emerging from the soil. The evidence forces you to the welcome realization that you also come from this complex ground... you'd toss out your life like some disposable product if this conviction of your origins wasn't so precarious, so threatened with extinction when the city takes you up again."

The cemetery figures prominently in "Flying a Red Kite," the title story of Hugh Hood's first collection. Hood, a profoundly Catholic writer, is preoccupied with the idea of immortality here. The main character, Fred Calvert, experiences a crisis of faith when, on a bus ride on a sweltering summer afternoon, he sits near a priest who, when the bus passes Notre Dame des Neiges cemetery mutters, "It's all a sham," adding, "They're in there for good." The following day, a Sunday, Fred takes his daughter, Deedee, on an outing to fly a kite on the mountain. It is an idyllic afternoon: "On either side of the dirt road grew great clumps of wild flowers, yellow and blue, buttercups, daisies and goldenrod, and cornflowers and clover.... The scent of clover and of dry sweet grass was very keen here, and from the east, over the curved top of the mountain, the wind blew in a steady uneddying stream." After several false attempts, Fred manages to get the kite aloft, and when it begins to soar, it flies over the cemetery that he had passed the previous day.

"He thought flashingly of the priest saying, 'It's all a sham,' and he knew all at once that the priest was wrong. Deedee came running down to him, laughing with excitement and pleasure and singing joyfully...and he knelt in the dusty roadway and put his arms around her, placing her hands on the line between his." The story ends on a note of exhilaration, and Fred's faith in an afterlife is reaffirmed.

Montreal seen from the mountain in the early 1960s.

The deeply Catholic foundations of Montreal are embodied in and emblazoned on the mountain by its great electric cross, built under the auspices of the Saint-Jean-Baptiste Society in 1924. The rationale for the monument is given in an account nearly contemporaneous with its construction: "Despite its cosmopolitan character, the city is pre-eminently Christian. Hence, to symbolize the faith, there was erected in 1924, on the summit of Mount Royal, 826 feet above sea level, a huge steel cross, 102 feet high, 30 feet across and six feet thick.... At night it is lighted by 280 lights, of 75 watts each, placed two feet apart, so that it is seen as a cross of fire for many miles by the sailors on the rivers and the people of the adjoining districts."

The cross has exercised a compelling hold over the imagination of writers. Its image opens A.M. Klein's poem "The Mountain": "Who knows it only by the famous cross which bleeds / into the fifty miles of night its light / knows a night scene..."

A strange, other-worldly night scene implicating the cross is to be found at

the heart of Jacques Benoît's quirky 1981 fantasy novel *Gisèle et le serpent*. The narrator, a totally rational physician, reports with amazement the surreal events to which he is witness in the city. "I was perhaps two hundred steps from the cross on Mount Royal, when, near the edge of the path, I suddenly saw something stir the leaves. A reddish snout peeked out. It was, believe it or not, a fox which darted out in my direction as if it were fleeing something.

"I laughed out loud for a moment and continued on my way. Between the trees, I saw the city, all in pastels on account of the evening, and beyond, the Jacques Cartier Bridge and the river. In the meantime, even though it was still quite light, the cross on Mount Royal lit up." At this point in the story, the narrator meets three fantastic characters – two women and a man – and witnesses a strange and obscene act which shakes him considerably. "At the same time, I heard a powerful crackling behind me, and instinctively covered my face with my arms. It was the cross on Mount Royal which, for no reason that I could tell, extinguished itself: its hundreds of bulbs all burned out at once."

The cross has also exercised a strong fascination for the noted Yiddish writer Chava Rosenfarb, casting a brooding shadow over Rosenfarb's novella, "Edgia's Revenge." In the story, Rosenfarb depicts a poisonous symbiotic relationship between two former concentration camp inmates who meet in Montreal after the war. Edgia, whose life the narrator, Rella, had saved in Auschwitz, now lives on Esplanade Street, facing Mount Royal. "The apartment was long and dark. Only the living room possessed a large wide window with a panoramic view, a view which gave out on a large sports field in the foreground and Mount Royal topped by its cross behind."

Much of the mysterious power of the novella rests upon the juxtaposition of Jewish suffering with the Christian symbolism of the cross on the mountain. On one of her visits to Edgia, Rella reports on a strange conversation, emblematic of the twisted relationship between the two women.

> "[Edgia] pointed her chin at the window, through which she could see the cross on top of the mountain. Illuminated by electric bulbs, it shone into the room through the navy blue darkness of evening. 'Do you see that cross up there?... I have the impression it's missing something. Guess what?'
>
> "'Jesus!' I exclaimed and burst into awkward laughter.
>
> "She nodded. 'Yes, Jesus. Every cross should have its Jesus, and every Jesus should have his cross.... The cross is the question and Jesus is the answer. Sometimes I believe that I am such a cross and that I carry my Jesus on my back.'"

The cross is also a primary symbol in Robert Majzels's dark and foreboding 1997 novel, *City of Forgetting*. Majzels's mountain stands in stark counterpoint to MacLennan's in *Two Solitudes*, published half a century earlier. For MacLennan the mountain was a symbol of greatness, a vantage point from which to survey Montreal as it reached a high-water mark in its development. In *City of Forgetting*, it is a place of refuge from the dissolution of the city, and, indeed, from all that society has to offer at the end of the millennium. Compare this description by Majzels of a view from the mountain with the earlier one from MacLennan: "The city, a dirty dishrag stretched out at her feet; the skyscrapers stacked up against the river; the trussed arch of the Jacques Cartier Bridge, as though the mountain crucifix had tipped over into the water. Briefly, a rain shower erupts, sweeps past her and across the river into the curving plain."

"Her" is Clytemnestra, heroine of Aeschylus's tragedy of the same name. Majzels has stocked his novel with an assortment of homeless and mentally ill people, real-life faces recognizable to people who frequent the city's downtown neighbourhoods. But in a clever conceit, he has assigned to them attributes of historical and literary figures and cultural archetypes. Appearing along with Clytemnestra are de Maisonneuve, Lady Macbeth, Che Guevara, Le Corbusier, and Suzy Creamcheez, a tough but vulnerable street child. Majzels takes full advantage of the rich literary and historical associations these characters offer him. The homeless de Maisonneuve lives on the waterfront in a trench that is threatened with inundation, as was the first settlement at Pointe à Callière. And, like the original de Maisonneuve, the reincarnation hoists a cross on his shoulder up the mountain. But this cross is "a jumble of metal, plastic, wood and glass, patched together with wire and rope: tin tubing from an oil furnace, half a car fender and a strip of blown tire, slices of broken window pane, brown-leafed branches scavenged from a dying maple, busted bits of a recycling bin, the jagged pole of a stop sign." The symbol of redemption is reduced to rubbish. And the characters, too, forgotten, ignored, or persecuted, in the manner of people of their station, have become society's detritus, cast up on the mountain's slopes.

In his novel City of Forgetting, *Robert Majzels sees Mount Royal in less heroic terms than some authors have.*

Still, the mountain doesn't have only lugubrious or elegiac associations. Its lighter and earthier aspects are also reflected in literature. In *St. Urbain's Horseman*, Mordecai Richler resurrects a teenaged Duddy Kravitz from his earlier novel, *The Apprenticeship of Duddy Kravitz*, to lead Jake Hersh, the protagonist of *St. Urbain*, astray. "They found some butts, lit up, and climbed Mount Royal in search of couples in bushes. 'Everybody's doin' it, doin' it,' Duddy sang, 'pickin' their nose and chewin' it, chewin' it.' He told Jake that once he discovered a couple stuck together, just like dogs, and had to summon the St. John's Ambulance man to get a kettle of boiling water to break them apart."

In Michel Tremblay's poignant love story, *The Heart Laid Bare*, the mountain appears in its guise as the "outside gayland of Montreal's nights, the famous bushes of Mont Royal, celebrated all over North America.... That's why hundreds of men of all ages and all convictions climb the steep slopes of Mont Royal every night, in the hope of ending up either as part of the wildest group of the century or in the most discreet, romantic spot in town, in the arms of a partner they'll never see again...."

From the vantage point of the various lookouts on the mountain, the city spreads out below in a series of intriguing panoramas. In a poem called "Lookout: Mount Royal," A.M. Klein gazes down on "the full birdseye circle to the river, / its singsong bridges, its mapmaker curves, / its island with the two shades of green, meadow and wood...."

The curve of the river is far more noticeable from above than it is in the centre of the town built on its shores. As Andrée Maillet notes in a short story, "Montreal sprawls in the middle of one of the most beautiful rivers in the world, but in order to see it, the inhabitants of its southern regions have to go perch high on the mountain, higher than the buildings, warehouses, and silos that almost hide it from existence for them."

Unlike the mountain, a kind of benign sentinel, the St. Lawrence has played a more ambiguous part in the city's story. It was, of course, the highway that brought both natives and Europeans to the island, and it was its rapids that helped determine the siting of Montreal. But the river also has had a more menacing aspect. Most notorious were its frequent floods, which plagued inhabitants from de Maisonneuve's time until near the end of the nineteenth century. Then, raised embankments and an ice bridge kept the water back, the bridge preventing the pileup of ice close to the low-lying harbour. Currents, shoals, and rocks played havoc with boats trying to navigate their way up the river. Particularly treacherous was the St. Mary's Current, caused by a narrowing of the river between Île Ste. Hélène and Montreal. Sailing ships often unloaded their cargoes and passengers rather than challenge the current, leaving the task of entering the port to smaller bateaux. The historian Kathleen Jenkins records, "So complicated was the passage that ships from Europe, it was agreed, seldom made more than one voyage a season up to Montreal."

There was also the difficulty of accessing Montreal from the mainland before the Victoria Bridge spanned the river. In summer and fall it might be

done by boat, and in winter by sleigh, but there could be weeks during each year when crossing the partly iced-over river was treacherous. The indefatigable Colonel George Landmann described his crossing in the dead of winter, having travelled from New York up the Richelieu Valley, the usual route for visitors from the south. He arrived at La Prairie on the south shore of the river and was ferried over, "amidst the most alarming confusion of floating ice rushing along at frightful speed." Dodging the ice floes and paddling furiously in the swift current of the river, Landmann estimated the paddlers covered nine miles and took six hours to reach Montreal.

Equally perilous but more scenic were the Lachine Rapids. Countless native and European fur traders and other river users lost their lives in the rushing waters. (General Jeffery Amherst nonchalantly records the loss of several dozen troops in the rapids while approaching Montreal in the campaign of 1760.) Like the mountain, the rapids were one of the natural wonders that had to be seen by all who visited. There are many descriptions of the river at this locale, including this one by Rosanna Leprohon in the novel *Antoinette De*

Ice jams on the St. Lawrence like this one in the late nineteenth century were one of the causes of spring flooding.

Shooting the Lachine Rapids in 1883.

Mirecourt, which describes her heroine's ride in the sleigh of the British officer, Colonel Evelyn, just after the Conquest: "At length they neared the Lachine Rapids, the roar of whose restless waters had been for some time previous sounding in their ears; and as the broad wreaths of foam, the snow-covered rocks with the black waters boiling and chafing up between them, or eddying around in countless different currents and whirlpools, burst upon their view, an involuntary exclamation escaped Colonel Evelyn's lips."

In *Two Solitudes*, MacLennan looks at the river through the eyes of the ruthless businessman Huntly McQueen atop his perch in the Royal Bank Building on St. James Street. MacLennan depicts the port of Montreal in 1917 as "one of the panoramas of the world." From his office McQueen "could look across the plain to the distant mountains across the American border. The Saint Lawrence, a mile wide, swept in a splendid curve along the southern bend of the island on which the city stood....

"McQueen's satisfaction constantly renewed itself through his ability to overlook all this. He felt himself at the exact centre of the country's heart, at the meeting place of ships, railroads and people, at the precise point where the interlocking directorates of Canada found their balance."

In Hugh Hood's story "Predictions of Ice," in the middle of a cloak-and-dagger plot set during a dockworker's strike, the author offers a loving description of the port of Montreal in the early 1960s:

"Supposing that we find ourselves on Bridge Street a few hundred feet south of the Mill Street intersection…, we'll be about at the beginning of the thickest and richest deposit of port and rail facilities imaginable. What you see from here are the immense grain elevators and some of the meat handling warehouses: rivers, bread, meat, nothing more human. The proof lies in the magnificence, the grand scale, of these buildings, among the noblest works of man, the means by which a people is fed….

"Farther east again, down a bumpy incline and under a tunnel, can be found the cheerful little dock where for fifty years excursion steamers put out for the celebrated Saguenay cruises, now unhappily a thing of the past. They used to leave to the sound of a brass band, with a happy crowd at dockside to bid all voyagers Godspeed, as if they were crossing the Atlantic instead of carting their golf clubs down to Murray Bay. Once at the end of a sweltering summer I stood at the extreme edge of that wharf and watched the wedding-cake shape of one of those steamers, the *Tadoussac* or the *Richelieu* float off illuminated into a soft gray twilight, all lights blazing, band playing, faint shouts of good cheer ringing across calm water. The river opened before her, under the great Jacques-Cartier she went, broad-beamed and dignified, softly outlined, gone."

A boat excursion also figures in Mairuth Sarsfield's 1997 novel *No Crystal Stair*, about Montreal's black community in the 1940s. A picnic is the highlight of a cruise organized by the Union United Congregational church. "By eight-fifteen, the Willow party was *en route*, squeezed cheerfully into Poppa Dad's noisy Chevy, greeting community people, mixed families, and friends from all over the Island of Montreal as, in their hundreds, they converged on foot, by bus, street car, taxi, bicycle, and private car on old Victoria Pier below Viger, near rue St. Denis, from where the boat *S.S. Belle Isle* would sail."

A wonderful description of the river at the easternmost stretch of the island is to be found in Jovette Marchessault's autobiographical novel, *Mother of the Grass*. Marchessault grew up in the 1940s in Pointe aux Trembles, an area known as Bout de l'Île, or Island's End. Of mixed Cree and French-Canadian origins ("We lived as a tribe, in a great congregation of nerve cells and blood cells"), Marchessault writes of her beginnings with an almost otherworldly lyricism.

RÉJEAN DUCHARME

One of Quebec's most original authors, Réjean Ducharme is also its most mysterious and reclusive. In 1965, Ducharme submitted the manuscript of his novel *L'Avalée des avalés* (*The Swallower Swallowed*) to a Montreal publisher, only to have it promptly returned. Not skipping a beat, he despatched the book – along with two earlier novels – to France's most distinguished house, Éditions Gallimard. Gallimard published all three in rapid succession.

The appearance of *L'Avalée des avalés* caused a literary sensation. It was immediately translated into four languages and its author hailed a genius. Hounded by journalists, Ducharme changed residence almost day by day. Rumours flew about the author and accusations were made that a youthful Quebecer could not have produced such a work of genius.

Ducharme was born in the small town of St. Félix de Valois in 1941. In a brief 1968 interview, he confided that, in the midst of a large family, he had spent a solitary childhood. He attended classical college in Joliette and, for a semester, Montreal's École Polytechnique. A grab bag of occupations followed: encyclopaedia salesman, theatre usher, proofreader. For a short period, he even trained in the Royal Canadian Air Force.

Given the sketchy outline of the author's life and the astonishing virtuosity of *The Swallower Swallowed*, the public's interest in Ducharme is not surprising. Nominated for France's prestigious Prix Goncourt, the book won a Governor General's Award in 1967. Ducharme has also received a string of other prizes – including a Governor General's Award for drama – culminating in the $100,000 inaugural Prix Gilles Corbeil in 1990 awarded by the Émile Nelligan Foundation for achievements in French-language literature by a North American.

Only two of Ducharme's novels and one play have been translated into English, his linguistic richness and playfulness stumping most attempts at crossing the language divide. But even in the original French, Ducharme's dense, often lyrical prose and brilliant shattering of the normal conventions of language pose a major challenge. The distinguished critic Gilles Marcotte once called his works "both the apotheosis and the negation of the novel."

Réjean Ducharme recognized that people other than French Canadians lived in Outremont.

"In those days we lived beside the river. An utterly beautiful river, with its depths turned in our direction. My grandmother said that the river was a baby-bottle for the whales and their children, formula which went to their heads and made them sing and snort out loud.... This river was a feast for the eyes, the ears, and the heart. Living beside a river, particularly one in a northern land, quickly teaches you the habits of eternity. You have the feeling that someone has personally handed you a flawless diamond, a secret, a gift."

The nourishing qualities of the river (similar to the attributes assigned to the mountain by Monique Proulx and Jacques Godbout) are poetically advanced by Réjean Ducharme in his novel *Le Nez qui voque.* "Where is my river, the Saint Lawrence? It is there. You can't hear it. It's like the horse that awaits you in the stable. You don't see it. But I can feel that it's there, that it flows while it pretends not to flow, that it embraces the city, that it carries a thousand cargoes on its back as if they were nothing."

We will give the last words to Geoffry Chadwick, the middle-aged and jaded gay lawyer created by Edward O. Phillips in *Sunday's Child*, the first of a series of comic thrillers set in Westmount, as he surveys the city from the home of his aunt Winnifred on the mountain in 1980. In a voice in which irony, pride, and love are commingled, Chadwick speaks for many a Montrealer: "I stood in the window of the guest bedroom…and looked across rooftops, across the city shimmering with streetlights to a black void which must be the river. Canada's own St. Lawrence. The mighty St. Lawrence. It is not the longest nor the most historic, not even the most mysterious. It undoubtedly carries the most industrial pollution, but it is mine. My river, my city, my life…. Seen through a luminous haze of alcohol and neon Montreal struck me as beautiful beyond belief."

Edward O. Phillips takes satiric jabs at Westmount's smart set.

EDWARD O. PHILLIPS

Born in Westmount in 1931, Edward O. Phillips was educated at McGill, at the Université de Montréal where he studied law, and at Harvard and Boston universities. He taught in public and private schools in Boston and Montreal and subsequently embarked on what with typical self-deprecation he has described as "a brief, undistinguished career as a painter. After I had sold to members of my family and friends on my Christmas card list, I tried my hand at fiction."

In 1981 Phillips launched *Sunday's Child*, the first of a series of comedies of manners featuring Geoffry Chadwick, a fiftyish homosexual lawyer who accidentally commits murder in Westmount. Subsequent novels in the series demonstrated Phillips's complete familiarity with the old anglo plutocracy of the town where he continues to live, and a biting wit. *Buried on Sunday*, Phillips's second novel, was awarded the Arthur Ellis Prize from the Crimewriters of Canada.

Chapter 7

THE MAIN AND THE PLATEAU

THE MAIN IS, unquestionably, the most famous street in Montreal, stretching across the width of the island and slicing both it and the city into its two major divisions: east and west. Aline Gubbay, a local historian who has chronicled many of Montreal's neighbourhoods, calls it the city's "strong, sinewy backbone," while fiction writer Andrée Maillet has described it as "the main street of the city, all the city in one street...."

It wasn't always called the Main. Its forerunner, named rue Saint-Lambert (after Lambert Closse, Maisonneuve's commander-in-chief, who died in an Indian attack in 1662), was laid out by Dollier de Casson in 1672 to run the short distance between Notre Dame and St. Jacques Streets. In the next century St. Lambert was lengthened beyond the walls of the old city in the direction of the parish of St. Laurent to the northwest, thus acquiring, outside the walls, the name of rue Saint-Laurent. In 1792, when the city limits were expanded, rue Saint-Laurent was declared the line of demarcation between the new east and west districts. In the early nineteenth century it became the main street of a burgeoning suburb known in French as Faubourg Saint-Laurent and in English as St. Lawrence Suburb. It was in this period that the street began to be called "the Main" or "la Main," abbreviated from "St. Lawrence Main" or "Saint-Laurent de la Main." To the west of this dividing line lay English Montreal; to the east, French.

But French and English were never alone on the Main. Scots and Irish were numerous enough in 1834 for Jacques Viger, Montreal's first mayor, to devise a city coat of arms in which the thistle and shamrock held equal sway with the fleur-de-lys and English rose. By the 1820s, there was a German Protestant church in the neighbourhood and two synagogues. After Montreal was declared the official point of entry for Lower Canada in 1832, the Main became, in Gubbay's words, "a cosmopolitan highway, a 'third city', neither French nor English, along which each ethnic group passed." The street was

Opposite: *Immigrants arriving in Montreal at the turn of the century. Many newcomers settled in the area known as the Plateau.*

characterized by a great deal of fluidity, communities replacing one another in quick succession as population patterns shifted.

Among the earliest and most numerous of the cosmopolitans were the Jews and the Italians. Both groups settled initially in the area of the Lower Main – the part running south of Ste. Catherine Street to the harbour – then staked out distinct portions of the street as their own.

Although since World War II Italians have overtaken Jews as the largest ethnic minority in the city, Jews were originally Montreal's quintessential trail-blazing "others." The earliest Jews in the province arrived with the British forces in 1759 and 1760. Merchants who imported food and other staples, they were English-speaking British subjects. Although they were a statistical anomaly, numbering a mere fifty-two settlers even after seventy years in the city, they founded the first synagogue in Canada, as early as 1768 at the corner of St. Lambert (the future Main) and Notre Dame Streets. Popularly known as the "Spanish and Portuguese," it followed the Sephardic ritual; in 1859 immigrants from Germany and Poland founded the Shaar Hashomayim synagogue nearby which followed the Ashkenazi service. When later Jewish immigrants arrived in greater numbers, it was natural that they gravitated toward the Main, where these earlier congregations had already taken root.

Significant migration began in the 1880s and peaked immediately before World War I. (In 1881, when the community was 120 years old, there were fewer than 1,000 Jews in Quebec. By 1921, there were nearly 48,000.) Hailing from eastern and central Europe, Jews brought diverse languages, religious customs, and political currents to the city. Their lingua franca was Yiddish, a language built on a Germanic grammatical structure, written in Hebrew characters, and, over the course of its nearly 1,000-year history, influenced by Aramaic, Russian, Polish, and some Romance languages. These immigrants worked in sweatshops or behind shop counters, peddled ice or rags, toiled as longshoremen, tinsmiths, and carpenters. They also crammed the seats of the newly constructed Monument National Theatre. Inaugurated in 1894 and designed as the headquarters of the Saint-Jean-Baptiste Society, the elegant Belle Époque building near the corner of St. Laurent and René Lévesque Boulevard contained shops, a museum, a trade school, and, most importantly, a theatre – a theatre which, incongruously, became an outlet for Jewish talent. In his 1990 essay "Montreal of Yesterday," Zachary Baker comments, "The popular culture of the immigrant quarter in that pre-electronic age, consisted of Yiddish theatre, vaudeville and primitive, silent motion pictures. The

Widening St. Lawrence Main Street about 1890. The view looks north from near the street's southern end in Old Montreal.

Monument National Theatre, where local and visiting troupes put on the best and worst Yiddish plays, also was, and still is [though no longer for Yiddish plays], a fixture on lower St. Lawrence Boulevard."

Three Jewish newspapers were published from offices on the Main in this period. The *Jewish Times* came out in English, and *Die Zeit* (The Times) and the *Keneder Adler* (Canadian Eagle, the only Yiddish daily in Canada) in Yiddish. Over time, Montreal also became an influential literary centre for Yiddish.

Before World War I, Jews lived in the area of the Lower Main (formerly the Faubourg St. Laurent), roughly occupying the district of present-day Chinatown. The corner of St. Urbain and Dorchester (now René Lévesque) was the heart of the neighbourhood. Small class and occupational differences governed the unwritten rules of settlement within the area. Unskilled workers lived mainly in the narrow lanes just west of the Main near Craig (now

The ethnic Main: St. Laurent Boulevard near the corner of Avenue des Pins.

St. Antoine) and Notre Dame Streets, for monthly rents between eight and ten dollars. Tailors lived a little farther uptown, the rents rising incrementally to reach twelve and fifteen dollars a month above Sherbrooke Street as far north as Duluth. A minority of prosperous Jews lived on Sherbrooke near University Street and McGill College Avenue.

Scores of writers have immortalized the Jewish Main, extolling its virtues as a shopping mecca, excoriating its ugliness, milking it for exotic local colour.

Mordecai Richler, one of Canada's most celebrated writers, is arguably the best-known author Montreal has ever produced. Caustic, controversial, and often crude, Richler shares with the title character of his 1989 novel *Solomon Gursky Was Here* "an unquenchable itch to meddle and provoke." But Richler's scatological inventiveness is fired by a secular moralism that is no less important to an appreciation of his work than is his gleeful ribaldry. Stupidity, hypocrisy, pretentiousness, and greed have always been the cardinal sins in his canon, targets of the savage wit that is as acidic and uproarious in his latest novel, *Barney's Version*, as it was when he began to write nearly fifty years ago.

Richler was born in 1931, the second son of an ill-matched couple. His father dealt in scrap metal, his mother was the daughter of a scholarly rabbi and had literary pretensions of her own. The family lived on St. Urbain, two streets west of the Main, until Mordecai was thirteen, when his parents separated. Though he left Canada at nineteen to spend some twenty years in Europe and now divides his time between Montreal, Quebec's Eastern Townships, and London, England, he has written that he feels "forever rooted in Montreal's St. Urbain Street. That was my time, my place, and I have elected myself to get it right."

And right he has got it in the novels *The Apprenticeship of Duddy Kravitz* and *St. Urbain's Horseman*, and in the collection of stories and essays called *The Street*, in which he wrote:

"St. Urbain was one of five working-class ghetto streets between the Main and Park Avenue.

"To a middle-class stranger, it's true, the five streets would have seemed interchangeable. On each corner a cigar store, a grocery, and a fruit man. Outside staircases everywhere. Winding ones, wooden ones, rusty and risky ones. An endless repetition of...peeling balconies and waste lots making the occasional gap here and there. But, as we boys knew, each street between the Main and Park Avenue represented subtle differences in income. No two cold-water flats were alike and no two streets were the same either....

"Of the five streets, St. Urbain was the best."

Richler is no less authoritative on the subject of the Main than he is about St. Urbain. In *The Street*, he focuses on its bazaar-like character, calling it "rich in delights, but also squalid, filthy, and hollering with stores whose wares, whether furniture or fruit, were ugly or damaged." The Main had "something for all our appetites": on one side of the street stood a synagogue, on the other, a theatre advertising "The Picture They Claimed Could Never Be Made." A little farther along were places of self-improvement such as the Workman's Circle – and strip joints.

"Around the corner there was the ritual baths, the *shvitz* or *mikva*, where my grandfather and his cronies went before the High Holidays, emerging boiling red from the highest reaches of the steam rooms to happily flog each other with brushes fashioned of pine tree branches. Where supremely orthodox women went once a month to purify themselves."

Richler recalls being taken to the Main, before the Jewish High Holidays, for the annual purchase of a new suit – "the itch of the cheap tweed was excruciating" – and new shoes – "with a built-in squeak." Fruit, meat, and fish were purchased on the Main as well, "and here the important thing was to watch the man with the scales."

The Winnipeg-born author Jack Ludwig, who has made his reputation in the United States, uses the Main as the backdrop for a short story set in the 1950s entitled "A Woman of Her Age." Once a week, on Fridays, septuagenarian Mrs. Doba Goffman has her chauffeur drive her from the upper reaches of Westmount down to the Main to recapture the days before tragedy befell her when she was still a hard-working young radical married to a shop owner on the street. Heartbroken and more than a little eccentric, Mrs. Goffman has the chauffeur drop her a couple of streets short of the prime market area and walks the rest of the way. She wears an old coat purchased years ago in Eaton's basement, lest she look out of place among the working-class shoppers. Her oversize nose inhales the ripe scents of the Main. "Doba, catch that goose roasting, her nose seems to say. Hey, poppyseed cookies! *Real* stuffed fish! St Lawrence Boulevard, I love you!

"Mitchell the 'Kosher Butcher' nodded...as she walked past his full window – fresh killed ducks and chickens hanging by their feet, cows' brains in pools, tongues like holsters, calves' feet signed by the Rabbi's indelible pencil." At the corner of Rachel and the Main, Mrs. Goffman stopped to allow a horse-drawn wagon to go past. "What a wonderful stink an old nag gave off! Wheels creaking was a melody to her deafish ears." Amidst the Rachel Street market stalls, Mrs. Goffman shopped for items she would never take back home to her antiseptic Westmount mansion. She "rubbed a cold slimy fish with her manicured fingernails, poked open a carp's small-toothed mouth, combed its still freezing fins with her wrinkled hand." Her final stop was Triminiuk's Delicatessen, where the air was like "a home-made mist – garlic pickles, pastrami, salami, sauerkraut, fresh rye bread...."

The novelist, short story writer, and poet Andrée Maillet, who wrote two collections inspired by the city in the 1960s, characterizes the Main between

Opposite: *Mordecai Richler, renowned chronicler of St. Urbain Street. The photo is from 1969.*

Ste. Catherine and Mont Royal Boulevard as resembling "the main artery of a ghetto: it's as picturesque as all hell, but not very clean." Observing men in Hasidic garb with a mixture of fascination and repulsion, Maillet's male narrator comments, "To tell the truth, I'm no anti-semite, but do they ever wash, these sallow Jews, and do they need to be dirty in order to practice orthodoxy? They walk by me as if I didn't exist..., wearing an air of humble pride like exiled kings or caged beasts, a people fallen from on high."

Writing of an earlier era in *The Fat Woman Next Door Is Pregnant*, Michel Tremblay intimately portrays the way that Jews and French Canadians lived cheek by jowl in the inner city in wartime and highlights the seeds of friction between them. He describes the route of what was once the longest streetcar ride in Montreal, the number 52, which started at the corner of Mount Royal and Fullum in the Plateau, then traversed the city to the west end, taking St. Laurent as its north-south thoroughfare. Housewives from the Plateau "would set off in a group on Friday or Saturday, noisy, laughing, tearing open bags of penny candy or chewing enormous wads of gum. As long as the streetcar was going down Mont-Royal, they were in their element, giving each other slaps on the back if they choked, calling out to other women they knew; sometimes they'd even ask the driver how come he wasn't in the army. But when the streetcar turned down Saint-Laurent, heading south, suddenly they'd calm down and sink back into the straw seats; all of them, without exception, owed money to the Jews on Saint-Laurent, especially to the merchants who sold furniture and clothes; and for them, the long street separating rue Mont-Royal from rue Sainte-Catherine was a very sensitive one to cross."

In her 1955 novel, *The Cashier*, Gabrielle Roy gives her beleaguered Everyman, the bank clerk Alexandre Chenevert, a moonlighting job on the Main in postwar Montreal. "In May he began to devote two evenings a week to the tangled accounts of a man named Markhous, a Jewish cloth merchant born in Hungary, who operated a wholesale store on the Boulevard St.-Laurent.... The shop was a junk pile. A small table served Alexandre as a desk. Bolts of cloth, bundles of samples, even dried skins...lay scattered upon it." Markhous wants him to dicker with the figures so he'll pay less income tax. He plies him with advice on how to get rich. "When Alexandre was free to go home, Markhous would detain him to recount his rise to fortune in the city, how he had landed in Montreal with only ten dollars in his pocket.... He would constantly put his hand on his shoulder, clasp his fingers; he would make him little presents of candy, of still-serviceable cloth. And Alexandre,

who had so often scolded Godias for his anti-Semitism, made it a point of honor not to admit that Markhous weighed on his nerves. But his effort to be friendly wore Alexandre down."

The Montreal-born playwright, filmmaker, and novelist Ted Allan, author of the award-winning screenplay *Lies My Father Told Me*, sets an anti-Semitic moment on the mountain in a short story also entitled "Lies My Father Told Me." Davie, Allan's fictional alter ego in the story, and his grandfather live in the area of the Main and are riding home in the horse-drawn wagon with which the grandfather carries on his trade as a peddler. "One Sunday on our ride home through the mountain, a group of young boys and girls threw stones at us and shouted in French, *'Juif... Juif...'* Grandpa held his strong arm around me, cursed back, muttering 'anti-Semites' under his breath. When I asked him what he said, he answered, 'It is something I hope you never learn.'"

Richler writes in *The Street*, "Looking back, it's easy to see that the real trouble was there was no dialogue between us and the French Canadians, each elbowing the other, striving for WASP acceptance." He gives a stinging description of the Jewish stereotype of the French Canadian:

> "Pea-soups were for turning the lights on and off on the sabbath and running elevators and cleaning out chimneys and furnaces. They were, it was rumoured, ridden with T.B., rickets, and the syph. Their older women were for washing windows and waxing floors and the younger ones were for maids in the higher reaches of Outremont, working in factories, and making time with, if and when you had the chance. The French Canadians were our schwartzes."

Prejudice and misunderstanding between ethnic groups were not restricted to Jews and French Canadians, nor was exploitation necessarily interethnic. In his 1992 novel, *Le Figuier enchanté*, the Italian-born Montreal playwright and novelist Marco Micone cites the sign "Pas de chiens, pas d'Italiens" in a Montreal window of the 1950s. The immigrant father figure in *Le Figuier enchanté* writes a pained letter home to his village in the Molise reporting on this sign and then adds, "I work for an Italian who treats his workers like dogs."

Although there have been Italians associated with the city since the seventeenth century – the Carignan-Salières regiment from France included several Italian soldiers – it wasn't until the last two decades of the nineteenth century that Italian arrivals became numerically significant. Economic and political upheavals precipitated by the Italian unification movement in the 1860s, as well as the pressure of overpopulation and chronic poverty in the south, encouraged large-scale emigration.

Italian immigration to Canada occurred in two main waves: from the turn of the century to World War I and from 1950 to 1970. The vast majority came from the impoverished south, the earliest groups working seasonally on the railways and canals. Many were recruited by unscrupulous labour agents who exploited them for a quick cash return. Subsequently they found jobs in the building trades, gardening, and landscaping, and became the progenitors of an Italian-based construction industry in Montreal.

The first district to be called "La Piccola Italia" was centred on the parish church of Madonna-di-Monte-Carmel below Ste. Catherine Street, between St. Laurent and Amherst, but the name Little Italy gradually became associated with a section of the Main much farther to the north. Commenting on the settlement patterns of turn-of-the-century immigrants, Aline Gubbay writes in *A Street Called the Main*, "In the fields and forests north of Jean Talon there were rabbits for the hunting, and everywhere wild fruits to be gathered, cherries and grapes, from which to make wine. New immigrants, dismayed at the limited choice of fruits and vegetables they found in the city markets, staked out allotments and spent most of their free time working their gardens, arriving, mostly on foot, from their homes on the Lower Main."

In the early 1900s Italians working at the CPR Mile End station (the Mile End name came from a racetrack that was once a mile away from the city limits) and freight yards at the corner of Bellechasse and St. Laurent began to close the gap between the area of their first settlement on the Lower Main and these Jean Talon fields. They surrounded their little homes with lush vegetable gardens and grapevines. A magnificent new parish church, Madonna-Della-Difesa was begun in 1911 in this new district and still stands today on the corner of Dante and Alma Streets in Little Italy.

With time these industrious immigrants created numerous businesses small and large – grocery stores, restaurants, shoe shops, and so on. In 1911, Charles-Honoré Catelli began a pasta business at the corner of Bellechasse and Drolet Streets

Shovelling up cabbage leaves in the Jean Talon Market, the heart of Montreal's Little Italy.

that bore his name, although it has since been bought out by Borden Foods Canada.

As the city's Italian population has grown, it has spread to many other neighbourhoods. But the area of the Jean Talon market just east of the Main at Jean Talon remains quintessentially identified with them. In Régine Robin's poetic and meditative 1983 novel, *The Wanderer,* about the clash of cultures in Montreal, the protagonist – like Robin, a woman with braided ethnic origins who comes to Montreal via Paris – roams the various neighbourhoods of the city. Fascinated by them, she is nonetheless unable to put down roots anywhere. In the company of a Paraguayan émigré, she discovers the northern section of the Main, in the vicinity of the market and the Italian quarter. Robin sets the scene in sensuous prose, piling detail upon detail: "There would be mounds of tomatoes, cauliflowers, lettuces, and peppers, straw baskets full of blueberries or strawberries, and further on, braids of garlic, red and white onions, shallots, herbs. There would be the scent of fennel, thyme, and mint amidst the flies and wasps, between the slightly sour watermelons and the prickly pears from who knows where. Still further, flowers and plants, mellow odours wafting over the voices speaking Italian and Greek. A cheerful confusion they'd feel at home in, delighting in the array of honey and natural jams, jars of wild garlic, sachets of lavender."

The global flavour of the Main was given ample play in a murder mystery set in the neighbourhood by the American writer Rodney Whitaker, who uses the pseudonym Trevanian for his thrillers. His 1976 novel, *The Main,* revolves around Claude Lapointe, an aging detective with a serious heart condition who is searching for a murderer in the area.

RÉGINE ROBIN

Born in Paris in 1939 of Jewish parents who left Poland for France before World War II, Régine Robin obtained a doctorate in history at the Université de Paris, before coming to Quebec in 1977.

A historian, essayist, and novelist, she is an important and original thinker, who has taught since 1982 at the Université du Québec à Montréal and been acclaimed as a significant voice in a new Quebec literature of hybridity and exile. In addition to *The Wanderer,* she has published another novel and a collection of short stories; her non-fiction titles won a Governor General's Award in 1987 and the Prix Jean-Jacques Rousseau in 1994. In all of her work – her books include a study of Socialist Realism and a biography of Kafka – there is a preoccupation with the relationship between personal identity and society. In recognition of her groundbreaking studies in literary theory, she has been hailed by *Le Devoir* as "Montreal's grande dame of postmodernism."

"The swearing, the shouting, the grumbling, the swatches of conversation are in French, Yiddish, Portuguese, German, Chinese, Hungarian, Greek.... Signs in the window of a bank attest to the cosmopolitan quality of the street:

HABLAMOS ESPANOL
OMI OYMEN EΛΛHNIKA
PARLIAMO ITALIANO
WIR SPRECHEN DEUTSCH
FALAMOS PORTUGUES

"And there is a worn street joke: 'I wonder who in that bank can speak all those languages?'

"'The customers.'"

The highlighting of the international aspect of the street by an American writer coincided with the beginning of an upswing in the fortunes of the Main, until then generally regarded by the mainstream as a slum inhabited by lowlifes and foreigners reeking of garlic. Even most immigrants eschewed the area once they prospered, returning to it only in order to procure a cherished delicacy or two unavailable in more upscale parts of town. In the 1980s, however, trendy boutiques, restaurants, and clubs began to spring up next to the stalwart old ethnic businesses, and it became fashionable to celebrate St. Laurent's character as a multicultural emporium.

Alongside this reputation as a cosmopolitan mecca, the Main has another, seamier persona based around the intersection of St. Laurent and Ste. Catherine and the streets running south toward the harbour. Here a sophisticated demi-monde jostled with strung-out poverty; risqué entertainment vied with bargain-basement brothels. Writers have picked up on both the air of menace and the outrageous beauty of some of the denizens of these streets. Constance Beresford-Howe, for instance, in her 1973 novel *The Book of Eve*, writes of "the weasel gangs of teen-agers, the raisin-eyed toughs, the belligerent drunks," while the poet Jean-Paul Daoust notes that "the transvestites with their high heels hobble in the slush of their make-up."

For the Paris-born critic and novelist Jean Basile, the Main is "our tragic dimension." In *La Jument des Mongols*, the first of a trilogy of novels in which Montreal is a virtual personage, he produces a masterful and relentless description of the Main's seediness, yet his narrator still somehow celebrates its dives, greasy spoons, and strip joints, extolling "the Midnight and the Savoy that are off limits to all those who earn more than one thousand dollars and two cents." "I adore the Savoy and the Midnight," says another character, "but if you frequent them, you'd better resort to American style hygiene and dust yourself generously with DDT powder."

The street people of the Main and its cheap glitter have a mythic quality for Michel Tremblay, who frequently uses them in the eleven-play cycle that begins with *Les Belles-soeurs* (1968) and ends with *Damnée Manon, sacrée Sandra* (1977). In the penultimate play, *Sainte-Carmen of the Main* (1976), the eponymous heroine performs in the Rodéo, a sleazy Western-style club on the Main. When Carmen refuses to sing the Nashville cowboy yodels that have always been her trademark and begins to substitute songs she has written herself in the idiom of the street, she elicits a diatribe from her lover, Maurice, the owner of the club: "People who end up on the Main don't want to be saved! I've been working the Main for twenty-five years, night and day.... The Main is my mother!... She gave me my first rap on the knuckles, my first kick in the ass and my first dose. There isn't a square inch of the Main that I don't know by heart. And believe me, kiddo, it's not you who's going to change her." He mocks Carmen's desire to give the people songs about themselves that they can identify with: "'The Main needs someone to talk to it about the Main'? The Main needs someone to give her a good screw!'"

As closely as Tremblay's writing has been associated with the prostitutes, transvestites, and cheap entertainers of the Main, he is most intimately identified with the streets of the Plateau Mont-Royal, the primarily residential and working-class neighbourhood whose boundaries extend roughly from the Mount Royal Park/Outremont area on the west, along Van Horne and the Canadian Pacific Railway tracks on the north and east (in the vicinity of Frontenac Street), and Sherbrooke Street in the south.

In the cycle of novels that carries the overarching title "Les chroniques du Plateau Mont-Royal," Tremblay's semi-autobiographical characters pepper the streets of his formative years (all of them east of the Main): Mont-Royal, Marie-Anne, St. Joseph, Papineau, Gilford, Calixa-Lavallée, de Lanaudière, and, above all, Fabre Street where he was born and grew up.

The Plateau is one of the city's old-new neighbourhoods. In the early part of the nineteenth century, it was largely uninhabited – a place of orchards and fields. A few hamlets dotted the area, home to stone cutters who supplied the greystone for the buildings in the city below the Sherbrooke Street escarpment. By mid-century, streets such as Coloniale and Hôtel-de-Ville were taking shape

Mile End Road (today Mount Royal Avenue) about 1875, when it was still a street in the village of St. Jean Baptiste.

as a burgeoning city spread northward. A reservoir on the east side, having proved inadequate to halt the great fire of 1852, was filled in and became St. Louis Square. Farther east, Lafontaine Park was created in 1888 from a military parade ground.

Development above Sherbrooke Street was spurred on after 1861 by the introduction of horse-drawn trams on St. Laurent, and by the completion of a railway in the Mile End area that defined the northern and eastern edges of the Plateau. At the end of the nineteenth century, the population of the villages was swelling with new immigrants from Europe. By 1900, with the annexation of municipalities such as Saint-Jean-Baptiste and Mile End, the Plateau began to resemble the neighbourhood it is today.

But by no means is the area one of uniform streets and blocks. As Hugh Hood writes in the 1967 story "Light Shining Out of Darkness," "South of

HUGH HOOD

Hugh Hood was born in Toronto in 1928 to parents who embodied Canada's linguistic duality. His father was an anglophone from Nova Scotia; his French-Canadian mother grew up in one of the earliest French communities of Toronto. Hood, the author of about thirty books, has remained faithful to his bicultural roots: he obtained a doctorate at the University of Toronto and subsequently taught English literature at the Université de Montréal.

Hood's reputation is largely based upon fiction, though he has also published essays, criticism, and biography. Recognized early in his career as a fine practitioner of the short story, he is today more closely identified with his projected twelve-volume New Age/Nouveau Siècle novel series, now almost complete. In it he set out to express nothing less than a fictional representation of the total Canadian experience in the twentieth century.

Key to an appreciation of Hood's art is his staunch Catholicism. Weaned on the Scriptures and educated in Catholic schools, he has described himself as "through and through a Catholic" writer, and sincerely searches in ordinary daily life for evidence of a higher meaning.

Hood's notable short story collections include *Around the Mountain: Scenes from Montreal Life* (1967), in which the boundary between fiction and essay is provocatively blurred; *The Fruit Man, The Meat Man and The Manager* (1971), and *None Genuine Without This Signature* (1980).

Hugh Hood saw redemption in the flight of a kite on the mountain.

Boulevard Mont-Royal as far as Rachel, from the Main eastwards past Papineau, lies the country of the *ruelles* [lanes]. Close to the Main are streets like Henri-Julien, de Bullion, Hôtel de Ville, one way north or south, which in another place might be considered slums, [but] not in Montréal.... They are narrow blocks, buildings fronting on parallel main streets and backing on a shared alley." Hood's eye alights on "a bare-bottomed infant creeping along the *ruelle* curb, already trained to evade the creeping delivery vans which sometimes bump along the pitted track."

When these streets were laid out in the nineteenth century, there was no automobile traffic to take into account, so houses crowd against each other. But there are nonetheless subtle gradations of status and elegance between streets or even between sections of the same street. Triplexes became the Plateau's dominant housing type when developers sought to get the most they could from land that was increasing in value as the population soared. On poorer streets, buildings might be constructed right up to the sidewalk, while elsewhere they were set back allowing for small gardens in front and the ubiquitous outside staircases of the Plateau. One theory about these external stairs is that they were adopted because they allowed maximum living space on the first two floors of a building.

Here is Hugh Hood once more, in 1967:

"The main streets east and west are...Marie-Anne, Rachel and Duluth, and a slow summer bicycle ride east along any of them will display the

A panoramic view of the Plateau neighbourhood in the early years of the twentieth century. The view is from above Lafontaine Park, with the St. Jean Baptiste Church in the centre of the photo.

variety of customs and of wealth. Go along Marie-Anne and your way east from the Main is at first narrow and crowded, the business in the small grocery stores done half in the street…. [But] if you were to ride as far as Fabre, you would spot on the southeast corner a line of half a dozen row houses which could have been built yesterday, they shine so with fresh paint and gleaming woodwork, and they aren't restored town houses for television executives either, though each has a television aerial. They are two storeys high, and the curtains have all been starched this morning.

"North and south are some big important streets like Saint-Hubert, and here again you'll find a kind of dwelling that is perhaps indigenous. I mean those long rows of tall broad uninterrupted buildings…approached by outside staircases – front and rear, so that…you climb an outside staircase and enter an independent dwelling, often totally separated from the rest of the building except by the plumbing…. There is something very *Montréalais* about such buildings…."

Indeed, there is something quintessentially *Montréalais* about the Plateau Mont-Royal. St. Denis Street and the area to the east is almost uniformly French and has many associations with French Montreal's literary culture. It incorporates such iconic literary landmarks as St. Louis Square where Émile Nelligan threatened to commit suicide.

The meteoric talent and tormented destiny of Nelligan (1879–1941) have long transfixed French Canada. His life has inspired an opera and a ballet, a prestigious poetry prize bears his name, and his writings have generated a veritable literary industry of critical texts.

Nelligan's life makes wonderful grist for both Freudian and historical mills. The son of an Irish-immigrant father and a *pure laine québécoise* mother, he presents classic oedipal and two-solitudes complexes. His unilingually English father, an inspector of postal services in the Gaspé, was intensely practical and often absent from the family home in Montreal. The sensitive young boy identified with his musically gifted, patriotically *canadienne* mother, going so far as to pronounce his name the French way and spelling it "Nelighan."

When Nelligan was eighteen, his father tried to derail him from his poetic aspirations by first sending him on a sea voyage to Britain, then by finding him a job as a clerk. Neither ploy worked. Nelligan threw himself all the more into his art, but the inner turmoil which bore fruit in his work also unhinged him:

Émile Nelligan was the Plateau's most famous poet.

the night of his greatest triumph as a poet – when he was borne through the streets of Montreal on the shoulders of his admirers – proved to be his last public appearance.

This drama unfolded on May 26, 1899, when, in response to some earlier criticism of his work by a visiting French critic, Nelligan gave a riveting recital of his newly minted poem, "La Romance du vin." Its lines include:

I dream of making poems that will find
Renown, and sigh the haunting dirge of winds
Moving in autumn through the distant haze.

Nelligan's brief moment of glory at the end of one century and the dawn of another was symbolic and timely: he was Canada's greatest nineteenth-century lyricist (in the 1960s the American literary critic Edmund Wilson called him "the only first-rate Canadian poet, French or English, that I have yet read"). Many also regard him, for reasons both of form and content, to be Canada's first modern poet.

In three years, between the ages of sixteen and nineteen, Nelligan produced some 160 poems that were dramatically different from any then written in this country. In nineteenth-century Quebec, patriotism, the glories of old France, ancestral fidelity to the land and Church were the accepted poetic themes. A poet was regarded as the mouthpiece of society's prevailing values.

In 1895 a group of students and intellectuals founded the *École littéraire de Montréal*, a literary society that met weekly to read poetry and discuss culture. Its honorary head was the establishment poet Louis Fréchette, but its most charismatic member proved to be Nelligan, who joined in 1897.

In his exploration of unusual symbols, sensitivity to the power of words, musicality, and preoccupation with personal melancholy and alienation, Nelligan stood in dramatic contrast to Fréchette, the poet laureate celebrating traditional values and historical themes. Nelligan looked for his inspiration to Edgar Allan Poe in the United States, and to the French Romantic and symbolist poets Baudelaire, Rimbaud, and Verlaine. He saw himself as a rebel artist with no future other than the writing of verse. In "A Poet" he pleads, "Let him live without doing him harm!/ Let him go, he's a dreamer passing by,/ An angelic soul opening to spring skies."

Nelligan, in his brooding, introspective verses, rarely looked beyond his studio window for inspiration, but in one poem, "Notre-Dame-de-la-Défaite,"

a glimpse of the city that nourished him shimmers before us:

Our Holy Lady, mantled in gold
From her flowering heath
  Comes each evening while her Jesus sleeps
In his Ville Marie

Our Holy Lady is enthroned on high
  Upon our Mount Royal
From whence her glance subdues the creatures
  Of the infernal abyss.
For she has decreed: "An angel
  With his gun protects
My silver city garlanded in snow."
  Our Lady of Heaven above!

No one can say what prompted him two months after his night of fame to climb a tree in St. Louis Square and threaten to do away with himself. Shortly thereafter he was committed to the Retraite Saint-Benoît, where he remained for twenty-five years. In 1925 he was transferred to Saint-Jean-de-Dieu Hospital, where he died in 1941. Diagnosed as a schizophrenic, he produced no new work during his confinement. Yet a writer friend who visited him in 1909 observed that he continued to show "an undeviating obsession with literature."

Many writers have grown up or lived in the Plateau (including Nelligan, who was raised on Laval Avenue, and Hubert Aquin, who attended nearby École Olier, Nelligan's alma mater) but Michel Tremblay is the Plateau's most famous and favourite son, its bard extraordinaire. The youngest of five children, he was born in 1942 to an elderly couple in a yellow brick house on rue Fabre. Poverty and a severe wartime housing shortage squeezed three families into seven rooms, with the result that he was brought up by no less than five women. His acute sensitivity to their sorrows and dreams has fed all of his writing.

Tremblay has mined both the emotional and physical terrain of his formative years in his plays and novels. He has raised a cast of working-class dysfunctionals to the level of universality and high art, even as they speak a *joual* whose cultural significance and linguistic validity have been a source of controversy in Quebec. An avowed separatist who refused to allow the performance of his plays in English in Montreal until after the Parti Québécois electoral win in

1976, Tremblay is the first Canadian playwright to find worldwide acclaim. (His nationalist fervour appears to have abated somewhat with the years, if his acceptance of the Order of Canada in 1999 is any measure.)

Translated into a variety of languages including Spanish, Polish, Yiddish, and even Scottish vernacular, Tremblay's first play, *Les Belles-soeurs*, has made a place for itself in the international repertoire of popular drama, to become a modern classic. Tremblay wrote *Les Belles-soeurs* in three weeks in 1965; it premiered at the Théâtre du Rideau Vert in 1968. On the surface, a naturalistic slice-of-life about a woman of Fabre Street who wins a million trading stamps and invites her relatives and friends to a stamp-pasting party, the play explores themes of "*la maudite vie plate*": the senseless daily routines and cultural impotence of the working class of east-end Montreal.

In much of his writing, Tremblay offers a harrowing view of both the Québécois proletarian family and the marginalized denizens of the Main. Yet some of his work, which is powerfully influenced by the hold on his imagination of his beloved mother, not only probes psychic pain but soars with a redemptive love.

Nowhere does this love show more than in *The Fat Woman Next Door Is Pregnant*, a novel that unfolds on a single spring day in May 1942. The title character is Tremblay's mother, pregnant with the author himself. In fact, all of rue Fabre seems in a state of expectancy, the fat woman only one of seven to be pregnant on the block. In the gentle climax of the novel, several brawny men are required to hoist the fat woman to the balcony overlooking the street, but when they succeed, the effort is worth it. "It's beautiful," the fat woman says, "the leaves haven't started to grow yet, but it won't be long now.... It smells of April or May, all at once.'" From the balcony, the fat woman begins to call the other pregnant women toward her, and the men sidle away. "Then from the balcony came laughter, whispers and shouts that were held back by hands placed over mouths. There were seven women. Six were in their early twenties and didn't know what was in store for them, while the seventh, who could have been their mother, explained it all to them."

This tender evocation is not only at variance with much of what Tremblay has written but with the general depiction of the area by other writers. Jacques Brault's poem "Rue St.-Denis" captures the grey melancholy of the street during the Depression years: "I know that the shadows under the staircases laugh at my dreams/...It was yesterday it is now the same cramped despair that limps along on the ice." To Irving Layton, wartime de Bullion is a "reptilian street whose scaly limbs/Are crooked stairways" where "rouged whores lean lips to narrow slits."

The most devastating description comes from the artist, playwright, and feminist Jovette Marchessault who grew up in the Plateau in wartime, after her family left behind the bucolic setting of Pointe aux Trembles, at the far eastern extremity of the island.

"One day we set up house in Boyer Street in Plateau Mont-Royal in a big casket with seven compartments.... In the fall and the winter in Boyer Street, we lived in the kitchen. In the evenings we would talk about the past and the future, about the latest obituary column in

JOVETTE MARCHESSAULT

Jovette Marchessault was born in 1938 into a working-class family of mixed Cree and French-Canadian origins. The two great positive influences of her childhood were periods spent in the semi-rural ambience of the Bout de l'Île section of Pointe aux Trembles, and her close relationship with her grandmother. The first rooted her in a love and first-hand knowledge of nature. The second gave her a mentor with unusual strength of character and a deep knowledge of native lore that would one day feed Marchessault's visual art and writing.

Marchessault grew up in poverty, terrorized and in rebellion against the cycle of family violence she witnessed in her Plateau Mont-Royal neighbourhood. She quit school at thirteen to work, first at a series of menial jobs, later in clerical positions. Though she had wanted to be a writer from childhood, it was only when her grandmother died in 1969 that Marchessault quit the jobs that hemmed her in and moved to a cabin in the woods to write. Defeated by the tyranny of the blank page, she turned to painting. She supported herself with her art for five years, exhibiting her masks, sculptures, drawings, and frescoes at galleries in Montreal, Toronto, New York, Paris, and Brussels. When she finally took another stab at writing in 1974, her writer's block had dissolved.

Like a Child of the Earth won the France-Quebec Prize in 1976. A highly original, lyrical, and often polemical novel, it begins and ends with the narrator's birth. As in the sequel, *Mother of the Grass* (1980), Marchessault stretches the boundaries of autobiography to include mythic and visionary experiences. In both these books, she is interested in reclaiming her Amerindian heritage, subtly linking the oppression of native people with the historical stifling of women's creativity.

In the late 1970s Marchessault began to write for the stage. Her plays, which have been performed in Montreal, Toronto, Vancouver, and New York, make inventive and freewheeling use of details from the lives of women writers and artists to reinterpret both religion and history from a feminist perspective. At first her writing was imbued with a radical lesbian sensibility, but in recent years it has become infused with a utopian world view that stresses interconnectedness and reconciliation. Marchessault won the Governor General's Award for drama for her 1990 play, *The Magnificent Voyage of Emily Carr*.

La Presse, about that vulture, Duplessis, about the fires on Papineau, Cartier, Christophe-Colomb, Beaudry, Ontario, Resther, Gilford, or Mentana. We would also talk about the water pipes which were about to freeze, about the windows we would have to stuff with newspapers against the draught, about tons of coal, about rationing, epidemics, my aunt Exilda's third marriage, my uncle Arthur's model widowerhood, more epidemics, and ever and always, with no opposition, about rats.

"This casket was literally infested with rats. Fat rats, noisy rats, snickering rats, rats that pillaged, rats that hung out, rats that harassed us, rats that skinned us very gently, and tasted us a bit at a time."

Some thirty years later the Plateau began another life, in the renovation and gentrification movement that has transformed many other inner city neighbourhoods all across North America. Its physical renewal was paralleled by the dynamic and upbeat literary outlook of Yves Beauchemin's immensely popular novel *The Alley Cat*, set in the mid-1970s, about an engaging young entrepreneur who wants to transform La Binerie, a (real) neighbourhood restaurant in the Plateau, located at Mount Royal near St. Denis. "It was a tiny place squeezed between two buildings that left it only fifteen feet of front, forcing it to stretch like a railway car.... There was room for only seventeen customers at a time, but they followed one another at a steady clip, for the restaurant was famous for its hearty country fare."

Florent Boissonneault's struggles to establish himself may be epic and uphill, he may be plagued by the nefarious machinations of the anglophone swindler Slipskin and the demonic immigrant Ratablavasky, but *The Alley Cat* is light years removed from the deep strain of pessimism and malaise that characterizes much of French-Canadian writing. And, at the conclusion of the story, Florent and his wife, Elise, "rented a lovely apartment on Sherbrooke Street near St-Denis (six rooms, stained-glass windows, fireplace) in an old stone building that stood three stories high." They have not yet reached the pinnacle of their ambitions – to own "a nice little house" in the South Shore suburbs – but the old-world elegance of refurbished turn-of-the-century Sherbrooke, bordering on the Plateau, is a sure sign of their incipient arrival.

Yves Beauchemin outside La Binerie, the short-order restaurant on Mount Royal Avenue that turns up in The Alley Cat.

Chapter 8

THE TOWN BELOW

O<small>F ALL OF</small> Montreal's neighbourhoods, the most geographically disadvantaged have been those in the city's southwest. Sprawling on both sides of the Lachine Canal, they lie below the escarpment that separated desirable land near the mountain from marshy terrain by the bank of the St. Lawrence. Here lay teeming working-class suburbs and slums afflicted by pollution, overcrowding, disease, and floods.

In the nineteenth century, St. Henri, Griffintown, and Pointe St. Charles shared a proletarian lineage that could be traced back to the building of the Lachine Canal. The industries that sprang up along the canal – brickyards, foundries, sugar refineries, breweries, clothing wholesalers, tanneries — attracted labourers, who, of necessity, settled close to their jobs. French, Irish, and English workmen first streamed to the districts close to Old Montreal, the French occupying St. Henri and the neighbouring villages of Ste. Cunégonde and St. Gabriel. Griffintown (named after a soap manufacturer whose factory was located on Wellington Street) was the preserve of the Irish. Pointe St. Charles belonged to a mixed bag of English-speakers, and, later, in the early years of the twentieth century, with the growth of heavy industries spawned by the railways – iron and steel, lumber, transportation equipment – to eastern Europeans: Poles, Ukrainians, Slovaks, and Czechs. By World War I, the banks of the Lachine Canal represented the largest concentration of industry in the country.

In 1897, a young shoe manufacturer named Herbert Ames, who in subsequent years carved out for himself a prominent career as a Montreal alderman bent upon civic reform, a Tory M.P., and an officeholder with the League of Nations, published *The City Below the Hill*, a landmark sociological study of life in the city's lower town. It depicted a bleak scene of unemployment, low wages, and deplorable living conditions. Among the families who lived in Griffintown, the average weekly wage was $11, dropping to as little as $1.75, or 25 cents a day.

Opposite: *Flooding was a persistent problem in low-lying areas near the river. The view here is of Little St. Antoine Street in Griffintown during the flood of 1886.*

Montreal's heavily industrialized southwestern neighbourhoods in 1902. The view is from the tower of Windsor Station.

Historian Terry Copp describes the way the district that Ames investigated looked at the turn of the twentieth century: "Rue Notre Dame bisected the City Below the Hill and was the axis of all the *quartiers* of the old city. It was paved for most of its length by 1897 with a mixture of cobblestones and wooden blocks. Like most of the other main streets, it was festooned with the overhead wires of the Montreal Street Railway Company. At night the glare of the arc lamps and the glow of the remaining gas lights cast dark shadows over most of the street. Notre Dame was lined with one- and two-storey structures, mainly brick, intermingled with the more substantial greystone and shanty-built

wooden houses." The side streets were narrower, with paving stones giving way to earth. Sewer lines served most of the area on either side of Notre Dame Street but, despite an 1887 municipal bylaw prohibiting construction of new houses served by so-called pit-privies, more than half the households in the lower town were so equipped. Ames's fierce campaign to suppress outhouses earned him the sobriquet of "Water Closet Ames." He also proposed a central charity board, slum clearance, improved housing, and other remedies, but his vision was too radical for the governing philosophy of the day.

Thirteen years after the publication of *The City Below the Hill*, in 1910,

Henry Vivian, a visiting British member of Parliament railed, "Unless preparations are constantly made for caring for your population, Montreal will become one of the greatest cesspools of human depravity in the world. Nothing in East London is worse than some of the conditions which I saw in Montreal yesterday, and immediate improvement is needed." Of health conditions and, in particular, infant mortality, Copp observes, "Montreal was the most dangerous city in the civilized world to be born in. Between 1899 and 1901, 26.76 per cent of all new born children died before they were one year old. This was more than double the figure for New York City, and it was customarily cited as being lower than only one large city – Calcutta."

Nevertheless, the economic boom of the early twentieth century brought a measure of prosperity to Montreal. But the upswing was twinned with new threats to the shaky existence of the poor: inflation and the influx of a giant wave of immigrants who competed with locals for jobs and cheap housing. Copp writes: "The working class population of Montreal found that growth in the size and aggregate wealth of the city did not result in a significant improvement in the standard of living.... During thirty years of great economic growth the urban-industrial working class in Montreal...lived within a culture of poverty, created primarily by subsistence incomes and an absence of job security...."

The great flaw in Montreal's economy lay in the importance of a harbour that was effectively closed for four months of the year because of the icing over of the St. Lawrence. Shipping companies, warehouses, the railroads, and all manner of trading establishments were locked into a reduced season that was devastating for wage earners.

Montreal was particularly hard hit during the Depression. No other major Canadian city was subjected to as much unemployment during the 1930s. In the absence of the social services safety net that later generations have come to take for granted, loss of jobs spelled utter destitution. As one immigrant later reminisced in an oral history of the Irish in Montreal, "We'd go to the Atwater market on Saturday night after the farmers would leave and take a piece of newspaper. We didn't even have a bag in those days. We'd pick up a piece of turnip if it was lying on the ground, or a carrot, or a cabbage leaf, bring it home, boil it and eat it. We were glad to get it." Recalled another old-timer of the same era: "It was so bad during the Depression that people burned their shutters and the adjoining doors to keep warm in the winter."

Of the working-class neighbourhoods of the southwest, none has gener-

St. Henri, in 1865, when it was still known as St. Henri des Tanneries.

ated as much fine literature as St. Henri. Before being absorbed by the city in the late nineteenth century, it was an outlying village called St. Henri des Tanneries, set well away from more populated areas because of the stench of its tanning businesses.

St. Henri launched two of French Canada's most influential writers, the earlier of whom was the pharmacist Émile Coderre, who used the pseudonym Jean Narrache. Coderre wrote popular poems in a kind of proto-*joual* that captured the energy and vitality of St. Henri where his pharmacy was located. In his collections, *Quand j'parl' tout seul...* (1932) and *J'parl' pour parler* (1939), he became the voice of workers and the unemployed hit hard by the Depression.

Although it is nearly impossible to capture the precise essence of Narrache's poetry in English, some sense of its spirit can be gained by comparing the French with a rough English translation:

J'parl' pour parler..., ça, je l'sai bien.
Mêm' si j'vous cassais les oreilles,
La vie rest'ra toujours pareille
Pour tous ceux que c'est un' vie d'chien.
J'parl' pour parler pas rien qu'pour moi,
Mais pour tous les gars d'la misère;
C'est la majorité su' terre.
J'prends pour eux autr's, c'est ben mon droit.

I talk just to talk - that's all I know how,
Though I yell and I holler
Life won't change no how
For all those po' guys who lead a dog's life.

I talk just to talk, not just for myself
But for all those po' guys who're hard up out there;
Mostly that's ev'ryone on the face of the earth.
I'm with them po' guys, it's my right to curse.

But it is Gabrielle Roy (1909–83) or rather Roy's outstanding first novel, *The Tin Flute*, that is synonymous with St. Henri, for the district was Roy's first muse. In 1941, she was a young and penniless freelance journalist living a marginal existence in a rooming house on what was then Dorchester Boulevard, near Greene Avenue. She had arrived in Montreal from St. Boniface, Manitoba, by way of London and Paris, where she had tried her hand at being an actress. But the author who, more than any other, has bridged Canada's duality through her total bilingualism and popularity with both French and English readers did not find her true vocation in the two great European capitals. For that she had to come to Montreal.

She spoke about those lonely and dark wartime days many years later. "For human warmth," she said to one interviewer, "I used to roam the streets, walk and walk and walk." She told another, "I used to choose as the goal of my walks the pretty avenues of Westmount and the slope of the mountain. One day, by pure chance, by caprice if you will, I instead went south on rue Saint-Ambroise and found myself before I knew it in the very heart of Saint-Henri. What can I say? How can I give you the deep impression I suddenly received? It was like the lightning that strikes lovers; it was a revelation, an illumination."

Roy began to write about the St. Henri district in a series of articles for one of her freelance markets, the *Bulletin des agriculteurs*, a farm publication. In 1945 she published *Bonheur d'occasion*, which was subsequently translated under the rather insipid title *The Tin Flute* ("Second-hand Happiness," the translation of *Bonheur d'occasion* and a neat summation of the theme of the book, would have been far more effective). The novel became a landmark of Quebec literature. It broke with a long tradition of drawing inspiration from the land and instead dealt with the grittiness of urban life, in language that freely mixed in *joual*, what Roy called "le langage canayen."

The Tin Flute was also a huge commercial success, selling over a million copies worldwide (it was translated into at least eight languages) and heaping

A street in St. Henri in the 1970s. The neighbourhood remains one of the city's poorest.

honours upon its author. "In the context of Quebec and Canada, nothing like it had ever been seen," writes Roy's biographer, François Ricard, in *Gabrielle Roy: A Life*. "It was a kind of miracle worthy of Cinderella or any Hollywood success story. Almost overnight an obscure journalist with an obscure agricultural magazine became a real live princess; she was admired across the country, applauded abroad, fawned over by the public, hounded by reporters, honoured with prizes and distinctions and (which did no harm at all) showered with money."

The international triumph of the book was grounded in the highly specific landscape of wartime St. Henri, to which Roy almost certainly bestowed immortality. "Nothing is as quiet as St. Ambroise Street on winter nights," begins a passage mapping out the backdrop of the novel and introducing Jean Lévesque, Roy's ambition-driven anti-hero. In earlier times, the street had been the boundary of the village, with fields lying fallow beyond it, but now, "textile mills, grain elevators and warehouses...[had] risen to face the frame houses, slowly, solidly, walling them in." Jean's rooming house "was just in front of the swing-bridge of St. Augustin Street. It could watch the passage of flatboats, tankers that stank of oil or gasoline, wood barges, colliers, all of them giving a triple blast with their foghorns just before its door...."

A few streets from St. Ambroise stood St. Henri's Church and St. Henri Square, "a vast area furrowed by the railway and two streetcar tracks.... A train rolled by. The acrid smell of coal filled the street. A swirl of soot rose just above the rooftops, then, as it began to swoop down, the belfry of St. Henri's Church appeared, floating, without a base, like a phantom arrow amid the clouds."

When Jean walks to the St. Henri train station, what he sees is the scene that inspired the author's original flash of insight for the book: "Beyond it, in a large notch in the suburb, the town of Westmount climbs in tiers toward the mountain's ridge in its stiff English luxury.... Here poverty and superfluity will stare tirelessly at each other, as long as Westmount lasts, as long as St. Henri lies at its feet."

Others had earlier noted the disparity between the town on the heights and the one below. Writing in the 1914 classic *Arcadian Adventures with the Idle Rich*, Stephen Leacock took deadly satirical aim at the "Mausoleum Club," a stand-in for the posh Mount Royal Club on Sherbrooke Street. The Mausoleum Club occupied "the quietest corner of the best residential street in the City...." Leacock called this street Plutoria and observed with silken malice the conspicuous consumption of its inhabitants:

Gabrielle Roy immortalized St. Henri in The Tin Flute.

STEPHEN LEACOCK

The third of eleven children of a well-born but feckless father, Stephen Leacock (1869–1944) was born in England and came to Ontario with his family when he was six. He had an unstable and impoverished childhood on an Ontario farmstead, but nonetheless was educated at Upper Canada College, where in 1888 he became a schoolmaster himself.

A career change in his thirties saw him enroll in graduate school in 1899. He obtained a doctorate in political economy and political science in 1903, when he was appointed sessional lecturer at McGill University. Five years later, he became head of the department of economics. The professorial life suited him, and in 1906 he published his first and most wildly successful book (it was translated into nineteen languages): a college text on political science. Leacock went on to write some sixty books in the next four decades, about half of which were satire, parody, or delicious nonsense, the other half essays, history, political science, and polemics. The most famous Canadian author of his day, he lectured internationally and became a sort of unofficial ambassador for Montreal and McGill.

His two best works are *Sunshine Sketches of a Little Town* (1912), a series of gently satiric interrelated short stories loosely based on the Ontario town of Orillia where Leacock had a summer home, and *Arcadian Adventures with the Idle Rich* (1914), a much harder-edged portrayal of hypocrisy, materialism, and corruption in a large American city for which Montreal was the model.

Stephen Leacock became an unofficial ambassador for Montreal and McGill University.

"Here you may see a little toddling princess in a rabbit suit who owns fifty distilleries in her own right. There in a lacquered perambulator, sails past a little hooded head that controls from its cradle an entire New Jersey corporation....

"...If you were to mount to the roof of the Mausoleum Club...you could almost see the slums from there.... And on the other hand, if you never went up on the roof, but only dined inside among the palm trees, you would never know that the slums existed – which is much better...."

The juxtaposition of wealth above and poverty below was also noted by poet Irving Layton. In his autobiography, *Waiting for the Messiah*, Layton wrote of the Depression years: "What stuck out in my mind was the contrast between the sleek comfort found in one neighbourhood and the squalor in which it was set like an emerald in a base-metal ring." "Excursion," an early Layton poem, holds the powerful image, "rich/ Suburban Westmount that squats upon a slum."

Closer to Old Montreal than St. Henri was Griffintown, adjacent to the old Récollets district. Griffintown owed its existence to the Victoria Bridge. The bridge's builders, mainly Irish immigrants, settled near the structure that would announce the city's entry into the industrial age and the unevenly distributed prosperity that it brought.

Between 1845 and 1848 some 100,000 Irish fled to Canada as a result of the Great Famine. Many settled in the west end of the city and in Griffintown, which was almost exclusively Irish in its makeup. Even as the bridge took shape in the 1850s, the "fever sheds" – roughly made quarantine barracks – still lined the river banks offering a grim reminder of the great typhus epidemic of 1847.

According to a nineteenth-century account, "Griffintown comprises a little world within itself – shops, factories, schools, academies, churches and asylums. The Irish population of Montreal take a high stand in business, politics and society."

The overall impression of life in Griffintown, however, is far more dismal. Its marshy, unhealthy terrain was particularly prone to the floods that caused so much hardship. Ontario novelist Jane Urquhart casts a memorable scene of *Away*, her haunting novel about the Irish diaspora, in a Griffintown "up to its arse in the river" in the spring of 1868. Eileen, one of the novel's main characters, travels by train from the Lake Ontario village where she lives in search of her lover in Griffintown. She finds Montreal ankle-deep in water, the only effectual method of transportation being by boat.

> "Eileen was having trouble distinguishing between that which was afloat and that which was grounded. They had entered a poorer section of the city, now, where ragged families were huddled on thatched or tin rooftops, surrounded by tables, chairs, and a few miserable chickens. The odd stone building emerged at infrequent intervals looking like a ship moored in a harbour otherwise filled with wrecked vessels. Clumps of sod from submerged huts joined dancing chunks of ice on the water's surface. 'Their huts,' the boatman explained, nodding in the direction of one particularly wretched collection of individuals, and then pointing to a small floating island of mud and wattle and straw, 'their huts melt each spring. The *Irlandais*, the Irish.'"

Even into the twentieth century, "Griffintown consisted of very old houses and the plumbing left something to be desired," recalled Charles Blickstead, a retired firefighter born in Griffintown in 1907, in Patricia Burns's *The*

Shamrock and the Shield: An Oral History of the Irish in Montreal. "There were no bathtubs in the houses unless you bought one and you stuck it in and you had to fill it up with buckets of water. Shortly before I was born, toilet facilities consisted of an outhouse in the back and the water would be supplied through a pipe." Blickstead's generation refused to put up with these hardships. He and many of his peers saw to the education of their children and grabbed the first opportunity to move their families to better neighbourhoods.

In the 1940s and '50s, many of the descendants of the original inhabitants of Griffintown moved away, some to Pointe St. Charles, one notch up the social scale, and then, with increased affluence, to Verdun and Nôtre Dame de Grace (N.D.G.), suburbs that were newly opening up. Eventually, what the depredations of nature and poverty were unable to accomplish, urban redevelopment did. Today Griffintown no longer exists. It was razed in the 1960s to make way for the Bonaventure expressway.

During the construction of the Victoria Bridge in the 1850s, "fever sheds" near Griffintown could be seen from the river.

Just east of the St. Henri immortalized by Gabrielle Roy lay the sections of historic St. Antoine ward known as Little Burgundy, the original domain of Montreal's black community. At the turn of the twentieth century, St. Antoine ward was the largest political division in the city, comprising the entire west end. The southwestern and northern parts of the ward were residential; the eastern sections bordering Griffintown, commercial. The area below the escarpment in the southwest core became home to a growing black community.

The derelict Redpath sugar refinery along the Lachine Canal in Pointe St. Charles: De-industrialization hit hard in the neighbourhoods of the southwest.

Black slaves were present in Montreal in both the French colonial period and after the Conquest, but blacks almost disappeared from the historical record between 1834 – when slavery was abolished in the British Empire – and the 1880s. Nevertheless, Montreal had a black police chief, Thomas Wily, between 1844 and 1849, and there is evidence of the arrival in town of one Frederick "Shadrach" Wilkins via the Underground Railway in the 1850s. Wilkins became a restaurateur and saloon keeper who operated, in the words of historian Dorothy W. Williams, "the renowned Shadrach restaurant."

But it was the advent of the railroad and the hiring of black men into service positions as sleeping car porters, cooks, waiters, and redcaps by both American and Canadian railway companies that linked the southwestern section of Montreal with a black population. Beginning in the 1880s, first black Americans, then Canadians, and finally West Indians were recruited and hired in Montreal, then sent on runs across the continent.

According to a contemporary account, the earliest American porters "were citizens of Montreal between the trains" who used company accommodation while in Montreal for brief stopovers. Because of fear and racism, the Canadian government at first actively discouraged the wives and families of these transient black men from entering the country. By contrast, Canadian and West Indian blacks were permanent workers who made Montreal their home, mainly in the area of St. Antoine in the blocks between the Windsor Depot (on the Canadian Pacific Railway tracks) and the Bonaventure Station (on Grand Trunk Railway tracks). They formed the nucleus of the city's Negro community.

In the early and mid-nineteenth century, St. Antoine Street had been the ward's elegant main thoroughfare, lined with the stately homes of professionals and financiers. When new neighbourhoods started up and the Square Mile became the most desirable residential address, the abandoned St. Antoine Street mansions were bought by real estate speculators and subdivided into flats and rooms. The area became a natural haven for blacks: the rail companies' yards were nearby and the housing was affordable.

Nevertheless, a century ago blacks were still a tiny minority of the city's population. In 1897, Montreal numbered over a quarter of a million inhabitants, of whom 37,500 lived below the hill in St. Antoine ward. Estimates of the day put the number of blacks in the whole city at three hundred, ninety per cent of whom were thought to be American. Rather than a ghetto then, Little Burgundy was actually an immigrant and somewhat cosmopolitan neighbourhood that included an international travelling public, French Canadians, and transient and resident blacks. It was primarily a poor district, with absentee landlords taking advantage of the high occupancy rate promoted by cheap rents and doing little to maintain their properties. Dorothy W. Williams writes in *The Road to Now: A History of Blacks in Montreal*: "Residents lived in dilapidated and dangerous housing that was sub-standard even for its day. In many cases the buildings had been condemned, and outdoor privy pits were breeding grounds for disease and death."

One of the defining events of the culture of poverty was moving day, an inevitable exercise in downward mobility for many of the poor, forced to vacate their lodgings for ever worsening ones as their funds shrivelled. The ritual of moving was similar for French-Canadian and black families and is described in the literature of both communities.

Gabrielle Roy evokes a tender portrait of Rose-Anna, the pregnant matriarch of the Lacasse family in *The Tin Flute*, as she rouses her brood of small children at dawn on May 1 – for many years Montreal's perennial moving day – to ready them for their new home.

"Home!

"That was an old word, one of the first the children had ever learned. You used it without thinking, a hundred times a day. It had meant so many different things! They'd used it once for a dank basement apartment on St. James Street, and again for the three-room place where they had stifled under the roof of a dingy building on St. Antoine. Home was

Moving day, a Montreal tradition, then and (opposite) *more recently.*

an elastic word and even meaningless at times, for it evoked not a single place but maybe twenty shelters scattered through the neighbourhood. It was rich in regrets and nostalgia, and it always meant uncertainty. It was related to the annual migration. It was coloured by the season. It sounded in your heart like an unforeseen departure, a flight, for when you heard it you could imagine that you also heard the shrill cry of migratory birds."

Writing some fifty years after Roy, Mairuth Sarsfield, who grew up in Little Burgundy in the 1930s and '40s and now lives in Ottawa, made Montreal's black community the focal point of her first novel, *No Crystal Stair*. Set in the same period as *The Tin Flute*, *No Crystal Stair* is a work of personalized social history as much as popular literature. It too has its moving day scenario, this one seen through the eyes of eleven-year-old Pippa:

"When the streetcar had passed the street-level window of their two-bed-room flat on St. Antoine, Pippa followed the shadows it threw along the ceiling and over the cardboard packing cases at the foot of the bed. Tomorrow her whole life would change and they'd be in their new house on rue des Seigneurs. Slowly its rattle had receded; the darkness dropped silently down again. Ruminating under her tightly braided hair and silk stocking cap, Pippa had conjured up portraits of people on that midnight streetcar run. What did they do after dark in those tall grey towers facing Notre Dame Cathedral on Place d'Armes, near the streetcar terminus?"

Intrigued by Little Burgundy in the 1950s, well before multiculturalism became an accepted Canadian social policy, Miriam Waddington hinted only obliquely at the presence of blacks as she strove to capture the spirit of the neighbourhood in the 1955 poem "Saint Antoine Street."

Opposite: *Rockhead's Paradise was a Montreal landmark. Morley Callaghan named it "the Café St. Antoine"; Mairuth Sarsfield called it "a den of iniquity."*

...the street is like a forest
Of white trees and negro underbrush
Full of furious growing
And the pavement spills
Its nameless colour, oh I wade
Ankle deep in it
Lost and puzzled.

Nervous with the noise of trains
The crash of stop, the gust of go,
I circle rising storms of soot...

A few years later, Al Purdy evoked St. Antoine's black citizens much more explicitly in the poem "Negroes on St. Antoine":

Here there's a blackness under the sun
where tracks cross and glum groceries are molars
set in slums that no forceps budge—
rooted deep in the continental jawbone.

Here...
  on holidays come black New Yorkers,
jazz combos and beat musicians,
the clean pride of Jomo Kenyatta
dulled on the face of a C.N.R. porter....

In one of his most acclaimed books, *The Loved and the Lost*, the Toronto-born novelist Morley Callaghan (1903–90) explored the sensitive subject of race relations in Montreal in the early 1950s. Once again St. Antoine Street figures as a major set, in particular the "Café St. Antoine," a nightclub modelled on the famous Rockhead's Paradise.

Rufus Rockhead was a Jamaican immigrant who, in the 1920s, worked as a railway porter on the Montreal-Chicago run. Supplementing his income with liquor smuggling during the Prohibition years, he was able to save enough money to go into the tavern business. By the 1940s, he was owner of one the biggest nightclubs in town.

Here is Rockhead's disguised as the Café St. Antoine, as described by

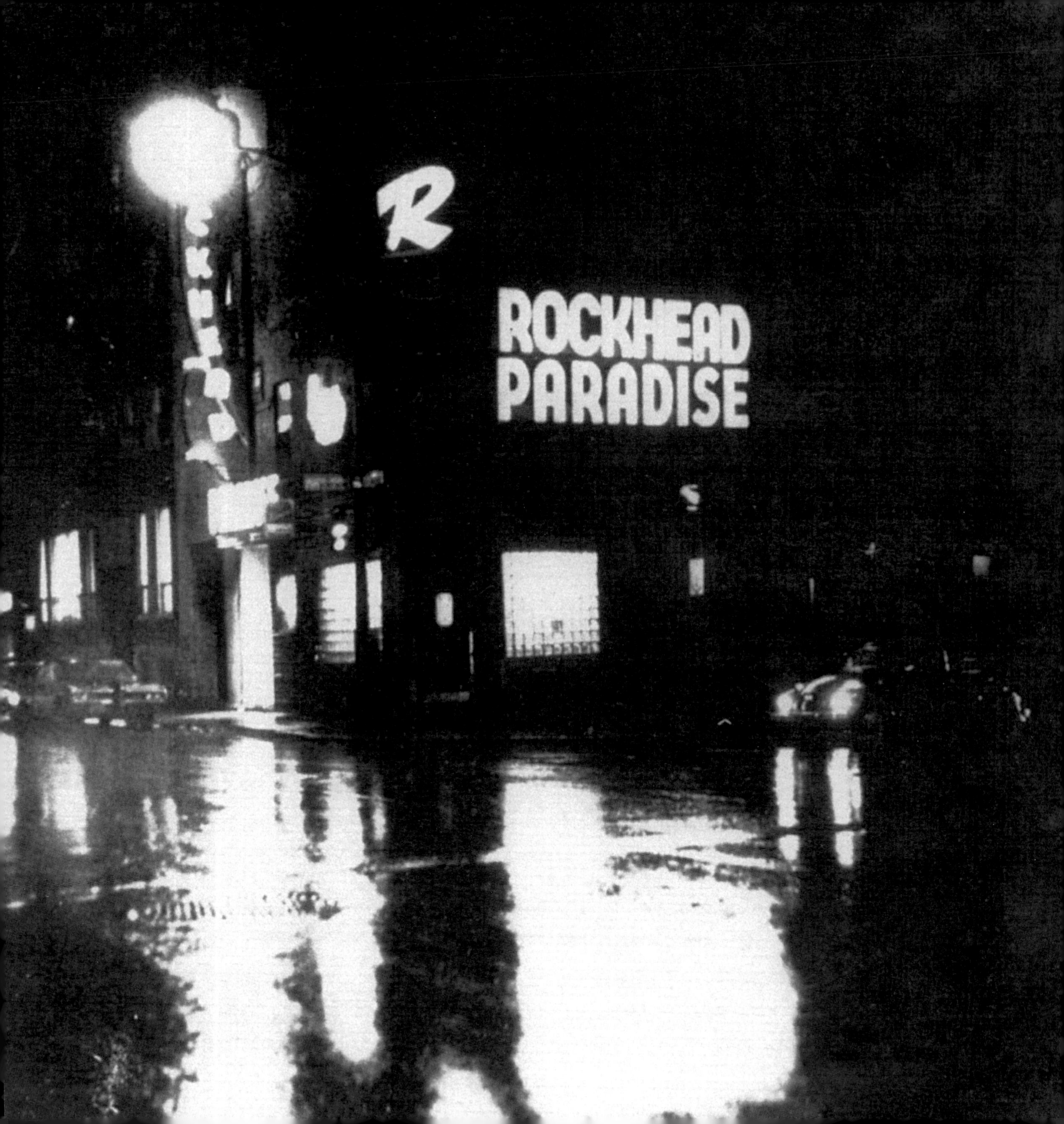
R
ROCKHEAD
PARADISE

Callaghan's Jim McAlpine, a recently hired columnist for the fictional Montreal *Sun* and a newcomer from Toronto, who peers in from a window:

> "Music came from the ground-floor open window, the music of a cello and a piano, and he could see three figures, one a Negro at a piano, another, who looked like a French Canadian, at the cello, and the third figure, the face hidden, was bending over the piano. The piano and the cello achieved an hypnotic effect in primitive counterpoint, repeating a simple theme over and over with curious discords;...the musicians were held in their strange rapture, and there was nothing in the world for them but the lonely little theme and that one room in the cold night and their own intensity. The shunting of engines in the station yard and the hum of the city and the gray shabby neighbourhood could never break the magic of their private, peculiar, and isolated rapture."

Sarsfield's Pippa, too, is fascinated by Rockhead's and especially the "beautiful brown chorus girls" of her imagination. To a sheltered preadolescent schoolgirl, "Rockhead's, the jazz cabaret on lower Mountain Street, was the 'den of iniquity,'...that Prohibition had made irresistible to American sportsmen and gamblers. At night, with its pulsating yellow and red neon sign, it marked the halfway point of the streetcar run along St. Antoine." But Pippa, a child with a social conscience, ponders not so much what happens at showtime, but afterwards. "When the last streetcar before morning arrived at Mountain Street, how many of those Black musicians, who wore mysterious dark glasses while entertaining white folks at Rockhead's, would climb aboard for the long ride home to their own families in the respectable working-class districts St. Henri and Verdun?"

In the 1960s, a sweeping urban renewal program in the west end of the city effectively razed the old neighbourhood. A new Little Burgundy of subsidized housing units was created with the boundaries of Atwater and Guy, the Lachine Canal and St. Antoine. At the same time, a gentrification policy attracted an influx of middle-class whites, so that today less than ten per cent of Montreal's anglophone blacks live within the historic enclave. Mairuth Sarsfield's homey and accessible novel pays heartfelt homage to the old locale.

The municipality of Verdun has ancient historical roots, at least in name. In 1671 Major Zacharie du Puy, commander of the forces of the island of

A street in Verdun offers a good
example of the outdoor staircases
common in Montreal houses.

Montreal, was granted Verdun, a fiefdom of 320 arpents near Sault St. Louis.
Development of the fiefdom, however, was stymied by frequent flooding of the
area and its distance from the centre of town. The building of a dike and the
advent of the electric tram system at the turn of the twentieth century caused a
mini population boom. In 1891, Verdun numbered 296 people; by 1911, the
figure jumped to 11,629.

William Weintraub evokes this neighbourhood in his 1979 satiric novel,
The Underdogs. Lampooning the nationalist program of the Parti Québécois
which swept into office for the first time in 1976, Weintraub projected a future
twenty years after the separation of Quebec when Anglo Montreal would be
squeezed into the lower-class neighbourhoods of the south.

Weintraub's hero, Paul, an urban peasant, returns home after a day of work
by bicycle:

"Standing on the pedals, swinging vigorously from side to side, Paul went up the long incline that led out of the tunnel and onto Rue Camille Laurin, which the Anglos stubbornly persisted in calling by its original name, Wellington Street. This was the main artery leading to neighbourhoods that once bore names like Point St. Charles, Verdun, Crawford Park, Lasalle. Now it was all lumped together and called the Région Sud-Ouest.

"It was a melancholy area of grimy streets and sordid back alleys. Many of the decrepit brick houses were a century old, with sagging floors and collapsing balconies. Here, in the summer, through the hot and crowded streets, the evening breeze carried a sour whiff of garbage with it. And it was here, and in the equally desolate areas farther out along the shores of Lake St. Louis, that most of Montreal's Anglos now lived, in varying degrees of poverty – the same Anglos who had once been the lords and masters of Quebec."

In contrast to Weintraub, who offers up biting fantasy, the work of play-wright David Fennario, the author most intimately associated with Verdun and Pointe St. Charles, is characterized by an emphasis on grim reality. Born David Wiper in Verdun in 1947 and raised in Pointe St. Charles, he took the pseudonym "Fennario" from a Bob Dylan song. Best known for caustic plays written out of personal experience, a preoccupation with the plight of workers, and doctrinaire Marxism, Fennario quit school at age sixteen and worked at a series of odd jobs. His writing career was launched when he returned to school as a mature student at Dawson College in 1969 and kept a journal for his creative-writing class. The diary evolved into the novel *Without a Parachute*, published in 1972.

Fennario's journal entry in *Without a Parachute* for December 20, 1969, a Saturday night, records his depressed mood after a long walk home from the Vogue theatre on Charlebois Street in the Pointe. Where, he asks himself, do people get the strength to keep on living in "that whole vast slum"? He paints the scene with both sadness and affection: "Little taverns hugging the corners of the street. Factory chimneys, match-box houses, solitary street lamps. Second-hand, everything is second-hand, including their lives." Then he seems to take heart from the pluck of those who came before:

"These houses were built a long time ago by our great-grandfathers. The plumbers, plasterers, brick-layers, carpenters, tinsmiths, house painters and architects of the 1880's. All gone to the grave one way or the other. Ate their suppers, drank their beer, made love to their wives, fed their children, smoked their pipes, enjoyed their summer nights and Christmas festivities. With little triumphs and many tragedies lived out their days of hard work and small pleasures."

Fennario's best-known and most accomplished play, *Balconville*, is considered Canada's first bilingual play; it debuted in 1979. Set on the balconies of tenements in the Point at the height of summer, it features eight characters, English and French, and shows with both compassion and humour that the struggles and suffering of the working poor cut deeper than their differences of language and ethnicity.

Writing some thirty years after Fennario, novelist Trevor Ferguson, in his detective novel *City of Ice* and under the pseudonym John Farrow, evokes the same world as Fennario's *Balconville*, though not in blazing summer, but in the depths of winter.

"They drove into the poor neighborhoods that spread south-west from the downtown. Made narrow by winter, the streets were lined by snowbound parked cars in igloos. Red-brick rowhouses were crammed together, never a gap between them, two- and three-story flats with crooked exterior staircases made of wrought-iron railings and worn wood steps, hard against the sidewalks. Some entranceways had been tramped smooth by boots, others had been shoveled out. Balconies holding mounds of snow were pitched in different directions, shifting with time and rot, and windows were sealed by plastic wrap and old newsprint to bar draughts. At the roof line, snow drooped like wisps of white hair on aging gentlemen. Trees, leafless, rose from snowbanks as knurly sentinels, their upper branches run through with electrical wire. In the front windows of a few homes, Christmas lights, off now, had been strung in the shapes of squares or circles or stars, a cheery defense against long winter nights."

We leave the Town Below with the Christmas lights that brighten winter dimmed. The neighbourhood remains, if not as miserable as it was a century ago, still identified with the culture of poverty.

Chapter 9

ON TOP OF THE CITY: WESTMOUNT AND OUTREMONT

THE WEALTHY RESIDENTIAL enclaves of Outremont and, in particular, Westmount are represented in Montreal's literature as the pinnacle of bourgeois affluence, snobbish exclusivity, and social conservatism in the city. Many writers have found the inhabitants of the two areas a trove of rich source material.

Almost from the outset, the two municipalities were defined by geography. Historian Walter van Nus writes in an essay on the development of Montreal's suburbs: "Height...determined gradations of prestige even within a single suburb. In Westmount...the most elegant district lay north of The Boulevard, on the steepest part of the slope above 120 metres in altitude. Similarly in Outremont, the toniest streets developed just next to the mountainside; exclusive Maplewood Avenue, for instance, rose to 101 metres, and the town sloped downward in both altitude and socio-economic status to the industrial fringe along its northern border, at 68 metres."

Given Westmount's diminutive size – it is a mere square mile and a half in area, an outcropping of the larger Mount Royal – its cachet and reputation have had a disproportionate influence on the city's heart and soul. Partly this has resulted from Westmount's long and colourful history. Endowed with mountain springs of clear water and a favourable southwest orientation, it was the site of Indian settlements, wells, and trails even before the arrival of Montreal's European founders in the seventeenth century.

In 1662 the Sulpicians established Fort de la Montagne, a mission to the Indians, several kilometres northwest of Ville Marie, just east of Westmount's current boundaries. The Sulpicians' success with the land (apple orchards in particular flourished) led to the arrival and settlement of French farming families along the Indian trail, which became known as Côte St. Antoine in the late seventeenth century.

English settlers – merchants, military men, and fur traders – arrived with the Conquest. The first to put down roots in the area of today's Westmount, the fur trader Simon Clarke, built his house in the 1770s at the corner of Côte St. Antoine and present-day Clarke Avenue, near the Sulpician Mission, to attract the trade of Indians on their way to the Montreal fur fairs. Clarke's daughter-in-law, Marianne, left an engaging portrait of her husband's parents. Their house, she wrote in the early nineteenth century, had "a great cherry orchard on the slope behind.... The orchard in season was a mass of lovely white blossoms and on summer evenings an old lady in a high-backed chair sat under the wide-spreading trees intent on her knitting, while her husband opposite busied himself reading to her."

Later, when the Anglo-Scots plutocracy settled into first the Square Mile and then Westmount, the architecture of the area began to differ markedly from the earlier indigenous French-Canadian farmhouses designed to cope with Canada's extreme climate. Towers, terraces, and galleries adorned these opulent and fanciful properties, whose boundaries did not adhere to the straight-line divisions of the French farms but instead set the pattern for the future town's curving avenues, drives, and crescents.

Westmount and Outremont figure prominently in the literary landscape of the city. Writers have not been content merely to describe the stately homes, formal gardens, and tree-lined streets of the two neighbourhoods – one

The Grand Séminaire grew out of a Sulpician mission begun in the seventeenth century. The setting was still rural in 1883 when this photograph was taken.

conveniently French, the other English – but have also acted as social critics and satirists, often bitterly pillorying the city's wealthy and powerful élites.

Hugh MacLennan evokes an atmosphere of calm and consolation, a kind of spiritual balm, when he has Paul Tallard, the schoolboy son of the recently deceased Athanase Tallard in *Two Solitudes*, take a walk in Westmount on a Saturday afternoon in 1919. The death of his father has left Paul not only bereaved but poor, living with his mother in a seedy district in the east end and no longer able to attend Frobisher, the English boys' private school that was designed to groom him for success in the world of St. James Street. "In the upper levels of town," his melancholy eases: "Here the streets were quiet as churches and canopied by stately trees: maples, and limes, and elms with fresh leaves, and horse-chestnuts spired with blossoms. Here he could smell the fresh earth of newly-turned flower-beds, look over hedges and see immaculate lawns and gardeners clipping them, the lawn-mowers singing high in the warm air." Paul recognizes the houses of his former Frobisher classmates: "enormous brick-and-stone structures, some shaped like castles with gargoyles at the corners of the roofs, all with huge conservatories on their sides."

Some fifteen years later, Paul and his sweetheart, Heather Methuen, drive by a Westmount bowling green at night, "its lawn as smooth as a billiard cloth. The lights gleamed on the bald heads of elderly, flanneled men and the bowls rolled slumbrously forward over the grass. It was quaint and dignified and very English."

While she wrote about the same genteel, haut-bourgeois English characters in roughly the same period, the French novelist and short story writer Marie LeFranc depicts them far less benignly than does MacLennan. In her 1934 collection, *Visages de Montréal*, in which Westmount figures as "Pleasant View," LeFranc displays an intimate knowledge of its inhabitants acquired by teaching them a desirable Parisian French, as opposed to the locally inflected Québécois variety. As she portrays them, they live in "aristocratic isolation" in the upper reaches of the city, descending the slopes by car only to transact business. When the stock market crashes, their Packards deliver a final service: "They shut themselves up with the car in the garage, on the pretext of fixing something. They opened the tool box and turned on the ignition, slid under the belly of the beast as if to see what ailed it.... This was the stylish way to go, the only one which kept up decent appearances, a kind of caste ritual to which the financiers of Pleasant View remained faithful. Unable to prove suicide, the insurance companies paid the widows handsome policies. This was their last killing at the Stock Exchange."

A number of the descriptions of Westmount, both in fiction and memoir, derive from the point of view of children and adolescents, for whom the neighbourhood appears to have had great symbolic importance, either in shaping their aspirations, or, more often, in arousing feelings of intimidation and alienation.

Growing up on east-end Ste. Élisabeth Street, Irving Layton fought frequent pitched battles with French-Canadian boys when he ventured across St. Denis Street. But, he recalled many years later, "when I found myself in Westmount, that once-upon-a-time enclave of unbelievably dull and self-complacent Bourbons, I'd feel a different kind of menace. One that was internal rather than external in its threat, its thrust.... Here I always felt myself to be a trespasser, not a warrior as I did when I crossed St. Denis street. At any moment huge mastiffs would be loosed on me or someone with a healthily tanned face would say to me with cold but perfect English diction, 'Get away from here.'"

Westmount Park with its memorial to the dead of the world wars.

In her memoir of growing up in the 1940s, *Une Enfance à l'eau bénite,* broadcaster and author Denise Bombardier, describes Sunday family outings to various posh Montreal neighbourhoods in her godfather's old Ford. Bombardier was raised in the north end of the city by lower middle-class parents. Her mother sent her to elocution lessons and dressed her like a little princess, dreaming that her child would one day scale the social ladder. Her father detested the Catholic Church and the English in equal measure, denouncing then premier Maurice Duplessis and calling those who voted for him "Culbéquois" (a scatological word play on Québécois and, *cul,* the French word for ass). The family's Sunday jaunts generally ended in Westmount, "this high place of world-class richness."

"This city within the heart of Montreal seemed to me as unreal as Hollywood, of which my mother spoke often. I doubted that these enormous stone manors which hung from the mountain and dominated the city were inhabited by 'real people'."

Bombardier's father rages that Duplessis has handed over the whole province to these people. When the family tour takes it back into a poverty-stricken neighbourhood, the father once again vents his spleen: "Now, here you're at home. This is French Canada! Look up at those balconies, don't they all look happy? A cross on their necks, and then a dozen kids in the house!"

The impressions left by Layton and Bombardier underscore the validity of an observation made by Toronto-born writer Gwethalyn Graham (1913–65) in her 1944 international best-seller about interfaith love, *Earth and High Heaven*: "Hampered by racial-religious distinctions to start with, relations between the French, English and Jews of Montreal are still further complicated by the fact that all three groups suffer from an inferiority complex – the French because they are a minority in Canada, the English because they are a minority in Quebec, and the Jews because they are a minority everywhere."

A heartfelt novel in which love challenges bigotry in wartime Montreal,

A quiet street in Westmount.

Earth and High Heaven follows a romance between Erica Drake of the "Westmount Drakes" and Marc Reiser, a small-town-Ontario Jewish lawyer. Erica's father, Charles, owns Drake Importing, a family business stretching back four generations and based on West Indian sugar, rum, and molasses. The prosperity this company generates puts the Drakes at the apex of Westmount society, a fact borne out by the view from the panoramic windows of the Drakes' drawing-room where Marc stands looking out.

"The whole city lay spread out below him, enchanting in the sunlight of a late afternoon in June, mile upon mile of flat gray roofs half hidden by the light, new green of the trees; a few scattered skyscrapers, beyond the skyscrapers the long straight lines of the grain elevators down by the harbor, further up to the right the Lachine Canal, and everywhere the gray spires of churches, monasteries and convents. Somehow, even from here, you could tell that Montreal was predominantly French, and Catholic."

Gwethalyn Graham with the poets Earle Birney (left) and E. J. Pratt.

In *The Favourite Game*, his semi-autobiographical novel about a priapic Westmount Jewish boy who finds his calling as a poet, Leonard Cohen sets several nighttime scenes circa 1950 in King George Park on Côte St. Antoine Road between Murray and Belmont Avenues.

"The park nourished all the sleepers in the surrounding houses. It was the green heart. It gave the children dangerous bushes and heroic landscapes so they could imagine bravery. It gave the nurses and maids winding walks so they could imagine beauty. It gave the young merchant-princes leaf-hid necking benches, views of factories so they could imagine power. It gave the retired brokers vignettes of Scottish lanes where loving couples walked, so they could lean on their canes and imagine poetry. It was the best part of everyone's life. Nobody comes into a park for mean purposes except perhaps a sex maniac and who is to say that he isn't thinking of eternal roses as he unzips before the skipping-rope Beatrice?"

A superficial portrayal of Westmount would have it that the area belonged solely to the British upper crust of Montreal. But, as the existence of the Cohens on Belmont Avenue indicates, there was a small Jewish presence as early as the 1840s. Temple Emanu-el, the impressive Byzantine home of liberal Judaism in Canada, was built on the corner of Sherbrooke and Elm in the early twentieth century. (It makes a cameo appearance as Beth-Adonai in Judith Kalman's collection of linked stories, *The County of Birches*.)

There were French-Canadian residents as well. In a remarkable chapter of Michel Tremblay's memoir of growing up on the Plateau Mont-Royal, *Douze Coups de Théâtre*, the author draws an unforgettable portrait of a Montreal francophone matinée idol who takes the sixteen-year-old Michel home to his Westmount mansion one evening "for tea, and other things if your heart so desires."

Tremblay's first visit to Westmount has a profound impact on him, putting him in "another city, another country, another world!" The unnamed actor's home "seemed incredible to me. Something out of the movies perhaps. Cream walls, unthinkable for me, for in our house the colour of blood reigned supreme in the living room – even on the ceiling – and the wallpaper every-where had been bought on sale."

But when the famous actor opens his refrigerator in search of milk for Michel's tea, Tremblay is shocked: save for a bottle of Welch's grape juice and a few lemons, the refrigerator, unlike the plentifully laden larder of his own grease-spattered kitchen, is completely empty. "I had heard of this actor since my infancy; he had made all the women of the household weep in his many radio soaps. My grand-mother had been crazy about him; my mother and aunts swooned over his voice; my cousins shat themselves – that's how they put it – since his face was made visible to us by television. But it was me who had ended up in his arms, without having wanted it, without ever having desired him. And I trembled with fear because his fridge was empty. And I was sickened by the sourness of his lemon tea."

Several writers have exercised a lighter touch in conveying the emotional coldness and untouchability of Westmount. In the 1953 short satirical poem "Calamity," F.R. Scott, who for decades lived in Westmount on Clarke Avenue, lampoons the starchiness of the neighbourhood, a starchiness tem-porarily dispelled when a laundry truck careens down the hill and crashes into the poet's maple tree.

> *Normally we do not speak to one another on this avenue*
> *But the excitement made us suddenly neighbours.*
> *People who had never been introduced*
> *Exchanged remarks*
> *And for a while we were quite human.*

Andrée Maillet in her short story collection *Les Montréalais* is less successful at satire when she creates the vapid Westmount family of Sir Alfred Barton. With the exception of Sir Alfred, who, though a snob, has a strong sense of noblesse oblige, the other members of his household, which includes a stereotypic English governess called Whitey, belong more to the realm of heavy-handed caricature than to lighthearted ridicule. For instance, appalled by the philistinism of his grandson Freddy ("he's a nothing, and the trouble is, he's proud of it"), Sir Alfred expresses his sense of frustration that "if my descendants want to partake of all these privileges which depend on the labour of so many others, they have to go down into the city and help the mountain, our home and all the other houses on it like ours, the ones which have such a commanding view of the river." This didacticism of Sir Alfred's must surely owe something to the political views of the author who, in 1966, the year that *Les Montréalais* was first published, ran in Westmount as the candidate for the separatist R.I.N.

By contrast, Edward O. Phillips, whose series of comedy-of-manners cum thrillers is centred on the bitchy and aging Montreal lawyer Geoffry Chadwick, skewers Westmount with authority and understatement. In *Sunday Best*, arriving for dinner at the invitation of a wealthy widow at the fictional Mayfair Crescent near the summit of the mountain, Geoffry observes, "To use a current buzzword, Mayfair Crescent was a power address. Listing your place of residence as the Salvation Army Hostel or the Old Brewery Mission suggests that perhaps you don't file an income tax return. Mayfair Crescent, on the other hand, hints at tax paid in quarterly instalments on that income which slides without fanfare through the letter slot. All traces of the recent blizzard had been cleared away. Judging from the political clout represented by the collective residents, I'd guess it was probably one of the first streets in the city to be regularly ploughed."

Though the reality of Westmount is more complex and variegated than its stereotype as the stronghold and haven of the affluent and privileged, reading Phillips one can't help but think of the phrase "Westmount Rhodesians" that received wide currency in the 1970s, when it was coined by Keith Spicer, the first federal commissioner of official languages, and popularized by René Lévesque.

In certain respects, Outremont's history parallels Westmount's. As with Côte St. Antoine, Côte Ste. Catherine Road, Outremont's main thoroughfare, likely began as an Indian trail that wound its way around the east side of the mountain. By 1800, land in the area was occupied by orchards and farmsteads

F.R. SCOTT

A poet, constitutional lawyer, professor, civil libertarian, social democrat, political theorist, and activist, F.R. Scott (1899–1985) had a profound influence on Canadian artistic and political culture. He was born in Quebec City, the sixth of seven children of an Anglican archdeacon. Educated at Bishop's College, and – as a Rhodes scholar – at Oxford, he returned from England to Canada in 1923 to teach at Lower Canada College and to write poetry, but he soon entered McGill Law School.

At McGill he met the poet and critic A.J.M. Smith, who became a lifelong friend and with whom he founded the McGill Movement, which gave birth to an influential literary magazine, the *McGill Fortnightly Review*. Leon Edel, the future biographer of Henry James, and the poets John Glassco, A.M. Klein, and Leo Kennedy were also associated with the group.

Through the 1920s and '30s Scott increasingly began to turn to Canadian sources of inspiration for both his poetic and political values. At about the same time, he was developing an iconoclastic wit that satirized the imitative nature of the Canadian literary world.

In 1928 Scott joined the staff of the McGill Law School, where he eventually served as dean from 1961 to 1964. As a constitutional jurist, he won three landmark decisions at the Supreme Court; in two of them he took on Quebec premier Maurice Duplessis: the Padlock Act, which Duplessis had introduced in 1937 permitting the police to padlock the premises of anyone thought to be a Communist, and Roncarelli vs. Duplessis in a defence of Jehovah's Witnesses. In the

third case, Scott quipped, "I went to bat for the Lady Chatte" and succeeded in having the ban lifted in Quebec of D. H. Lawrence's *Lady Chatterley's Lover* because of obscenity charges.

Running parallel with his writing, teaching, and legal careers, Scott was in on the ground floor of the founding of the socialist movement in Canada. He was president of the Montreal branch of the League for Social Reconstruction in 1932, one of the framers of the Regina Manifesto, and national chairman for eight years of the CCF party, which was the precursor of the NDP.

For more than forty years Scott's Westmount home on Clarke Avenue was a meeting place for Montreal literati of both languages. A gifted translator of French poetry, he stimulated contact between English and French writers.

Despite the breadth of his achievements, according to Hugh MacLennan who eulogized him in print in 1985, "Frank often said that he would like to be remembered best as a poet."

F.R. Scott was a jurist, professor, and civil libertarian, as well as a writer.

fronting on what had become a county road. A community began to take shape after 1907 and by 1911 it had reached 5,000, mostly anglophones wanting to escape from the crowded city. This accounts for the many English street names in a municipality that today is mainly francophone.

As Walter van Nus writes, Outremont was (and to some extent still is) "two towns, a working-class district to the northeast (where the CPR had a marshalling yard) and an increasingly upper-class area as one walked south or west." Zoning laws varied according to the ward one lived in. From its inception until the late 1920s, Outremont remained predominantly anglophone. But as Westmount evolved into a staunchly English bastion, elements of the francophone bourgeoisie, made wealthy by the post-war boom, sought their own place on the mountain's heights. They turned to Outremont.

In the literature of Montreal, Outremont, like Westmount, is a powerful symbol of social and economic success, but with a telling difference: Outremont figures primarily in the writings of francophone writers to whom it often represents a pinnacle that falls short of the true summit.

In the 1949 novel *Le Poids du jour*, Ringuet tracks the progress up the social ladder of the industrialist Michel Garneau by means of his Outremont addresses: at first the Garneaus live in an apartment on Bernard, then a house on Dollard Avenue, and "finally! – a *cottage* on rue Pratt, in a brand new section of Outremont." This new section boasts a variety of styles: "In keeping with the taste of his clients, and probably his own as well, the architect had made the walls in the Norman style with the frame exposed. The newest fad was to mimic poverty while using lavish proportions and materials. There were English cottages with windows so low the mid-day sun could barely penetrate them; stupefying Italian villas, given the snowy conditions of a Canadian winter; California missions with unusable arcades. Somewhere there was even a miniature mosque."

To furnish the house, Garneau's wife scours auctions where the spoils are particularly rich given the Depression conditions of the 1930s and the excess number of "nouveaux pauvres." Having acquired what she calls a "Turkrish carpet" from a mansion on Westmount Boulevard, she takes even greater pride in being invited to some tony addresses. "The élite, those whose fortunes dated back two generations, didn't acknowledge them yet, but it would come. Madame Garneau had been invited to 'play the bridge' with Madame John Galarneau, on Belvedere Road."

It's a similar story in Robert Choquette's *Les Velder*, a novelization of the author's popular wartime radio serial, *La Pension Velder*. Mina Latour, wife of J.B. Latour, "a rich businessman with a residence on [Côte] Sainte-Catherine Street in Outremont and a country house in Laval-sur-le-Lac," schemes that "one day, 'a little later'" she will arrive "not just in Outremont, but in Westmount, that worldly Gibraltar.... Because, even though the Latours had penetrated those circles where, when they were poor, they could never have set foot, they were shut out of the real world."

Writing in the mid-1960s of a decade earlier, Pierre de Grandpré creates in *La Patience des justes* an idealistic hero in Étienne Merrin, the son of a wealthy newspaper publisher. Étienne belongs to that crème-de-la-crème minority of Outremonters whom the Garneaus and Latours of *Le Poids du jour* and *Les Velder* would ape. The vast Merrin residence on Mount Royal Boulevard which he sees with fresh eyes when he returns from five years of study in France's best universities "had been built at the end of the nineteenth century of grey freestone, each block of which had kept its pristine form; this still seemed to Étienne, no matter what, the exemplary material for shelter, solidity, dignity."

But to the young Denise Bombardier, a child of the poor north end, "Outremont seemed less normal than the Town of Mount Royal or Westmount." The dream homes "of rich French Canadians: of lawyers, doctors, wholesalers. Houses of brick or stone...the length of Côte-Sainte-Catherine...as grand as convents" were a troubling sight, not the objects of envy on Sunday family outings in the 1940s.

"So there were some people of our 'race' who were as rich as the English," Denise thought. Schooled by nuns, she had been taught that French-Canadian bosses were more virtuous than English ones, that they treated their employees with paternalistic consideration. But driving by the imposing homes on Côte Ste. Catherine Road, the bantering adults implied that wealthy French Canadians were corrupt, that they had acquired their riches "by the sin of impurity." "In this neighbourhood, I saw proof that it was possible to be 'other,' since all these people spoke French like me and, at the same time, were wealthy. But contrary to what my school taught, our riches, too, could be tainted by immorality...."

A convent education and impoverished background have inculcated a different lesson in Mary (a.k.a. Maryse) O'Sullivan, the title character of Francine Noël's coming-of-age novel of the Quiet Revolution, *Maryse*. The nuns have instructed Maryse that "charity supplied the keys to knowledge, but these keys

didn't necessarily open the gates of the wealthy." Twenty years old in 1968, Maryse is infatuated with Michel Paradis and Marité Grand'maison, both of whom have grown up in Outremont. She believes that "everything that came from the peaks of Outremont was marvellous" and is bowled over by Marité's mother, who "presided with elegance over a well-ordered, comfortable home, full of expensive fabrics, the home of a judge, where she, Mary O'Sullivan was allowed in, she who at the convent had never hoped to be invited home by the other boarders."

A more ironical view characterizes the vignette of Outremont to be found in *Wild to Mild*, the English translation of Réjean Ducharme's *L'Hiver de force*. Ducharme, a joyous postmodernist master of language, sets *L'Hiver de force* in the 1970s and follows the meanderings of a pair of dropouts from society – André Ferron and his sister Nicole – in the streets of Montreal. Their view of Outremont acknowledges the reality that others besides francophones live there; their perspective is of the outsider who does not want in. "We pass by the corner of Bernard Street and Park Avenue where things are Jewish and where things really move. On Côte Sainte-Catherine Road everything is dead, houses rise on fenced-in squares of lawn, like a double row of tombs...."

The most striking outsiders in Outremont are undoubtedly the Hasidim, ultraorthodox Jews whose style of dress makes them particularly noticeable. Hasidic men are characterized by flowing beards, dark suits, and fur-trimmed hats; women dress conservatively in long sleeves, stockings, and head coverings even in the height of summer.

Hasidim (the term means literally "pious ones" in Hebrew) came to North America in large numbers after World War II, when their Eastern European communities were decimated by the Holocaust. Over 6,000 are to be found in Outremont, particularly in the north-south streets west of Park Avenue.

By the 1980s, other visible minorities from the larger world began to impinge on the small and inbred French enclave of Outremont. The Haitian-born novelist Gérard Étienne, for instance, situates much of *Une Femme muette*, a surrealistic novel centred on a black couple from Haiti, in Outremont. Kept a prisoner by her husband, the underworld-linked, voodoo-practising Gros Zo, Marie-Anne wanders the streets of Outremont, deranged and half naked: "The wind swells the torn scraps of her garments.... She runs. Her braids bounce against her forehead. In front of the City Hall she takes a couple of gulps of air. She coasts along McEachran Street, goes up Lajoie

Hasidic Jews form a substantial community in Outremont.

Avenue once more until she reaches Joyce Park where she halts, breathless and exhausted. She lies down on a bench and falls asleep."

This is surely a far cry from the ambitions of the Garneaus and Latours a half century earlier. Reflecting on the social history of Outremont, the college professor Jean-Marc who narrates Michel Tremblay's novel *The Heart Laid Bare* and who lives on Bloomfield, one of Outremont's more modest streets, observes as he strolls through the neighbourhood, "Immutable Outremont, hated by some, secretly dreamed of by others, former fortress of wealthy French Canadians, cradle of most of the influential politicians of the sixties and seventies, both far right and moderate left, of both the federalist and the nationalist persuasion, favourite target of east-end workers,... Outremont, for so long had been not a place to live but a way of life, a social status...."

Judging by Étienne and Tremblay, in literature at least, the preoccupations of those who inhabit contemporary Outremont go beyond the parochial narcissism of social-climbing parvenus or élites to the manner born.

Chapter 10

NEIGHBOURHOODS

Montreal has been described as a city of neighbourhoods, and it is easy to see why. Even today, after many amalgamations have seen the city gobble up dozens of outlying communities, there remain twenty-eight municipalities on the island of Montreal and dozens more in the off-island metropolitan area. With different bylaws, architecture, and ethnic and socio-economic compositions, these communities often retain a distinctiveness that hearkens back to their beginnings. This can be seen easily, for example, in the Rivière des Prairies neighbourhood, at whose heart is still discernible the "rue Principale" of a Quebec village.

Though perhaps lesser known than Tremblay's Plateau or Richler's Main, these areas too have been commemorated in literature. In this final chapter, we traverse the island from east to west, dropping in on a number of neighbourhoods and their writers.

THE EASTERN ISLAND

Pointe aux Trembles
The eastern tip of Montreal Island is known as Bout de l'Île, or Land's End, one of the few geographical allusions to the city's being surrounded by water. Along with Longue Pointe and Rivière des Prairies, Pointe aux Trembles' origins date back nearly as far as the founding of Montreal, when settlers created fortified outposts to protect their farms. Pointe aux Trembles remained isolated and rural in character until well into the twentieth century, as Jovette Marchessault, who grew up in the 60th Avenue area in the 1940s recalls in her autobiographical novel, *Like a Child of the Earth*:

> "When I was born…we were living in Pointe-aux-Trembles, a few steps from the river. I had a little dog, some hens, some frogs, a plot of raspberry bushes, a room with wavy cardboard walls, a grandmother, a fine

Opposite: *The main street of the old part of Rivière des Prairies still has the aspect of a Quebec village.*

Jovette Marchessault remembered the rural character of the eastern end of Montreal Island as it existed during her childhood.

coal-furnace, and a wood stove. In those days, Pointe-aux-Trembles or Longue Pointe was in the country, surrounded by oat fields, rows of trees, silvery poplars, cherry trees, and cows. They used to say about us, 'They live at Island End,' or Bottom of the Island."

Rivière des Prairies

Railways and a major thoroughfare, Notre Dame Street East, eventually drew Pointe aux Trembles and Longue Pointe into the larger city, but Rivière des Prairies, on the north shore of the island, remained in splendid isolation rather longer. Not until the 1960s did Montreal begin to encroach on what was by then one of the last distinct villages on the island.

It seems appropriately named because of the grassy meadows that for so long characterized the area. However, according to the Jesuit *Relations*, Rivière des Prairies was actually named not for its fields but for a seventeenth-century settler named des Prairies. (He apparently took a wrong turn when he came to the tip of Montreal Island while sailing up the St. Lawrence.)

For a sense of the countrified aspect of the city at its edges, there remains no better source than Patrice Lacombe's classic nineteenth-century novel *La Terre paternelle*. This prototype of the Quebec *roman paysan* (a better-known classic of the genre is *Maria Chapdelaine*) captures a vision of Rivière des Prairies in its original, pristine state.

"Among all the pleasant places a visitor might encounter along the north shore of Montreal Island during the fair-weather months, the area known as the Gros-Sault is among the most fetching, appealing in the freshness of its fields and picturesque views of the surrounding countryside.

"The branch of the Ottawa River, at this spot called the Rivière-des-Prairies, flows deep and vigorously toward the end of the island where it reunites with the St. Lawrence. By general consensus, the beautiful woods lining the river banks have been spared the farmer's axe. Some trees, pulled up by the force of the current, lean out of the stream, seemingly stuck in the limpid waters that bathe their roots. A rich carpet extends under the trees whose dense foliage casts an impenetrable shadow over lovers of the sun.

"This charming spot never failed to attract nature lovers; as well each year, during the hot-weather months, it was a place to go for large numbers of Montrealers who wished to exchange the cares of the world and burning streets of the city for a few relaxing hours in the fresh, pure country air."

Since the 1980s and '90s, parts of Rivière des Prairies have become as densely built up as any place on the island outside of downtown, because the area had contained one of the few remaining pieces of undeveloped riverfront land.

Montreal East
This community embodies another set of contradictions. Cheek by jowl with the most rural part of the island sat its most industrialized municipality. Montreal East is occupied more by oil refineries than by people. Paradoxically, it was conceived by real estate developer Joseph Versailles to be quite the opposite. In the early twentieth century, Versailles persuaded the Quebec legislature to create a town before anyone actually lived there. Influenced by the Garden

Montreal East in the mid-1920s was already taking on the look of an industrial suburb.

City concept (Town of Mount Royal is a Montreal example), he intended to develop a model community, "even more green and peaceful than Westmount," according to the promotional literature. But a collapse in the real estate market in 1913 and the onset of World War I dashed those hopes. Instead, Versailles made the land available to a number of oil companies. By 1960, it was the most noxious spot on Montreal Island, its small residential area confined to one corner downwind from the stinking refineries.

In Pierre de Grandpré's novel *La Patience des justes*, Étienne Merrin, the scion of a well-to-do Outremont family, reflects on some of his impressions of the city in 1955: "From Bout de l'Île to Hochelaga, a persistent odour of gasoline permeated the air. This industrial flatland had, in spite of everything, more melancholy grandeur than you'd expect of a chilly hell comprised of junkyards, bituminous hovels, smoky switching stations. It was the cesspool of a city that had prospered faster than had the imagination of its inhabitants."

The east end still contains some of Montreal's poorest neighbourhoods.

Montreal North

Montreal North might be the most anonymous of the city's districts, were it not for the words of Victor-Lévy Beaulieu, several of whose novels are set in its precincts. (Beaulieu was born in St. Jean de Dieu, near Rimouski in 1945, but moved at the age of twelve to Montreal North.) Through the eyes of his narrator in the novel *Satan Belhumeur*, this working-class municipality, a product of post-war suburban sprawl, is a surreal and desperate no man's land, a literal dead end, summed up by the deliberately misspelled, *joual*-inflected name, Moréal-Mort, that Beaulieu has given it. It is a place corrupt from the top down, "beginning with His Honour, mayor Pollux Ryani, that old salesman of spaghetti and baked beans, famous in all of Moréal-Mort for the number of mistresses he kept in the four corners of the town. And, next to him, the infamous Caligula Trudel, Liberal Member of Parliament for twenty years, a little nigger chieftain of mafia bars and night clubs, seen only when completely soused...." Satan Belhumeur castigates the mayor, whose "electoral coffers are greased by speculators who have deforested all the outskirts of Rivière-des-Prairies, replacing green spaces by big, rambling houses. So that from Pie-IX to Langelier, all of Gouin Boulevard is hereafter disfigured.... It's a decadent Babylon of every species of architecture, Greek next to Roman, Byzantine sitting on top of Italian, with plenty of plaster deer, copper lions and sawfish bought at Kresge's."

Ville d'Anjou

The great post-war expansion of the city gave rise to two communities to the south of Montreal North, Ville St. Léonard and Ville d'Anjou. These sprawling residential districts in the east, and similar suburbs on the western side of the island, owed their growth to two trends. Higher employment – a booming economy and the prosperity it brought – meant one could own a house rather than rent in the crowded neighbourhoods of the inner city. The automobile made possible the commute between home and work. At the same time, thousands of new citizens poured into the city from rural Quebec and war-ravaged Europe. In particular, Italians, both those moving from the old country and those who came from the crowded Italian district on the Main, gave St. Léonard an ethnic cast.

In her collection of linked stories, *The County of Birches,* Judith Kalman shows the optimism of new immigrants of the 1960s through the viewpoint of her narrator, Dana Weisz, a Hungarian-Jewish child recently transplanted from the old-world elegance of Budapest and London to Ville d'Anjou, a suburbia of "bungalows, carports and duplexes."

> "Spring in the suburb was for children. The pavement dried quickly and you could bring out the bikes when the first strong sunny afternoon made pools of the yards. Jump ropes were pulled from the bottom of toy chests. Ball-o-bats appeared instantly on store shelves, and we doffed our coats at lunchtime to walk back to school in pullovers, under the wide blue sky. Snow melted off driveways that sloped towards the street. After school we tied a rope end to the garage door handle and skipped our first jumps of the season. The world in a suburban spring was spacious and full of promise.
>
> "The town smelled like running water. Melting snow cascaded in the gutters. We heard it spill down the sewers. The drugstore displayed spring candy: sponges like honeycomb that welded to our teeth, wax lips we sucked for their red sap then chewed into candle wax we spit into the street.... The town matched us in age, grew with us, drew from us its inspiration.... [It] was ours. Our spinning bicycle wheels possessed its streets, skimmed through puddles and left snake-like trails."

Pie IX and Hochelega-Maisonneuve

Dividing the outer suburbs from the inner-city neighbourhoods on the metropolis's east side, Pie IX Boulevard, one of Montreal's great arteries, bears a name that rings strange in anglophone ears. (It is called after Pope Pius IX – Pie being the French name for Pius – and rhymes with "tea.") Hugh Hood offers a depiction of driving on Pie IX in the 1960s:

> "The prospect of the city changes as you go north, heading off the island. The lights of the Metropolitan [expressway] recede, a pale stippled line away behind to the west. On your left there's nothing but dark space belonging to Saint-Michel de Laval, half-developed industrial park...with spur lines jutting off into fields, and here and there an occasional abandoned boxcar, and a taxi park or gas station. Pie-IX was just a ribbon development a few years ago, but now there is beginning to be a bit of a spread eastwards towards Ville de Saint-Léonard. There are Dairy Queens, closed for the winter, on our right, and used-car lots, small restaurants and raw new shopping centers all the way to Rivière des Prairies."

On Pie IX's west side lie the neighbourhoods of Maisonneuve and Hochelaga, usually joined as one large hyphenated entity.

Maisonneuve, created in 1883 as an industrial suburb, was dubbed "le petit Westmount de l'Est" because of its extravagant public spending programs, which attempted to improve the character of the town. Projects included tree planting along Pie IX Boulevard, the city hall and public market buildings on Morgan Boulevard, the Public Baths and Gymnasium, and the Frank Lloyd Wright-inspired fire station. The town was annexed by Montreal in 1918, in part because of insolvency brought on by its free-spending ways.

The latter-day additions of the Olympic Stadium and Olympic Village complexes have not diminished the area's reputation for grandiose projects. Still, for the underclass who lives in the neighbourhood it's a different story, as Ronald Sutherland suggests in his 1971 bilingual novel *Lark des Neiges*. The stream-of-consciousness narrative of a disturbed young mother of four and self-avowed "mental case," *Lark des Neiges* is set in a cheerless Maisonneuve that is probably as true to life today as it was thirty years ago: "The lights are still on in the candy store at the corner of the street, like an aquarium in a dimly lit room. But the street is deserted. People are suffocated out of the tenement houses on the balmy summer nights, when the humid air sucks generations of

Pie IX at Ste. Catherine Street in 1915–16, when the broad boulevard was just beginning to take shape.

odours from the cracks in floors and from under the layers of linoleum, and they sit on their stairs and balconies until early morning. But now the autumn winds are beginning to blow down over Sherbrooke Street and sweep across the empty lots on the hill. Curtains are drawn in the rows of windows, making the street cold and sterile, shut off from the hot vibrations of life inside the catacombs of east-end Montreal."

Slightly to the west of Maisonneuve but distinct from it, the working-class neighbourhood of Hochelaga is evoked by Jean Hamelin in an autobiographical collection of stories set in the 1930s, *Les Rumeurs de Hochelaga*: "If one took the trouble of approaching the grey-painted wooden balustrade that overhangs Cuvillier Street, what sort of panorama would one discover from that bird's eye view on the street? A string of symmetrical houses three stories high, all stuck one against the other, all fronted by exterior staircases turned in on themselves like spinning tops and hooked on to balconies teeming with children...."

This quintessentially French neighbourhood where, "once and for all, one was French Canadian, Catholic and Liberal, which meant that one was French Canadian twice over," nonetheless had its multicultural aspects. Enfolded by a "halo of mystery," Tching Lee, the Chinese laundryman, is harassed by the children of the neighbourhood who give expression to the xenophobia of the populace at large "that instinctively distrusts all that is not directly identified with itself." But "if the Chinaman can't hope for anything but a marginal existence, that doesn't mean he isn't an essential figure in the human landscape of these streets.... Despite everything, the Chinaman is as characteristic an ornament of Hochelaga as is the Jew who owns a butcher shop practically opposite him, and the Italian shoemaker a little to the west on Ontario Street. And when the Chinaman will die – because even the Chinese, for all that they look it, are not immortal – when none of his compatriots will be tempted to succeed him, when thirty years hence his shanty will be razed by bulldozers to make way for new housing, a bit of old Hochelaga will die with him."

Pied du Courant

Move on to the neighbourhood west of Hochelaga and you are in Montreal's most downtrodden district. The communities of Ste. Marie, St. Eusèbe, Papineau, and Bourget are collectively known as Pied du Courant (literally, foot of the current), taking their name from the spot where the St. Lawrence narrows and the swift waters of the St. Mary's Current make further upstream navigation difficult. This once heavily industrialized district is the heart of working-class French Montreal, the equivalent of English-speaking districts such as Pointe St. Charles and Verdun to the west. It is here that Hector Berthelot installed his heroine, Ursule, and her working-class family in his version of *Les Mystères de Montréal*.

One of the earliest big businesses to set up here was the Molson brewing concern, which opened its doors under that name in 1786. Other industries, including tanning and tobacco, followed, along with small manufacturing, brickyards, and foundries. Sugar from the West Indies was made into molasses, a staple for the working class. The odour of molasses in the area led to its being given the nickname Faubourg m'lasse. A royal commission in the 1880s found two hundred children working for McDonald Tobacco eleven hours a day, six days a week. At the time, W.C. McDonald was one of the city's thirty millionaires. (McDonald began spelling his name as Macdonald after he was knighted in 1898.) The area was devastated by the great fire of 1852 and ravaged by the epidemics of the nineteenth century, particularly the smallpox outbreak of 1886.

Ninety years later, the neighbourhood was captured by Brian Moore in *The Revolution Script*, a novelistic reconstruction of the October Crisis of 1970. Two of the kidnappers of James Cross, Jacques Lanctôt and Marc Charbonneau, are heading in Charbonneau's taxi "towards the waterfront,

moving through the residential slum streets of French Montreal, old streets of uneven little red-brick houses with small windows, double-paned to keep out the terrible winter winds, streets of uneven façades amateurish as a drawing by a six-year-old, streets in which many and multifarious families are crammed into airless, pokey Dickensian warrens which remain unchanged amid the fine false fronts of the Expo 67 years...; streets like Ontario.... To stare into the windows of Ontario Street is to see into the lives of the French poor who shop there: all is cheap, all is gaudy, all is old-fashioned. There are plastic flowers and imitation mahogany sideboards and shiny bedroom suites and strangely lapelled men's suits of cheap fabric.... It is a street of People's Credit Jewellers, and Bagues de Mariage, et Fiançailles; it is Caisse Populaire banks on the corner, and the one building which has size, stature, and some sense of graystone grandeur is, you can be certain, called the Church of Sacre Coeur, or Visitation, or St. Jean Baptiste. The food stores are crammed with cheap comestibles, with specials on beer and ground chuck. There are restaurants: they sell pizza and Chiens Chauds Stimés...and Mets Chinois...and Les Hamburgers, everything ticketed in that special dogsbody language which results when French Canadians literally translate from the English or the American."

Described at about the same time in Constance Beresford-Howe's novel *The Book of Eve*, the area has a much more benign aspect for Eve, the aging heroine. She has walked out on a sterile marriage of long duration in Notre Dame de Grâce and taken a room on Rue de la Visitation.

"Not more than two crow miles from N.D.G., but a different world. You could immerse in it, become invisible. Rue de la Visitation, let me hide myself in thee.

"In this district all the streets below Sherbrooke are narrow rows of senile, eccentric houses peering out of grimy dormer windows set high under fanciful mansard roofs. Iron lace and absurd crenellated towers crown them; they haven't been painted for at least a generation and couldn't care less. In every downstairs window sags a yellow sign: 'Appartements à louer.'...

"In this neighbourhood, where a lot of shift workers lived, there wasn't the same prim barricade between night and day, the shops seemed to stay open indifferently, the neon signs blinked colour into the bitter air, the traffic ground away even when the streets were dark and deserted....

"The quiet old side streets were left to such nightbirds as me."

Brian Moore reconstructed the October Crisis in fiction.

In recent years, at least the western end of the neighbourhood has experienced something of a revival, thanks to gay men, the foot soldiers of gentrification. Michel Tremblay vividly portrayed life in Montreal's "gay village" in the mid-1980s in *The Heart Laid Bare*:

> "It was dinner time and Montreal's gay village was springing to life. Mustachioed clones, skimpily clad or dressed to kill, were on the prowl, their faces fierce as hunting dogs, hard on the heels of the first passing figure that tempted them. It was a warm blue evening, the night was

"All is cheap, all is gaudy, all is old-fashioned," Brian Moore writes in The Revolution Script.

young, all hopes were allowed. Leather, though it was early in the humid month of September, gleamed in the neon glow, strides were virile, there was serious cruising in the air, the sort that's pursued without a hint of humour.... Open air restaurants...were already crammed full of guys sprawled in their chairs, feigning coolness, looking vague and super-laid-back, fingers encircling the first glass of beer but perfectly aware of anything that moved and everything that could be hunted in the area."

THE NORTHERN SUBURBS

Villeray, Little Italy

"At the end of the '50s, my parents moved to the north end of the city on Delorimier right next to Jean-Talon, to a district that seemed without history, where it was possible, even at night, to walk around without the least fear of attack."

The neighbourhood to which the poet and fiction writer André Major refers is Villeray, part of a populous and amorphous district north and northeast of the mountain above the Canadian Pacific Railway tracks. Montreal had expanded north of the rail line near the turn of the century, aided by the growth of the tramway network. As the century progressed, the city advanced to Jean Talon Boulevard, Villeray Street, Crémazie Boulevard, and finally, by mid-century, to the river skirting the back side of the island.

Until the twentieth century, the northern section of the island was farmland, divided up, like the rest, by the "côtes" or country roads with farms fronting on them. Little knots of settlements grew up here and there, near a quarry or close to the post hotel on the road leading to the north end of the island (the future St. Laurent Boulevard).

On the east side of the Main, quarries and tramway stables drew people to the area. Shops and small factories followed and gradually gave rise to a number of working-class parishes crammed with the families of masons, carpenters, quarrymen, and the like. By the 1930s, the locality had become the vast residential district it is today.

The prolific novelist and playwright Claude Jasmin, who was born in 1930, recalls the St. Denis/Jean Talon section of Villeray in his memoir of a childhood during the Depression, *La Petite patrie*. In this passage he describes a sight every Montrealer will be familiar with to this day – snow-clearing. The nature of the horsepower on the equipment has changed, but the impression made by the operation holds true:

"The frightful machine was a monster with two heads, its four nostrils steaming in the premature cold and snow of December. The bells on its harnesses rang out. It approached us, chest muscles constricting and expanding. Behind this enormous mount, there appeared a terrifying man wearing a cap with fur-lined ears and enormous mitts with stiffened thumbs. This man with the red face and blue nose, with brows coated with frost, steered a creaking vehicle that cleared the snow off the wide sidewalk of Saint-Denis Street.

"If we stayed there, the monster would undoubtedly crush us pitilessly. A cry of terror, and there we were, perched on the stairs for safety, watching wide-eyed the progress of this gigantic team. The eyes were hidden behind visors of dark leather, their jaws were decked with icicles, as the high rumps pulled that pitiless, unstoppable plough. And mounted upon it was this *bonhomme*, this rigid giant who clucked bizarre commands in a cavernous voice at regular intervals.

"When the infernal red machine had gone by, what joy to discover the long bank of snow heaped up on the curb of Saint-Denis Street. A glance to check the horizon of Jean Talon Street where the apocalyptic beast receded, then, once more safe, the virtues of a small shovel of red enamelled iron to dig trenches, secret passages and corridors, became manifest. From time to time a car passed by and the tramways continued their eternal shuttles. Men came and went, oblivious to us little urchins uncovering the possibilities of serried banks of snow, the pleasure of newborn winter, the joy which henceforth would always come in the wake of the terrifying municipal scraper and its noisy ringing."

While the northeastern suburbs were mostly French in Major's and Jasmin's childhoods, they have become more multi-ethnic in recent years as Haitians, Latin Americans, and Asians established themselves in the area. These days this is their neighbourhood. Dany Laferrière's impressionistic chronicle of his first year in Montreal in 1976, *A Drifting Year*, shows the young Haitian immigrant ("still vaguely a virgin") on the make in the Villeray area:

Fifty Crémazie is the name of the place.
A crummy bar at 50 Crémazie Street.
Full of immigrants on a Saturday night.
Girls too.
The youngest must be
sixty-five.

The guy who brought me to this hole
told me to be patient,
the girls were bound to show up
any minute now.
There they are!
Between them, they must
have a hundred and thirty-six years of living.
I'm not even twenty-three.

The body may be older than it used to be.
The skin more wrinkled.
The bones drier.
The voice hasn't changed.
Close your eyes and you're with a girl of sixteen.

Park Extension and Town of Mount Royal

Moving west of St. Laurent Boulevard, ethnic diversity is still apparent, but the original language of the area is as likely to be English as French. Here two neighbourhoods border each other, divided by the railway line that gave birth to one and helped support the working-class residents of the other. One, Town of Mount Royal, is as rich as the other, Park Extension, is poor. T.M.R., as the former is commonly known, has been for most of its history a bastion of upper-middle-class anglophones; the other neighbourhood is a constantly shifting polyglot. Originally sheltering English and Irish, Jews and displaced eastern Europeans, more recently Park Ex's long, straight streets lined with modest brick homes house south Asians, north Africans, and Middle Easterners. The "Extension" of the name refers to the neighbourhood's location north of the Park Avenue axis, but another image conjured up is of an extended arm beckoning the world's immigrants and refugees to its confines.

DANY LAFERRIÈRE

The best known of Montreal's Haitian writers, Dany Laferrière has found a broad English-speaking audience in translation. Technically no longer a Montrealer – he has lived in Miami since 1990 – Laferrière continues to identify and to be identified with the city where his publishers, VLB and Lanctôt, and translator, David Homel, are located.

Laferrière was born in Port-au-Prince in 1953, where he became a journalist. The murder of a friend during the era of Jean-Claude Duvalier prompted his departure for Montreal in 1978. While he was trying to establish himself as a writer, he worked in a tannery.

The first of Laferrière's eight novels, *How to Make Love to a Negro* (1985), a work of fictionalized autobiography, features a poor young black writer who shares his digs with a ruminative African. Seemingly a lighthearted romp, the book is a subtle attack on racism and stereotyping as it shows how the two young men attract the sexual attention of white women who use them for casual adventures but won't invite them home to meet the family.

The zany eroticism and cheerful willingness to shock which were the hallmarks of Laferrière's early work have ripened into a larger vision over the years. Along with his flair for dialogue and humour, he cares deeply about his characters. His lyrical and sensitive novel/memoir *The Aroma of Coffee* (1991), in which a ten-year-old boy describes his relationship with his grandmother, the central figure in a small Haitian village, is widely regarded as his best work.

Dany Laferrière is the best known of Montreal's Haitian writers.

TREVOR FERGUSON

Born in Seaforth, Ontario, the son of a clergyman and a teacher, Trevor Ferguson arrived at the age of three in Montreal's Park Extension, a neighbourhood that has figured extensively in several of his seven novels, and from which he ran away at the age of sixteen. He has estimated that he crossed Canada seventeen times during his wandering years, finding shelter in Salvation Army hostels and in jails. He worked in bush camps in the North West Territories, British Columbia, and Alberta, these experiences giving him material for the novels *High Water Chants* (1977), *The Fire Line* (1995), and *The Timekeeper* (1996), all characterized by his trademark rugged, male-dominated prose.

It was at the end of one of these bush episodes that Ferguson realized he was meant to be a writer. Having walked away from a job, he was left hanging around a flophouse in High Level, Alberta, waiting for a final cheque. He has said, "I wrote out a statement in a Gideons' Bible that I was going to be a writer and not going to let anything stop me. I was not going to take jobs I liked because they might suck me into staying with them."

He kept his promise. He returned to Montreal in 1970 ("just in time for the October Crisis. Eventually we all mature and come back home") and worked as a cab driver and bartender for several years. His artistic breakthrough novel, *Onyx John* (1985), a comic and fantastic coming-of-age saga, exhibited Ferguson's flair for the dramatic and his linguistic energy. (Leon Rooke called it one of the two best novels ever written in Canada.)

Ferguson's commercial breakthrough, however, came in 1999 with the publication of his pseudonymous suspense novel, *City of Ice*, which prompted a bidding war among New York publishers and was bought by Random House for close to half a million U.S. dollars.

Park Extension has figured in several of Trevor Ferguson's novels.

Park Extension serves as a kind of holding pen for Trevor Ferguson's protagonist, Sparrow Drinkwater, in the 1993 quest-for-identity novel *The True Life Adventures of Sparrow Drinkwater*.

"Railway tracks limited Park Extension on two sides, east and south, and only...daring recalcitrant adolescents...crossed into the nether and French speaking regions beyond. To the north, Crémazie Street, the extension of a dirt highway thick with traffic, barricaded our settlement from wild and boundless fields and scruffy woods. The west side was restricted by the golf course. While the fairways were considered a natural adjunct to our range, the affluent town beyond it – called Town of Mount Royal, commonly referred to as 'The Town' – was inherently hostile to our ragamuffin presence.... This was the domain of the rich...."

Town of Mount Royal was conceived as a "garden city." The idea originated with the British urban planner Sir Ebenezer Howard, who believed that employment opportunities were as integral to new urban developments as housing and green space. In the case of T.M.R., the notion was promoted by executives of the Canadian Northern Railway before World War I; they saw it as one part of a huge development scheme that would bring the railway into central Montreal via a tunnel under Mount Royal.

For decades T.M.R. was a preserve of anglo starchiness that did not readily welcome either Jews or French Canadians, a fact to which Denise Bombardier alludes in her account of family outings by car in her 1985 memoir, *Une Enfance à l'eau bénite*. "We crossed Town of Mount Royal first, where the new English middle class lived, the parvenus. Immense colonnades like those of the White House, split levels with porticos made of Carrara marble. Through the uncurtained picture windows, like displays in department stores, we could make out luxurious furnishings: armchairs in garnet velvet, floor-lamps as grand as street lights.... We cruised slowly to get a better glimpse of the interiors. Sometimes we caught sight of the owners while they washed their cars or watered the lawn, looking smug. They raised their head in our direction but didn't smile, and I turned away, afraid of catching their eye. 'They're rich, but they look stupid,' my aunt lashed out by way of a commentary."

St. Laurent

As early as the late seventeenth century, Montreal was ringed by a string of fortified hamlets, joined to the main town by the "côtes." One of these settlements was St. Laurent. For most of its history, it remained a village, until dramatic changes began around 1950.

St. Laurent lies just north of the main east-west axis that runs through the centre of the island. This road, called Côte de Liesse, Côte St. Laurent, Côte St. Michel or Côte St. Léonard, depending on what parish it was passing through, became an increasingly busy thoroughfare until finally, at the end of the 1950s, it became the Metropolitan Boulevard, the city's main east-west expressway. The Met's role in the twentieth century was akin to that of the Lachine Canal a century earlier, drawing industry to both sides of the corridor it created. St. Laurent was among the beneficiaries, and it remains home to one of the largest industrial parks in the city.

Hugh Hood discovered traces of an earlier history in suburban St. Laurent, in the 1967 short story "The Village Inside."

"Sometimes the overlay of city on remote village can be traced, building by building, along an old main street. In August, ranging wider and wider on my bike in the evenings, trying to crowd in all the sunshine coming to me before August, I discovered *rue Sainte-Croix* out in Saint-Laurent, not really remote, simply the continuation of Lucerne after it passes under the elevated highway. True enough, it's no more than five miles from the centre of town, but you can detect the ancient village inside the suburban growth, like an attenuated ghost, traceable by houses spotted along the street as you ride north, interrupted by modern installations of a qualified beauty and utility....

"Up the street there's a superb stone farmhouse of the kind you still see all over the richer farmland of western Québec, two storeys and an attic, of immensely solid irregular stones, maybe a hundred and twenty years old and now the offices of a small local construction company. Further along there's a Victorian mansion with a tower surrounded by balconies, red brick with a pattern of darker, almost bluish, stone let into the wall. Who can have lived there? An early mayor, the richest man in the village? Houses like these, about ten of them set among gas stations and gravel yards, suggest the tidal-wave movement of an enormous city's advance in every direction, like débris surfacing from a sunken wreck."

Côte des Neiges

On the northwest flank of the mountain, Côte des Neiges, another humble village, has existed since the early days of the French régime. It was linked to Montreal by a road that separates the Westmount side of the mountain from the more rugged summit to the east, the road itself earlier having been an Indian trail that led to the Rivière des Prairies.

In the nineteenth century, Côte des Neiges village was a favourite summering place enjoyed by anglophones who had the means to escape the oppressive heat (and diseases) in the crowded town on the St. Lawrence shore. Lumkin's Hotel became the village's most famous resort. In the mid-nineteenth century, the city's two great cemeteries – the Catholic Notre Dame des Neiges and Protestant Mount Royal Cemetery – were established nearby.

Despite its attractions, Côte des Neiges was not a prosperous place, at the turn of the century lacking even the essential service of a proper fire department. As a result, it was annexed by the city in two stages, in 1907 and 1910. Urbanization of the area began in earnest about the time of World War I. Between the wars, the area's big institutions – the Université de Montréal and St. Joseph's Oratory – were begun. By mid-century, Côte des Neiges had become a densely built, cosmopolitan community. Today it is the city's most ethnically diverse neighbourhood. Its three hospitals – Ste. Justine's, St. Mary's, and the Jewish General – reflect the area's earlier makeup, while packed cheek-by-jowl on Côte des Neiges Road are shops proclaiming their owners' origins in South Asia, Vietnam, and the Caribbean.

An excerpt from an essay by Jean Éthier-Blais catches the heart of the neighbourhood, near St. Joseph's Oratory, in a state of architectural transition in the late 1960s: "Côte-des-Neiges was a garden. Near the Oratory whose cupola...stood up against the horizon like a latter-day tribute to Brunneleschi, the old Rockhill Apartments nestled gently against the rising slope of Mount Royal, prefaced by a garden. A gentle stroll led to brick buildings fashioned for a life of good fortune. You looked upon apartment buildings which gave the

Côte des Neiges Road about 1900. The neighbourhood was being integrated into the city, but it was still possible to see a cattle drive along the main street.

impression of family homes, all to be demolished and replaced by a twenty-three storey building. It projects against the Montreal skyline like a shriek of glass and concrete; a fitting symbol for the disappearance of a calm and radiant life and its replacement by a completely geometric conception of human evolution."

Notre Dame de Grâce and Snowdon

Today's N.D.G./Snowdon neighbourhood was originally known as Côte St. Pierre and included all the territory between the vicinity of Côte des Neiges in the east and Lachine in the west. One of the first residents was Jean Décarie, who arrived in the colony in 1650, with other settlers recruited by Jeanne Mance.

In the late eighteenth century, a Loyalist named William Powell built a splendid country house near present-day Décarie Boulevard between Monkland Avenue and Côte St. Luc Road. He then sold this imposing property to James Monk, a fellow Loyalist, in 1795. Called Monklands, the mansion served as the governor general's official residence between 1844 and 1849, when for a brief period Montreal was capital of the United Province of Canada.

After the central government moved to Kingston in 1849, the residence was briefly converted into a posh sixty-room hotel but was purchased in 1854 by the Congregation of Notre Dame, which had sold off much of its property in Pointe St. Charles to the Grand Trunk Railway. The Sisters proceeded to build the magnificent Villa Maria complex on the site, which nestles in sixty hectares of parkland and houses a fine private Catholic girls' school.

There were some seventy families living in the area in the mid-nineteenth century when the parish of Notre Dame de Grâce was created, extending from the escarpment in the south, north to Côte St. Luc Road, and including today's municipalities of Westmount, Hampstead, Côte St. Luc, and Montreal West.

The neighbourhood remained essentially rural through the nineteeth century and was renowned for its apple orchards, fruit from which was exported to England. Also famous were "Décarie melons," which were highly regarded in the luxury hotels of Montreal and New York.

Snowdon may be considered a northern continuation of N.D.G., since the Montreal Park and Island Tramway line, whose western station was in

Snowdon, was extended southward to N.D.G. in 1908. From World War I onward, through the link by tramway and railway to the city, development of N.D.G. grew apace. Its evolution into a largely anglophone neighbourhood at around this time was remarked upon by Hugh MacLennan in disparaging terms in 1954, recalling his arrival in the area twenty years earlier.

"Where Royal Avenue joins Sherbrooke in Notre Dame de Grâce I looked around. It reminded me of the Cowley Road in Oxford, or any modern, semi-suburban street that has grown up in England since the English have lost their taste. I knew even without seeing beyond the window curtains that most of these modest duplex houses and three-and-four-storey apartments would have cramped rooms, an air of strained respectability and photographs of the King and Queen (cut from magazines) hanging on their tan-coloured walls."

N.D.G. feels equally claustrophobic to the irreverent, aging housewife of

By 1871 Monklands, the former governor general's estate, had been turned into the Villa Maria convent with the vice-regal mansion as its centrepiece.

Beresford-Howe's *Book of Eve.* Eve has abandoned her husband and previous existence in favour of the east end, but makes a quick foray home by bus to reflect on what she has left behind.

"On your left, Ladies and Gentlemen, is N.D.G., a very neat suburb of hell. Note those rows of bright, ugly, cheap shops – cleaner's, shoe-repair place, Greek restaurant, costume-jeweller, drugstore – comments, every one, on how limited, after all, are the needs of the human spirit. Observe the pot-holes and unremoved snow: much city graft in Our Lady's domain.

"So this was the land of lost delights, I thought, staring curiously out of the dusty bus window. Every inch, every block was familiar –- I grew up here, when the trees in N.D.G. Park were just new-planted twigs; never lived anywhere else all my married life. It was a solemn thought. Nearly seventy years in philodendron-land; Reader's Digestville; two-storeydom. On streets called Draper, Wilson, Harvard, and Grove Hill Place, where, till recently, the French language was never heard, and people were too respectable to sit out on the front porch in the evenings."

A generation later, the N.D.G. of the Haitian-born novelist Émile Ollivier is a complex, multi-hued, and multicultural district, divided more by race than by language. In this excerpt from Ollivier's prize-winning novel of exile and identity, *Passages*, Leyda, the Haitian-born female main character, wanders through N.D.G. Park in autumn.

"In this enclosure ringed by birches, the contrasting colours struck the eye: crimson maples, gilded yellow poplars, insolent green conifers beneath a tattered sky pierced by light.... Recently this park was the theatre of violent conflict between black youth who for the most part live to the south, below Sherbrooke, and Jewish teens who in the main live to the north. Since then it has become a buffer, a point of demarcation, a fault line between two solitudes.

"Eleven o'clock sounded from the belfry of Saint Augustine Church. Leyda began to hurry. She circled a brightly coloured little kiosk, the relic of the last Caribbean festival. The district had resonated with boisterous rhythms, outrageous performances, supreme mirth. Leyda

Constance Beresford-Howe called N.D.G. "a neat suburb of hell."

retained in her memory an image of every shade of skin colour clustered together in a riot of motley outfits, a laughing throng of bodies slick with sweat beneath the sun; this whole part of the city suddenly gone mad: blinding lights, sirens, cars and buses paralyzed, the passengers trapped; people everywhere, in the street, on the sidewalks, at windows, in lanes, on the grass. And...a cacophony of sounds which suddenly became the rhythms of méringue, reggae, calypso...."

Lachine

Lachine owes its name to a common-place old Ville Marie joke made at the expense of the explorer Robert Cavelier, sieur de La Salle, who was obsessed with finding a passage to China by way of the St. Lawrence. La Salle's seigneury, St. Sulpice, was located at the western end of the trail that linked Montreal with Lake St. Louis, circumventing the Lachine Rapids. (The site of La Salle's property was just below where the Lachine locks are today; the municipality immediately east of Lachine is named after him.)

The most notable event in the town's history is an infamous one – the Lachine massacre of 1689, in which an Iroquois war party of 1,500 warriors crossed Lake St. Louis and attacked the village while its inhabitants slept. Governor Louis de Buade, Comte de Frontenac, reported: "They burned more than nine miles of territory, sacking all the houses as far as the very doors of the city, carrying off more than 120 men, women and children, after having massacred more than 200 others, who were either brained, burnt or roasted." Notwithstanding the inhumanity of the event, it appears that the scale of horror was exaggerated by contemporaries. Later research suggests that twenty-four settlers were slaughtered straight off, and ninety taken prisoner, of whom forty-two were never seen again.

From its earliest days, Lachine was the jumping-off point for fur traders, explorers, and missionaries making their way into the interior. In the eighteenth and early nineteenth centuries, it was a destination for day trips by sleigh and carriage from Montreal. The canal, whose entrance was near the town, brought industrialization which, in the later nineteenth century, joined Lachine with the rest of the city. The first railway on the island connected Lachine and Montreal in 1846.

The history of Lachine forms the backdrop to Julien Bigras's 1983 semi-autobiographical novel, *Ma Vie, ma folie*. Bigras, a psychoanalyst as well as writer, enters into a search for his family roots, while treating an aboriginal patient. "François Bigras, the first ancestor, arrived in 1682, at the age of twenty, a loner and romantic from La Rochelle." Bigras's researches "leave no doubt about the life of a pariah that he led. His descendants followed in his footsteps, all of them drinkers, drifters incapable of taking root. Installed in...Lachine, they only lived there a few days a year, just enough time to get thoroughly drunk, to consort with the prostitutes of the town, to get their wives pregnant, and then take off for the West and indulge themselves with the debaucheries awaiting them there! Many of them...at certain times lived like animals eager for one thing only: sexual gratification."

The Lachine Rapids figure in a vignette of the 1920s in Saul Bellow's novel

Herzog. The Nobel Prize-winning novelist was born in Lachine in 1915 and, like the title character, Moses Herzog, spent the first nine years of his life in Montreal. Here Herzog, a species of intellectual Everyman, is depicted as a child in the toilet of a moving train heading west from Montreal: "The train crossed the Saint Lawrence. Moses pressed the pedal and through the stained funnel of the toilet he saw the river frothing. Then he stood at the window. The water shone and curved on the great slabs of rock, spinning into foam at the Lachine Rapids where it sucked and rumbled. On the other shore was Caughnawaga, where the Indians lived in shacks raised on stilts. Then came the burnt summer fields."

In Irving Layton's poem "Lachine, Que." the suburb takes on many of its contemporary aspects:

The Lachine Canal in Lachine today has become part of a park.

Here, the skies
crimson with sunset
disappear
into blast furnaces:
emerge
rows of red-bricked
houses,
whose guardians,
their bellies
full of apples and lard,
wave shirtsleeves at the summer.
And all day long
the trains
coming and going
expel soot
upon this workmen's suburbia
which lies glistening
at the foot
of the highway
like a safe
used by an idiot.

The Lakeshore/West Island

Like the eastern end of the island, communities on the western extremity, including Pointe Claire and Ste. Anne de Bellevue, began as defensive redoubts during the early colonial period. Pointe Claire received its name because, from this small, treeless peninsula jutting into Lake St. Louis, French soldiers could easily spot Iroquois raiding parties. By 1765 Pointe Claire was a hamlet in a parish of some eight hundred people.

For most of their histories, the first communities on the West Island were isolated farming villages, but in the nineteenth century they became popular resort areas for people from the city. Urbanization of the Lakeshore became a phenomenon only after World War II, when the rise of the automobile made commuting relatively easy to such bedroom communities as Beaconsfield, Dollard des Ormeaux, Baie d'Urfé, and Kirkland. Flight from the inner city neighbourhoods and immigration – before the Quiet Revolution much of it from the British Isles – led to the present-day anglophone character of the area.

IRVING LAYTON

Issie Lazarovitch tried out several names (Isadore Lazarre, Irving Lazarre, Pete Lazarovitch) and several occupations (including Fuller Brush man and insurance salesman) before he became Irving Layton and one of the great poets of the twentieth century. The eighth and youngest child of an orthodox Jewish couple who arrived in Montreal from Romania in 1913 when Issie was a year old, he grew up in extreme poverty on Ste. Elisabeth Street. The parlour of the family's four-room shack was converted into a grocery store from which his mother eked out their living, while his father devoted himself to otherworldly studies and meditations; he died when the boy was twelve.

Layton wrote his first poem (inspired by the cleavage of his grade six teacher) at around the same age, but it was not until he was nearly thirty that he became actively involved in the poetry scene in the city, beginning to contribute to the groundbreaking little magazine *First Statement* in 1942, and co-editing it for several years with John Sutherland and

Louis Dudek. More than anyone else, he helped to dispel the puritanism and effeteness that stultified Canadian literature in the 1940s and '50s, and broke down barriers of subject, style, and language.

In the nearly fifty years that his career has spanned, Layton has produced a body of poetry that reflects all facets of his bohemian life: his five wives and assorted love affairs; his children; his mercurial political views (from a youthful flirtation with Communism to support of the Vietnam War and of the War Measures Act during the October Crisis of 1970); his friendships and feuds; his atheism and his Judaism.

The critic Mervin Butovsky has written that "his life-long act of writing has produced no single poem more impressive than his assertive, hectoring self, a self-conscious mock figure who invented just the kind of person he had to become if he was to deliver himself from the obscurity and ineffectuality that had engulfed others around him. Layton brought to his chosen literary vocation much the same raw, dynamic energy that his peers from the first immigrant generation were to demonstrate when they elbowed their way out of Montreal's urban slums into the often inhospitable fields of law, medicine, commerce, and manufacturing."

Irving Layton in 1957. Layton's bohemianism represented a break with traditional attitudes in Canadian poetry.

Ste. Anne de Bellevue writer Kenneth Radu picks up on a historical echo of the area in a short story titled "Real Men." The story's protagonist, Vincent, a Franco-Italian West Islander, passes a summer's day poolside in Ste. Anne, "legs stretched out, his fifty-dollar red bikini eye-catching and protuberant."

In his imagination, Vincent conjures up an incident from three hundred years before, when "a band of twenty-six Iroquois Indians, having attacked the settlement at LaSalle where they left two people dead, one soldier and one blacksmith, and the wooden palisade in flames, took to their canoes and paddled along the St. Lawrence river to what is now Lake St. Louis. They quickly disembarked, hoisted the canoes over their heads, and portaged around the rapids which pleasure boats avoided today by using the lock in Ste. Anne de Bellevue, a popular village on the shore of the lake. Within minutes they re-entered the water and stroked their leisurely way through the Lake of the Two Mountains. By the time they beached their ingenious craft near a clearing in the mixed forest, built a campfire and, exhausted, drifted into their private dreams, a contingent of French soldiers had been mustered, dispatched by land through the black-fly infested forest and waited in ambush for 'les sauvages.'"

Although an English-speaking enclave today, the Lakeshore before World War II was almost exclusively French-Canadian, but for the occasional family from Montreal that rented a summer cottage there. This was the case of the family in Joyce Marshall's story "The Little White Girl." "Though we rented a house just outside the city on what Montrealers called the lakeshore every summer, my parents never got organized in time to find one that had enough bedrooms, was properly furnished – or anywhere near the beach.... This year's was the pokiest and least convenient – a derelict farmhouse a long way back from the village on St. John's Road. My mother...talked a great deal about...the frustration of being married to a man who preferred dull, flat old Lake St. Louis to the ocean. For us children, trips to the beach now began with a hilly trudge down a dirt road, leaps every now and then across ditches to avoid farmers in their rigs, but daily miracles along our way – devil's paintbrushes, chicory and vetch, and once, overnight, a whole broad field of quivering blue-eyed grass."

In her 1995 novel *The Tragedy Queen*, Linda Leith shows a contemporary yet timeless Pointe Claire with documentary exactitude through the eyes of the con man Vince Carlson:

"Pointe Claire village.... The silver-spired church, the greystone convent

Linda Leith offers a contemporary but timeless picture of the suburb Pointe Claire.

and the windmill on the point look no different from this distance than they looked thirty years before.

"The point itself – the cape – juts out into the St. Lawrence and affords a clear view up and down river – west to Ste. Anne de Bellevue on the tip of the island of Montreal, and east to the Lachine Rapids and, beyond them, to the centre of Montreal. Far away in the distance a black tanker is churning its way slowly down the Seaway past the long line of trees on the far shore.

"The Indians were the first to admire the view up and down river. The Indians who never were Indian. Lachine which is not China – nor India either, for that matter. And – Vince realizes for the first time – the lake which is not a lake. It's steaming, now, sullen in the accumulating heat of the summer morning. Vince must have always known that this was the St. Lawrence, at least to the extent that he would probably have been able to give the right answer if someone had insisted that he explain exactly what Lake St. Louis was. A bay in the St. Lawrence."

*

A great city, we began this book by observing, is twice built: first out of building materials and then through myriad expressions of the imagination. In attempting to map Montreal through its literature, our approach has been more eclectic than exhaustive, the idiosyncratic choices of two unabashed lovers of this city. We leave the whimsical last word to Gwethalyn Graham, who also loved Montreal (where she lived for many years) and who gave it a romantic cast in the 1940s, in a vision which no longer fully holds and is all the more poignant for that.

"These are some of the things you would remember if you had to go away and live somewhere else –... the incredible tropical green of this northern city in summer, the old gray squares, the Serpentine in Lafontaine Park with little overhanging casinos and packed with little boats; the harbor, the river; the formalized black-and-white figures of the nuns taking the air just at dusk among the trees around the Mother House of the Congregation of Notre Dame, the narrow gray streets of downtown Montreal like the streets of an old French provincial town, the figure of the Blessed Virgin keeping watch over the harbor from her place high up on the Bonsecours, the sailors' church; the steep terraced gardens of Westmount, and the endless narrow balconies of endless walled convents and monasteries, where nobody ever walks."

SOURCES

Every effort has been made to trace ownership of copyright material; however, we will welcome any information that allows us to rectify any reference or credit for subsequent editions.

Hubert Aquin: Excerpts from *Prochain Episode* by Hubert Aquin. Used by permission, McClelland & Stewart, Inc. The Canadian Publishers.

Yves Beauchemin: Excerpts from *The Alley Cat* by Yves Beauchemin translated by Sheila Fischman. Used by permission, McClelland & Stewart, Inc. The Canadian Publishers. Excerpts from *Juliette* by Yves Beauchemin translated by Sheila Fischman. Used by permission, McClelland & Stewart, Inc. The Canadian Publishers.

Claude Beausoleil: "Endless Montreal." Translated by D.G. Jones. *Ellipse* 56 (1996). By permission of D.G. Jones.

Saul Bellow: Excerpts from *Herzog* by Saul Bellow, published by Viking, by permission of Penguin Putnam Inc.

Constance Beresford-Howe: Excerpts from *The Book of Eve* copyright © 1973 by Constance Beresford-Howe reprinted by arrangement with Bella Pomer Agency.

Morley Callaghan: Excerpts from *The Loved and the Lost*. Copyright © Morley Callaghan, 1951. Reprinted by permission of Macmillan Canada, an imprint of CDG Books Canada Inc.

Leonard Cohen: Excerpts from *Let Us Compare Mythologies* by Leonard Cohen. Used by permission, McClelland & Stewart, Inc. The Canadian Publishers.

Réjean Ducharme: Excerpt from *Le Nez qui voque*, © Paris: Gallimard, 1967, by kind permission of Editions Gallimard.

David Fennario: Excerpts from *Without a Parachute* by David Fennario, by permission of the author.

Trevor Ferguson: Excerpts from *City of Ice* and *The True Life Adventures of Sparrow Drinkwater* by Trevor Ferguson, by permission of the author.

Mavis Gallant: Excerpts from *The Selected Stories of Mavis Gallant* by Mavis Gallant. Used by permission, McClelland & Stewart, Inc. The Canadian Publishers.

Hugh Hood: Excerpts from *Flying a Red Kite* and *Around the Mountain: Scenes from Montreal Life* by Hugh Hood, by permission of the author.

Judith Kalman: Excerpts from *The County of Birches* by Judith Kalman, by permission of the author.

Dany Laferrière: *A Drifting Year* copyright © 1994 by Dany Laferrière, translation copyright © by David Homel. First published in French by VLB Éditeur. Published in English by Douglas & McIntyre, 1997. Reprinted by permission of the publisher.

Irving Layton: Excerpts from *Collected Poems* by Irving Layton. Used by permission, McClelland & Stewart, Inc. The Canadian Publishers. Excerpts from *Waiting for the Messiah* by Irving Layton, by permission of the author.

Linda Leith: Excerpts from *The Tragedy Queen* by Linda Leith, by permission of the author.

Jack Ludwig: Excerpts from "A Woman of Her Age" by Jack Ludwig, reprinted with permission of the author.

Hugh MacLennan: Excerpts from *Thirty and Three*, *Two Solitudes*, and *The Watch That Ends the Night* by Hugh MacLennan, by permission of McGill University.

Robert Majzels: Excerpts from *City of Forgetting* by Robert Majzels, by permission of the author.

Jovette Marchessault: Excerpts from *Like a Child of the Earth* and *Mother of the Grass* by Jovette Marchessault, translated by Yvonne Klein, by permission of the author.

Joyce Marshall: Excerpts from *Any Time at All and Other Stories* by Joyce Marshall. Used by permission, McClelland & Stewart, Inc. The Canadian Publishers.

Brian Moore: Excerpts from *The Revolution Script* copyright © 1971 by Brian Moore, published by Holt Rinehart & Winston, reprinted by permission of Curtis Brown, Ltd.

Edward O. Phillips: Excerpts from *Sunday Best* and *Sunday's Child* by Edward O. Phillips, by permission of the author.

Monique Proulx: *Aurora Montrealis* by Monique Proulx, translation copyright © 1997 by Matt Cohen. Copyright ©1996 by Les Éditions du Boréal. Published in English by Douglas & McIntyre. Reprinted by permission of the publisher.

Al Purdy: Excerpt from "Negroes on St. Antoine Street" by Al Purdy, by permission of the author.

Kenneth Radu: Excerpts from "Real Men" by Kenneth Radu, by permission of the author.

Mordecai Richler: Excerpts from *Barney's Version*, *St. Urbain's Horseman*, and *The Street* by Mordecai Richler, by permission of the author.

Régine Robin: Excerpts from *La Québécoite* by Régine Robin, translated by Phyllis Aronoff as *The Wanderer*, by permission of the translator.

Chava Rosenfarb: Excerpts from "Edgia's Revenge" by Chava Rosenfarb, by permission of the author.

Gabrielle Roy: Excerpts from Gabrielle Roy's *The Cashier*, translated by Henry Binsse, and *The Tin Flute*, translated by Alan Brown, Copyright: Fonds Gabrielle Roy, by permission of Fonds Gabrielle Roy.

F.R. Scott: Excerpts from *The Collected Poems of F.R. Scott* by F.R. Scott. Used by permission, McClelland & Stewart, Inc. The Canadian Publishers.

Raymond Souster: The excerpt from "St. Catherine Street East" by Raymond Souster is reprinted from *Collected Poems, Volume III*, by permission of Oberon Press.

Michel Tremblay: Excerpts from *The Heart Laid Bare* by Michel Tremblay translated by Sheila Fischman. Used by permission, McClelland & Stewart, Inc. The Canadian Publishers. Excerpts from Michel Tremblay's *The Fat Woman Next Door Is Pregnant*, translated by Sheila Fischman, and from his *Sainte-Carmen of the Main*, translated by John Van Burek, by permission of the author.

Jane Urquhart: Excerpts from *Away* by Jane Urquhart. Used by permission, McClelland & Stewart, Inc. The Canadian Publishers.

Miriam Waddington: Excerpts from "East on Dorchester Street" and "Saint Antoine Street" from *Collected Poems* by Miriam Waddington. Copyright © Miriam Waddington 1986. Reprinted by permission of Oxford University Press Canada.

William Weintraub: Excerpts from *The Underdogs* by William Weintraub, by permission of the author.

SELECTED BIBLIOGRAPHY

Unless indicated in the bibliography below, translations from the French are by Bryan Demchinsky and Elaine Kalman Naves.

Abboud, Christiane (director). *Les Rues de Montréal*. Montreal: Méridian, Ville de Montréal: 1995.

Abley, Mark. *Glasburyon*. Kingston: Quarry Press, 1994.

Allan, Ted. *Don't You Know Anybody Else?* Toronto: McClelland & Stewart, 1985.

Ames, Herbert. *The City Below the Hill*. (1897). Toronto: University of Toronto Press, 1972.

Anburey, Thomas. *Travels Through the Interior Parts of America*, 2 vol. London: William Lane, 1789.

Aquin, Hubert. *Prochain Episode*. Translated by Penny Williams. Toronto: McClelland & Stewart, New Canadian Library, 1972.

Basile, Jean. *La Jument des Mongols*. Montreal: Éditions de l'Hexagone, 1988.

——. *Les Voyages d'Irkoutsk*. Montreal: HMH, 1970.

Beauchemin, Yves. *The Alley Cat*. (1981). Translated by Sheila Fischman. Toronto: McClelland & Stewart, 1986.

——. *Juliette*. (1989). Translated by Sheila Fischman. Toronto: McClelland & Stewart, 1993.

Beaulieu, Victor-Lévy. *Satan Belhumeur*. Montreal: VLB Éditeur, 1981.

Beausoleil, Claude. "Endless Montreal." Translated by D.G. Jones. *Ellipse* 56 (1996).

Bellow, Saul. *Herzog*. New York: Viking, 1965.

Benoît, Jacques. *Gisèle et le serpent*. Montreal: Libre Expression, 1981.

Benoît, Michèle, and Roger Gratton. *Pignon sur rue : les quartiers de Montréal*. Montreal: Guérin, 1991.

Beresford-Howe, Constance. *The Book of Eve*, Toronto: Macmillan, 1973.

Berthelot, Hector. *Les Mystères de Montréal*. Montreal: A.P. Pigeon, 1901.

Bigras, Julien. *Ma Vie, ma folie*. Montreal: Boréal, 1983.

Birney, Earle. "Montréal 1945." *Ellipse* 56 (1996).

Bliss, Michael. *Plague: A Story of Smallpox in Montreal*. Toronto: HarperCollins, 1991.

Boissevain, Jeremy. *The Italians of Montreal*. Ottawa: Minister of Supply and Services Canada, 1970.

Bombardier, Denise. *Une Enfance à l'eau bénite*. Paris: Éditions du Seuil, 1985.

Borrett, George Tuthill. *Letters From Canada and the United States*. London: Groombridge and Sons, 1866.

Brooke, Frances. *The History of Emily Montague*. (1769). Toronto: McClelland & Stewart (New Canadian Library), 1995.

Brooke, Rupert. *Letters From America*. (1931). London: Sidgwick & Jackson, 1987.

Brown, Thomas Storrow. "Montreal in 1818." *The New Dominion Monthly*, March, 1870.

Burns, Patricia. *The Shamrock and the Shield: An Oral History of the Irish in Montreal*. Montreal: Véhicule Press, 1998.

Butler, Samuel. *The Note-Books of Samuel Butler*. (1921). Edited by Henry Festing Jones. London: Sidgwick & Jackson, 1987.

Callaghan, Morley. *The Loved and the Lost*. Toronto: Macmillan, 1951.

Charlevoix, Pierre de. *History and General Description of New France*. New York: F.P. Harper, 1900.

Choko, Marc H. *Les Grandes Places Publiques de Montréal*. Montreal: Méridien, 1987.

Choquette, Robert. *Les Velder*. Montreal: Bernard Valiquette, 1941.

Cohen, Leonard. *Let Us Compare Mythologies*. (1956). Toronto: McClelland & Stewart, 1966.

——. *The Favourite Game*. London: Secker & Warburg, 1963.

Collard, Edgar. *All Our Yesterdays*. Montreal: The Gazette, 1988.

——. *Montreal: The Days That Are No More*. Toronto: Doubleday Canada Limited, 1976.

—— *The Story of Dominion Square/Place du Canada*. Toronto: Longmans Canada Limited, 1971.

——. *Call Back Yesterdays*. Toronto: Longmans Canada Limited, 1965.

Colombo, John Robert. *Canadian Literary Landmarks*. Willowdale, Ontario: Hounslow, 1984.

Copp, Terry. *The Anatomy of Poverty: The Condition of the Working Class in Montreal 1907-1929*. Toronto: McClelland & Stewart, 1974.

de Grandpré, Pierre. *La Patience des justes*. Ottawa: Le Cercle du livre de France, 1966.

de LaGrave, Jean-Paul. *Voltaire's Man in America*. Translated by Arnold Bennett. Montreal: Robert Davies Publishing, 1997.

de Lamothe, H. *Cinq Mois Chez les Français d'Amérique*. Paris: Librairie Hachette, 1880.

Desjardins, Pauline, and Geneviève Duguay. *Pointe-à-Callière: From Ville-Marie to Montreal*. Translated by Käthe Roth. Quebec City: Septentrion/Le Vieux-Port de Montréal, 1992.

DeVolpi, Charles P., and P.S. Winkworth. *Montréal: Recueil Iconographique/A Pictorial Record, 1535-1885*, 2 vol. Montreal: Dev-Sco Publications, 1963.

Ducharme, Réjean. *Le Nez qui voque*. Paris: Gallimard, 1967.

——. *Wild to Mild*. (1973). Translated by Robert Guy Scully. St. Lambert, Quebec: Héritage, 1980.

Dumas, Evelyn. *Un Événement de mes octobres*. Montreal: Biocreux, 1979.

Dupré, Louis, Bruno Roy, and France Théoret, eds. *Montréal des écrivains*. Montreal: Éditions de l'Hexagone, 1988.

Éthier-Blais, Jean. "La Côte-des-Neiges d'antan." *Morceaux du grand Montréal*. Edited by Robert Guy Scully. Montreal: Éditions Noroît.

Étienne, Gérard. *Une Femme muette*. Montreal: Éditions Nouvelle Optique, 1983.

Fennario, David. *Without a Parachute*. (1972). Toronto: McClelland& Stewart, 1974.

Ferguson, Trevor [John Farrow, pseud.]. *City of Ice*. Toronto: HarperCollins, 1999.

——. *The True Life Adventures of Sparrow Drinkwater*. Toronto: HarperCollins, 1993.

Flenley, Ralph, editor and translator. *A History of Montreal, 1640-1672, From the French of Dollier de Casson*. Toronto: E. P. Dutton & Co., 1928.

Fournier, Roger. *Moi, mon corps, mon âme, Montréal, etc*. Montreal: Les Éditions la Presse, 1974.

Fréchette, Louis. From *La Légende d'un peuple*. Paris: La Librairie Illustrée, 1890.

Führer, Charlotte. *The Mysteries of Montreal: Memoirs of a Midwife*. (1881). Vancouver: University of British Columbia, 1984.

Gallant, Mavis. *The Selected Stories of Mavis Gallant*. Toronto: McClelland & Stewart, 1996.

Gélinas, Pierre. *Les Vivants, les morts et les autres*. Ottawa: Le Cercle du livre de France, 1959.

Godbout, Jacques. *Knife on the Table*. Translated by Penny Williams. Toronto: McClelland & Stewart, New Canadian Library, 1968.

Gournay, Isabelle, and France Vanlaethem, editors. *Montreal Metropolis, 1880-1930*. Toronto: Canadian Centre for Architecture/Stoddart Publishing, 1998.

Graham, Gwethalyn. *Earth and High Heaven*. Philadelphia and New York: J.B. Lippincott, 1944.

Grant, George Monro. *Picturesque Canada*. Toronto: Belden Bros., c1882.

Gubbay, Aline. *A Street Called the Main: The Story of Montreal's Boulevard Saint-Laurent*. Montreal: Meridian Press, 1989.

——. *A View of Their Own: The Story of Westmount*. Montreal: Price-Patterson, 1998.

Hamelin, Jean. *Les Rumeurs de Hochelaga*. Montreal: Hurtubise HMH, 1971.

Hamilton, Robert M. and Dorothy Shields. *The Dictionary of Canadian Quotations and Phrases*. (1979). Toronto: McClelland & Stewart, 1982.

Hood, Hugh. *Flying a Red Kite*. Toronto: The Ryerson Press, 1962.

——. *Around the Mountain: Scenes from Montreal Life*. Toronto: Peter Martin Associates, 1967.

Irving, Washington. *Astoria, or Anecdotes of an Enterprise Beyond the Rocky Mountains*. Vol. 1. New York: Putnam, 1897.

Jasmin, Claude. *La Petite patrie*. Montreal: Éditions La Presse, 1972.

Jenkins, Kathleen. *Montreal: Island City of the St. Lawrence*. New York: Doubleday, 1966.

Kalm, Peter. *Travels Into North America*. 2 vol. London: T. Lowndes, 1772.

Kalman, Judith. *The County of Birches*. Vancouver and Toronto: Douglas & McIntyre, 1998.

Kemble, Fanny. Letter Dec. 21, 1834, to Charles Mathews in his *Memoirs of Charles Mathews, 1838-39*. Vol. 4. Philadelphia: Lea & Blanchard, 1839.

Kenton, Edna editor. *The Jesuit Relations and Allied Documents*. (1896). Toronto: McClelland & Stewart, 1925.

Klein, A.M. *The Rocking Chair and Other Poems*. Toronto: The Ryerson Press, 1948.

Lacombe, Patrice. *Terre paternelle*. Montreal: Beauchemin, 1912.

Laferrière, Dany. *A Drifting Year*. (1994). Translated by David Homel. Vancouver and Toronto: Douglas & McIntyre, 1997.

Lambert, John. *Travels through Lower Canada and the United States of America in the Years 1806, 1807 and 1808*. London: Richard Phillips, T. Gillet, 1810.

Landmann, George. *Adventures and Recollections*. Vol. 1. London: Colburn and Co., 1852.

Larouche, Pierre. *Montreal 1535: La Redécouverte de Hochelaga*. Montreal: Éditions Ville Nouvelles-Villes Anciennes, 1992

LaRue, Monique, and Jean-François Chassay. *Promenades littéraires dans Montréal*. Montreal: Éditions Québec/Amérique, 1989.

Layton, Irving. *The Collected Poems of Irving Layton*. Toronto: McClelland & Stewart, 1971.

——. *Waiting for the Messiah*. Toronto: McClelland & Stewart, 1985.

Lazar, Barry, and Tamsin Douglas. *The Guide to Ethnic Montreal*. Montreal: Véhicule Press, 1993.

Leacock, Stephen. *Leacock's Montreal*, edited by John Culliton. Toronto: McClelland & Stewart, 1948.

——. *Arcadian Adventures with the Idle Rich*. (1914). Toronto: McClelland & Stewart, New Canadian Library, 1959.

LeFranc, Marie. *Visages de Montréal*. Montreal: Éditions du Zodiaque, 1934.

Leith, Linda. *The Tragedy Queen*. Montreal: Nuage Editions, 1995.

Lenoir, Joseph. *Oeuvres*. Edited by John Hare and Jeanne d'Arc Lortie. Montreal: Les Presses de l'Université de Montréal, 1988.

Leprohon, Rosanna. *Antoinette De Mirecourt, or Secret Marrying and Secret Sorrowing*. (1864). Edited by John C. Stockdale. Ottawa: Carleton University Press, 1989.

Lighthall, W.D. *Montreal After 250 Years*. Montreal: F.E. Grafton, 1892.

Linteau, Paul-André. *Histoire de Montréal depuis la Confédération*. Montreal: Boréal, 1992.

Ludwig, Jack. "A Woman of Her Age." (1965). In *Canadian Short Stories*. Second series selected by Robert Weaver. Toronto: Oxford University Press, 1968.

MacKay, Donald. *The Square Mile: Merchant Princes of Montreal*. Vancouver/Toronto: Douglas & McIntyre, 1987.

MacLennan, Hugh. *The Watch That Ends the Night*. Toronto: Macmillan, 1959.

——. *Thirty and Three*. Toronto: Macmillan, 1954.

——. *Two Solitudes*. Toronto: Collins, 1945.

Mailhot, Laurent, and Pierre Nepveu. *La Poésie québécoise des origines à nos jours: Anthologie*. Montreal: Éditions de l'Hexagone, 1986.

Maillet, Andrée. *Les Montréalais*. (1966). Montreal: Éditions de l'Hexagone, 1987.

Major, André, Paul Chamberland, Ghislain Côté, Nicole Drassel, and Michel Garneau. *Le Pays: poésie canadienne*. Montreal: Librairie Déom, 1963.

Majzels, Robert. *City of Forgetting*. Toronto: The Mercury Press, 1997.

Marchessault, Jovette. *Mother of the Grass* (1980). Translated by Yvonne Klein. Vancouver: Talonbooks, 1989.

——. *Like a Child of the Earth*. (1975). Translated by Yvonne Klein. Vancouver: Talonbooks, 1988.

Marsan, Jean-Claude. *Montreal in Evolution*. (1974). Montreal: McGill-Queen's University Press, 1981.

Marshall, Joyce. *A Private Place*. Ottawa: Oberon, 1975.

Micone, Marco. *Le Figuier enchanté*. Montreal: Boréal, 1992.

Moore, Brian. *The Revolution Script*. Toronto: McClelland & Stewart, 1972.

Morin, Marie. *Histoire simple et véritable: les annales de l'Hôtel-Dieu de Montréal, 1659-1725*. Montreal: Presses de l'Universite de Montreal, 1979.

Moritz, Albert and Theresa. *The Oxford Illustrated Literary Guide to Canada*. Toronto: Oxford University Press, 1987.

Naves, Elaine Kalman. *Putting Down Roots: Montreal's Immigrant Writers*. Montreal: Véhicule Press, 1998.

———. *The Writers of Montreal*. Montreal: Véhicule Press, 1993.

Nepveu, Pierre and Gilles Marcott. *Montréal imaginaire: ville et littérature*. Quebec City: Fides, 1992.

Noël, Francine. *Maryse*. Montreal: VLB Éditeur, 1983.

O'Brien, Kevin. *Oscar Wilde in Canada: An Apostle for the Arts*. Toronto: 1982.

Ollivier, Émile. *Passages*. Montreal: Éditions de l'Hexagone, 1991.

Olmsted, Frederick Law. *Mount Royal*. New York: G.P. Putnam's Sons, 1881.

Palmer, John. *Journal of Travels in the United States of North America and in Lower Canada, performed in the Year 1817*. London: Sherwood, Neely, and Jones, 1818.

Panetton, Philippe [Ringuet, pseud.]. *Le Poids du jour*. Montreal: Les Éditions Variétés, 1949.

Parizeau, Alice. *Rue Sherbrooke ouest*. Ottawa: Le Cercle du Livre de France, 1967.

Pendergast, James F., and Bruce G. Trigger. *Cartier's Hochelaga and the Dawson Site*. Montreal: McGill-Queen's University Press, 1972.

Phillips, Edward O. *Sunday Best*. Toronto: Seal Books, 1990.

———. *Sunday's Child*. Toronto: McClelland & Stewart, 1981.

Pinard, Guy. Montréal: *Son Histoire, Son Architecture*. Montreal: Méridien, 1992.

Prévost, Robert. Montréal: *A History*. (1991). Translated by Elizabeth Mueller and Robert Chodos. Toronto: McClelland & Stewart, 1993.

Proulx, Monique. *Aurora Montrealis*. Translated by Matt Cohen. Vancouver and Toronto: Douglas & McIntyre, 1997.

Purdy, Al. *Poems for All the Annettes*. Toronto: House of Anansi, 1968.

Radu, Kenneth. "Real Men." In *Telling Differences: New Fiction From Quebec*. Edited by Linda Leith. Montreal: Véhicule Press, 1988.

Rémillard, François, and Brian Merrett. *Montreal Architecture: A Guide to Styles and Buildings*. Translated by Pierre Miville-Deschênes. Montreal: Meridian Press, 1990.

Rhys, Horton. *A Theatrical Trip for a Wager*. London: C. Dudley, 1861.

Richardson, John. *Eight Years in Canada*. Montreal: H.H. Cunningham, 1848.

Richler, Mordecai. *Barney's Version*. Toronto: Alfred A. Knopf Canada, 1997.

———. *St. Urbain's Horseman*. Toronto: McClelland & Stewart, 1971.

———. *The Street*. Toronto: McClelland & Stewart, 1969.

Robert, Jean-Claude. *Atlas Historique de Montréal*. Montreal: Art Global/Libre Expression, 1994.

Roberts, Leslie. *Montreal: From Mission Colony to World City*. Toronto: Macmillan of Canada, 1969.

Robin, Régine. *The Wanderer*. (1983). Translated by Phyllis Aronoff. Montreal: Alter Ego Editions, 1997.

Robinson, Ira, Pierre Anctil, and Melvin Butovsky, eds. *An Everyday Miracle: Yiddish Culture in Montreal*. Montreal: Véhicule Press, 1990.

Rosenfarb, Chava. "Edgia's Revenge." In *Found Treasures: Stories byYiddish Women Writers*. Edited by Frieda Forman, Ethel Raicus, Sarah Silberstein Swartz, and Margie Wolfe. Toronto: Second Story Press, 1994.

Roy, Gabrielle. *The Cashier*. (1954). Translated by Henry Binsse. New York: Harcourt, Brace and Company, 1955.

———. *The Tin Flute*. (1945). Translated by Alan Brown. Toronto: McClelland & Stewart, 1980.

Sangster, Charles. *The St. Lawrence and the Saguenay and Other Poems*. Kingston, (Ont.) : John Creighton and John Duff ; New York: Miller, Orton & Mulligan, 1856.

Sarsfield, Mairuth. *No Crystal Stair*. Norval, Ont.: Moulin, 1997.

Scott, F.R. *The Collected Poems*. Toronto: McClelland & Stewart, 1981.

Silliman, Benjamin. *A Tour to Quebec, in the Autumn of 1819*. London: R. Phillips, 1822.

Sleigh, B.W.A. *Pine Forests or Hacmatack Clearings; or Travel, Life and Adventure in the British North American Provinces*. London: R. Bentley,1853.

Souster, Raymond. *Collected Poems, Vol. III, 1962-74*. Ottawa: Oberon, 1982.

Sutherland, Ronald. *Lark des Neiges*. Toronto: New Press, 1971.

Symons, Scott. *Place d'Armes: A Personal Narrative*. Toronto: McClelland & Stewart, 1978.

Talbot, Edward Allen. *Five Years Residence in the Canadas*. Vol. 1. London: Longman, Hurst, Rees, Orme, Brown and Green, 1824.

Thériault, Yves. *Aaron*. (1954). Montreal: Éditions de l'Homme, 1965.

Thoreau, Henry David. *A Yankee in Canada*. (1866). Montreal: Harvest House, 1961.

Traill, Catharine Parr. *The Backwoods of Canada*. (1836). Ottawa: Carleton University Press, 1997.

Tremblay, Michel. *Douze Coups de Théâtre*. Montreal: Leméac, 1992.

———. *The Fat Woman Next Door Is Pregnant*. (1978). Translated by Sheila Fischman. Vancouver: Talonbooks, 1981.

———. *Sainte-Carmen of the Main*. (1976). Translated by John Van Burek. Vancouver: Talonbooks, 1981.

Trollope, Anthony. *North America*. 2 vol. London: Chapman & Hall, 1866.

Urquhart, Jane. *Away*. Toronto: McClelland & Stewart, 1993.

Villemaire, Yollande. "Amazon Angel." Translated by Judith Cowan. *Ellipse* 56 (1996).

Waddington, Miriam. *Collected Poems*. Toronto: Oxford University Press, 1986. By permission of Oxford University Press.

Weintraub, William. *City Unique: Montreal Days and Nights in the 1940s and '50s*. Toronto: McClelland & Stewart, 1996.

———. *The Underdogs*. Toronto: McClelland & Stewart, 1979.

Whitaker, Rodney [Trevanian, pseud.]. *The Main*. New York: Harcourt, Brace, Jovanovitch, 1976.

Williams, Dorothy. *The Road to Now: A History of Blacks in Montreal*. Véhicule Press, 1997.

Wood, Col. William, editor in chief. *The Storied Province of Quebec*. 5 vol. Toronto: The Dominion Publishing Co., 1931.

INDEX

Italic page numbers indicate the presence of an illustration.

PICTURE CREDITS